Economics for Real People

An Introduction to the
Austrian School

Economics for Real People

An Introduction to the
Austrian School

Gene Callahan

MISES
INSTITUTE

Published by The Ludwig von Mises Institute, 518 West Magnolia Avenue,
Auburn, Alabama 36832-4528.

ISBN: 0-945466-35-8

ACKNOWLEDGMENTS

Dedicated to Professor Israel Kirzner, on the occasion of his retirement from economics.

My deepest gratitude to my wife, Elen, for her support and forbearance during the many hours it took to complete this book.

Special thanks to Lew Rockwell, president of the Ludwig von Mises Institute, for conceiving of this project, and having enough faith in me to put it in my hands.

Thanks to my friend Rob Dodson, who surprised me one day by mailing me a cover design he put together on his own initiative. That design is essentially the cover of the book you are holding.

Thanks to Jonathan Erickson of *Dr. Dobb's Journal* for permission to use my Dr. Dobb's online op-eds, "Just What Is Superior Technology?" as the basis for Chapter 16, and "Those Damned Bugs!" as the basis for part of Chapter 14.

Thanks to Michael Novak of the American Enterprise Institute for permission to use his phrase, "social justice, rightly understood," as the title for Part 4 of the book.

Thanks to the many commentators on the book (and sections of it as they appeared in article form), whose efforts improved this book tremendously and drove me to greater precision and clarity of expression. These include Walter Block (Loyola University), Peter Boettke (George Mason University), Sam Bostaph (University of Dallas), Colin Colenso (Shanghai, China), Harry David (New Haven, Conn.), Brian Doherty

(*Reason*), Richard Ebeling (Hillsdale College), Roger Garrison (Auburn University), Jeffrey Herbener (Grove City College), Sanford Ikeda (SUNY Purchase), Stephan Kinsella (Houston, Texas), Peter Lewin (University of Texas at Dallas), Stan Liebowitz (University of Texas at Dallas), Jeanne Locklair (Laboratory Institute of Merchandising), Robert Murphy (New York University), Marcel Popescu (Romania), Joseph Salerno (Pace University), Jeff Scott (Wells Fargo), Glen Tenney (Great Basin College), Jeff Tucker (Mises Institute), Christopher Westley (Jacksonville State University), Rich Wilcke (University of Louisville), Marco de Wit (University of Turku), James Yohe (University of West Florida), Sean Callahan (my brother), and my parents, Eugene and Patricia Callahan.

Any errors that remain are, of course, entirely mine.

Thanks to Pete Kavall, for teaching me what science is, and to Chogyam Trungpu and Tarthang Tulku, for continuing inspiration.

CONTENTS

The harm done . . . was that they removed economics from reality. The task of economics, as many [successors] of the classical economists practiced it, was to deal not with events as they really happened, but only with forces that contributed in some not clearly defined manner to the emergence of what really happened. Economics did not actually aim at explaining the formation of market prices, but at the description of something that together with other factors played a certain, not clearly described role in this process. Virtually it did not deal with real living beings, but with a phantom, "economic man," a creature essentially different from real man.

—Ludwig von Mises
The Ultimate Foundation of Economic Science

PART III: INTERFERENCE WITH THE MARKET

PART IV: SOCIAL JUSTICE, RIGHTLY UNDERSTOOD

APPENDICES

Stayin' Alive

WHY READ THIS BOOK?

*P*ERHAPS, AT SOME point, you have heard about the Austrian School of economics and are curious as to what it is. Or you may be discouraged by the economics you have encountered in textbooks and newspapers, and are searching for a more realistic view of economic life. The dominant school of economics, often referred to as the *Neoclassical School*, seems to describe people behaving in ways that are hard to relate to the human activity we see around us every day. The textbook humans seem robotic, rigidly obeying a set of equations that "maximizes their utility" based on a set of parameters. The equations themselves are said to "cause" supply and demand to meet at an equilibrium price— one that sets the quantity demanded equal to the quantity supplied. What place do humans have in such a system of equations? It seems difficult to relate those mathematical constructs to the world in which we live. How is the idea of man as a utility equation solver relevant to an Islamic revolution, to Mother Teresa, to Jimi Hendrix, or to your own decision to take a vacation that you "really can't afford," but really need?

11

Yet, you feel that economics *ought* to be relevant to real life. Doesn't it deal with jobs, money, taxes, prices, and industry: stuff of everyday existence? Why should the subject seem so obscure?

The Austrian School of economics is an alternative to the mainstream approach. It places economics on a sound, human basis. It avoids the traps that plague most of modern economics: the assumption of selfishness as the basic human motivation, a narrow definition of rational behavior, and the overuse of unrealistic models. This book is an attempt to introduce you to the main ideas of the school.

The Austrian School is so-named because most of its early members hailed from—you've probably guessed by now—Austria. The Nazi occupation of that country, however, scattered the practitioners. Today we can find prominent Austrian School economists all over the world. I will use "Austrian economist" to mean a member of the Austrian School, whether or not the person in question ever lived in Austria.

My focus will not be on the history of the school, although I have included an appendix with a brief overview of that history. Nor is my goal to convince professional economists of other schools to "convert." It is instead intended to be the proverbial "guide for the intelligent layman." While I have always tried to be precise, I have tried to avoid entering into the fine details of esoteric debates from the economics profession, which would only create a schizophrenic book.

The Austrian School is not monolithic, and there are disagreements among Austrian economists on various theoretical points. To complicate matters further, there is not even a universally accepted criterion for just who is an Austrian economist. There are "semi-Austrians," "Austrian fellow travelers," and even economists who call themselves Austrian but are denied the title by other writers. I have tried to give an overall view of the school's views, but the understanding of the subject reflected in these pages is necessarily my own.

Because of the nature of this book, it cannot explore Austrian economics in the same depth as do systematic treatises such as Murray Rothbard's *Man, Economy, and State* or Ludwig von Mises's *Human Action.* If this book succeeds in interesting you in this subject, it will have done its job; I urge you to then pick up one of these masterworks on the topic. (There is also a bibliography at the end of the book recommending further reading.)

But there are advantages to the approach taken by this book. First of all, Rothbard's and Mises's tomes are huge: you don't really want to be hauling a book like that to the beach, now, do you? Second, most people are not attempting to become professional economists. You probably have a very limited amount of time and effort you are willing to put into the subject, at least until you sense of how it might benefit you to know more. Last, neither of those great works has anything about the hit TV show *Survivor*[1] in it, nor does either of them so much as mention the actress Helena Bonham-Carter. I guarantee that this book will be free of both of those flaws.

---

[1]For those who don't follow what's on TV, or who might be reading this book twenty years after its publication: *Survivor* was a show where a number of contestants were placed, by a TV network, on a desert island. Then they were presented with a series of "survival" challenges. A voting process eliminated contestants until only the winner was left. This turned out to be a fellow named Rich. The particular details of the show are unimportant to this book, as Rich is merely used as an example of an isolated individual and the economic problems he faces. (Hey, using Robinson Crusoe has become a cliché, so I had to think of *something* else.)

Speaking of *Survivor* (see, you didn't even have to wait long before I took care of the first problem!), I'm going to ask you to imagine a slightly different conclusion to the series. In the original television show, the winner—the fellow who "survived" the longest—was a guy named Rich. In our alternate universe Rich is still the winner, but, as the film crew packs up, they decide that they are fed up with his antics. Instead of transporting him home, they quietly slip off of the island while Rich is getting in a last session of nude sunbathing.

Rich arises to find that he is alone. He is now facing the most elementary human problem, how to survive, in the most basic of settings. What can economics say about his situation? Is our science rooted in man's nature, or is it just a creation of certain social arrangements that we can change at will? If someone isn't concerned with becoming as wealthy as possible, or rejects consumerism, is economics still relevant to them? These are some of the questions that this book will attempt to answer.

We will come back to Rich in Chapter 2, but first, we will examine the question of what, exactly, economics is.

PART I

THE SCIENCE OF HUMAN ACTION

What's Going On?

O N   T H E   N A T U R E   O F   E C O N O M I C S

> [Economics] is universally valid and absolutely and plainly human.
> —LUDWIG VON MISES, *HUMAN ACTION*

WHAT ARE WE STUDYING?

*W*HEN WE FIRST approach a science we want to know, "What does it study?" Another way of approaching the same issue is to ask, "What basic assumptions does it bring to its examination of the world?" As a first step in tackling a new subject, you usually try to gain an idea of what it is all about. Before buying a book on biology, you determine that you will be reading about living organisms. At the beginning of a chemistry course, you learn that you can expect to study the ways in which matter combines in different forms.

Many people feel that they are generally familiar with economics. However, if you ask around, you will find that people have difficulty in defining the subject. "It's the study of money," some might tell you. "It has to do with business, profit and loss, and so forth," someone else asserts. "No, it's about how society chooses to distribute wealth," another person argues. "Wrong! It's the search for mathematical patterns that describe the movement of prices," a fourth insists. Professor Israel Kirzner points out, in *The Economic Point of*

View, that even among professional economists, there are "a series of formulations of the economic point of view that are astounding in their variety."

The primary reason for this confusion is that economics is the youngest of the sciences known to man. Certainly there has been a proliferation of new branches of existing sciences in the several centuries since economics came to be recognized as a distinct subject. But molecular biology, for example, is a division of biology, not a brand-new science.

Economics, however, is different. The existence of a distinct science of economics can be traced back to the discovery that there is a predictable regularity to the interaction of people in society, and that this regularity emerged without being planned by anyone.

The inkling of such regularity, standing apart from both the mechanical regularity of the physical universe and the conscious plans of any specific individual, was the first emergence of the idea of *spontaneous order* into the Western scientific consciousness. Before the emergence of economics as a science, it was simply assumed that if we found order in things, then those things must have been put in order by someone—God in the case of physical laws, and specific humans in the case of man-made objects and institutions.

Earlier political philosophers proposed various schemes for organizing human society. If the plan did not work out, the plan's creator generally assumed that the rulers or the citizens had not been virtuous enough to execute his plan. It didn't occur to him that his plan contradicted universal rules of human action and could not succeed no matter how virtuous the participants were.

The increase in human freedom that began in Europe during the Middle Ages and culminated in the Industrial Revolution exposed a tremendous gap in the existing scheme of knowledge. Increasingly, Western European society was not being explicitly ordered by the command of a ruler. One by one, restrictions on production were falling. No longer was the entry into trades strictly controlled by a guild. Yet somehow there seemed to be about the right number of carpenters, blacksmiths, masons, and so on. No longer was a royal license necessary to enter into some line of manufacturing. And yet, although anyone could open a brewery, the world was not flooded with beer. Once again, the amount made seemed just about right. Even without anyone creating a master plan for a city's imports, the mix of goods that showed up at the city gates seemed roughly correct. In the nineteenth century, French economist Frédéric Bastiat remarked on the wonder of that phenomenon by exclaiming, "Paris gets fed!" Economics did not create that regularity, nor is it faced with the task of proving that it exists—we see it in front of us every day. Economics, rather, must explain *how* it comes about.

Many scholars contributed to the dawning realization that economics was a new way of looking at society. The origins of economic science stretch back earlier than is frequently thought, certainly back to at least the fifteenth century, when work done by the *Late Scholastics* at the University of Salamanca in Spain later prompted Joseph Schumpeter to dub them the first economists.

Adam Smith may not have been the first economist, as he is sometimes called. But more than any other social philosopher he popularized the notion that human beings, left free to pursue their own goals, would give rise to a social order that none of them had consciously planned. As Smith famously put it in *The Wealth of Nations*, free man acts as if "led by an invisible hand to promote an end which was no part of his intention."

The Austrian economist Ludwig von Mises said in his *magnum opus, Human Action,* that this discovery left people filled with

> stupefaction that there is another aspect from which human action might be viewed than that of good and bad, of fair and unfair, of just and unjust. In the course of social events there prevails a regularity of phenomena to which man must adjust his actions if he wishes to succeed.

Mises described the initial difficulties in determining the nature of economics:

> In the new science everything seemed to be problematic. It was a stranger in the traditional system of knowledge; people were perplexed and did not know how to classify it and to assign it its proper place. But on the other hand they were convinced that the inclusion of economics in the catalogue of knowledge did not require a rearrangement or expansion of the total scheme. They considered their catalogue system complete. If economics did not fit into it, the fault could only rest with the unsatisfactory treatment that the economists applied to their problems. (*Human Action*)

For many, the feeling of stupefaction was soon replaced by one of frustration. They had ideas for reforming society, and now they discovered that the emerging science of economics stood in their way. Economics advised these reformers that some plans for social organization would fail regardless of how well they were carried out, because the plans violated basic laws of human interaction.

Stopped in their tracks by the achievements of the early economists, some of these reformers, such as Karl Marx, attempted to invalidate the entire subject. Economists, Marx contended, were simply describing society as they found it under the domination of the capitalists. There are no economic truths that apply to all men in all times and places; most specifically, the laws formulated by the classical school, by writers such as Smith, Thomas Malthus, and David Ricardo, will not apply to those living in the future socialist utopia. In fact, said the Marxists, these thinkers were merely apologists for the exploitation of the masses by the wealthy few. The classical economists were, to phrase it in the style of the Chinese Marxists, running dog lackeys of the imperialist warmonger pigs.

The extent to which Marx and like-minded thinkers succeeded in their goal of undermining the foundations of economics reflected the fragility of those foundations. The classical economists had discovered many economic truths, but they were plagued by certain inconsistencies in their own theories, such as their inability to construct a coherent theory of value. (We will address this specific difficulty in more detail later.)

It was Mises, building on the work of earlier Austrian economists such as Carl Menger, who finally reconstructed economics "upon the solid foundation of a general theory of human action."

For some purposes it might be important to differentiate between the general science of human action, which Mises called *praxeology,* and economics as the branch of that science that deals with exchange. However, since the term praxeology has not gained widespread use, and a sharp delineation of economics from the rest of praxeology is unimportant in an introductory book, I will use *economics* as the name for the entire science of human action. Mises himself often uses it in this manner: "Economics . . . is the theory of all human action, the general science of the immutable categories of action and of their operation under all thinkable special conditions under which man acts" (*Human Action*).

What does Mises mean by "human action"? Let him tell us:

> Human action is purposeful behavior. Or we may say: Action is will put into operation and transformed into an agency, is aiming at ends and goals, is the ego's meaningful response to stimuli and to the conditions of its environment, is a person's conscious adjustment to the state of the universe that determines his life. (*Human Action*)

In a similar vein, the British philosopher Michael Oakeshott described human action as the attempt to replace what is with *what ought to be*, in the eyes of the person acting.

The wellspring of human action is *dissatisfaction*, or, if you want to see the glass as half full, the idea that life might be better than it is at present. "What is" is judged to be deficient in some way. If we are completely satisfied with the way things are at this moment, we have no motivation to act—any action could only make matters worse! But as soon as we perceive something in our world that we judge to be less than satisfactory, the possibility of acting in order to remedy this situation arises.

For example, you lie on a hammock, perfectly happy with the world, letting everything pass you by. But your idle is disturbed by a buzzing sound. It occurs to you that you would certainly feel more relaxed if this sound stopped, in other words, you can envision circumstances that you feel ought to be. You are experiencing the first component of human action, dissatisfaction.

However, in order to act, dissatisfaction is not enough. First of all, you must understand the *cause* of the uneasiness. Well, the noise, of course. But we cannot simply wish noises away. We must discover what is causing the noise. In order to act, we must understand that each cause is the *effect* of some other cause. We must be able to follow a chain of cause and effect until we reach a place where we feel our intervention, our action, will break the chain and eliminate our dissatisfaction. We must see a plan for moving from what is to what ought to be.

If the buzzing is from an airplane passing overhead, you will not act. (Unless your house has an anti-aircraft gun installed, there is nothing that you'll be able to do about the plane.) You must believe that your action can cause an effect in your world. In order to act, it's not necessary that you are correct in your belief! Ancient man often believed that performing certain rites could improve his environment, perhaps bringing rain during a drought or causing the herds he hunted to increase. As far as I know, those approaches did not work. But the belief that they would was enough to lead people to act on them.

So you look around to find the cause of the noise and see a mosquito. Perhaps you *can* do something about the buzzing—you can swat the little bugger. You are contemplating an *end*, that of being rid of the mosquito. You see that achieving the end will bring you a *benefit*—the noise will be gone, and you can rest undisturbed.

So, you could get up and kill the mosquito. But you had come outside with another end in mind—just loafing around on the hammock. You are now grappling with another component of human action—you have to make a *choice*. Being rid of the mosquito would be grand, sure—but you'll have to get up. And that's a bummer. The benefit you expect to receive from being rid of the mosquito comes at the *cost* of getting up. If the benefit from your action exceeds your cost, you will *profit* from the action.

Although we often use profit to refer to monetary gain, it also has a wider sense, as in, "How does it profit a man to gain the world but lose his soul?" We perform all of our actions, whether buying a stock or retreating to a mountain to meditate, with an eye to profiting in this psychic sense. As the above quotation indicates, if we choose to lead a pious life in poverty, it is because we expect the end result to benefit us more than the cost of surrendering the pursuit of worldly goods: we expect to profit from the choice.

Choices involve considering the means necessary to achieve our ends. I wouldn't mind being the strongest man in the world. But if I contemplate pursuing this end, I must also think about what I would have to do to achieve it. I would need to have access to strength-training equipment, to buy nutritional supplements, and I would have to spend many hours each day in training. In our world, everything we desire does not appear simply by wishing for it. Many things that we want, even things that we need to stay alive, can be had only after an expenditure of time and effort. Strength-training equipment does not simply fall from the sky. (Thank God!) And if I'm spending several hours a day weight lifting, I can't spend those hours writing a book, or playing with my kids.

For mortal man, time is the ultimate scarce item. Even for Bill Gates, time is in short supply. Although he can afford to charter private jets to both Aruba and Tahiti on the same morning, he still can't fly to both places simultaneously! To be human is to know that our days on Earth are numbered, and that we must choose how to use them. Because we live in a world of scarcity, the use of means to pursue an end involves *costs.* To me, the cost of spending my time weight training is determined by how much I *value* the other ways I could spend that time.

For economics, the value of the particular ends we might choose is subjective. No one else can tell me whether an hour spent weight lifting is more or less valuable *to me* than one spent writing. Nor is there any possible way to objectively measure the difference in my valuation of these activities. No one has invented a "value-ometer." Expressions such as "That dinner was twice as good as last night's" are simply figures of speech. They don't imply an actual ability to measure satisfaction. As Murray Rothbard pointed out, the way to verify this is to ask, "Twice as much of what?" We don't even have a unit by which we might measure satisfaction.

The subjective nature of value was one of Carl Menger's major insights. For the classical economists, value was a paradox. They attempted to base their theory of value on the labor involved in producing a good or the usefulness of the good, by some objective measure. But consider such a simple case as finding a diamond lying on the ground during a stroll. No labor was required to produce the diamond, nor is it more useful, at least to directly maintaining life, than a cup of water. And yet a diamond is generally considered much more valuable than a cup of water. Menger cut this Gordian knot by basing his theory of value on just that fact—things are valuable because acting humans consider them to be so.

Economics does not attempt to decide whether our choice of ends to pursue is wise. It does not tell us that we are wrong if we value a certain amount of leisure more than some amount of money. It does not view humans as being only worried about monetary gain. There is nothing "noneconomical" about someone giving away a fortune, or turning down a high-paying job to become a monk.

The question of whether or not there are objective values does not concern economics. Again, that should not be taken to mean that Austrian economics is hostile to any religion or system of ethics. I personally know of Austrian economists who are Catholics, atheists, Orthodox Jews, Buddhists, Objectivists, Protestants, and agnostics, and, if I only knew more economists, I'm sure I could mention Muslims, Hindus, and so on. Economics should, quite properly, leave comparing values to ethics, religion, and philosophy. Economics is not a theory of everything, but simply a theory of the consequences of choice. In studying economics, we take human ends as an ultimate given. People, somehow, *do* choose ends and *do* act to pursue them. The goal of our science is to explore the implications of these facts.

Mises said in the introduction to *Human Action*:

> Choosing determines all human decisions. In making his choice man chooses not only between various material things and services. All human values are offered for option. All ends and all means, both material and ideal issues, the sublime and the base, the noble and the ignoble, are ranged in a single row and subjected to a decision which picks out one thing and sets aside another. Nothing that men aim at or want to avoid remains outside of this arrangement into a unique scale of gradation and preference. The modern theory of value widens the scientific horizon and enlarges the field of economic studies.

WHY SHOULD WE STUDY ECONOMICS?

*O*NCE WE HAVE an idea what our subject is, the next question is whether it is worth studying. Given that you've picked up this book, you must have some notion that it could be useful. But if you don't intend to become a professor of economics, what can you gain from learning about it?

One of the benefits of studying economics is a deeper understanding of our own situation as acting humans. For instance, people often fail to properly account for the cost of their choices. Once we understand that our costs are measured in terms of our foregone alternatives, we might have a very different view of some common choices.

Let's look at a mundane example. We all know someone who has spent a great deal of time on some home improvement project. Perhaps this person undertook the project for sheer enjoyment. Economics will not attempt to recommend something else that would have been more enjoyable—it is not a self-improvement guide!

But often, the "do-it-yourselfer" will say that he is doing the work to "save money." "Look," he'll tell you, "it would have cost me $5,000 to get my roof done professionally. I managed to do it for only $1,000 in materials." An economist is able to point out that his calculation is faulty, and that he may have acted contrary to his own purpose. He has not taken into account the cost of his foregone opportunities. If the job took him 100 hours, and he could have put this time in at work and earned an additional $8,000, he has actually suffered a large monetary loss by doing the job himself. This example turns on dollars and cents, but in other cases, it is psychic costs that we fail to account for properly. When a philanderer cheats on his wife, we may wonder if he has fully considered the costs involved. Perhaps he has, in which case economics can turn the problem over to ethics and religion. But all too often, people take account of the immediately visible profit from an action and fail to account for the less visible, more distant costs. Bastiat referred to this as the problem of what is seen and what is not seen. He felt that it was an important task of economics to teach us "not to judge things solely by *what is seen*, but rather by *what is not seen*."

Another benefit of an understanding of economics is that it is crucial to evaluating questions of public policy. Should we raise the minimum wage, leave it alone, or even eliminate it? Can we lift our standard of living by protecting domestic industries? What would be the result of privatizing Social Security? These are all economic questions.

Some people feel that these questions should be answered on a "practical," case-by-case basis. They claim to disdain the use of theory in resolving them. The English economist John Maynard Keynes saw the error in such thinking:

> The ideas of economists and political philosophers, both when they are right and when they are wrong, are more powerful than is commonly understood. Indeed, the world is ruled by little else. Practical men, who believe themselves to be quite exempt from any intellectual influences, are usually slaves of some defunct economist. (*The General Theory of Employment, Interest, and Money*)

HOW SHOULD WE STUDY ECONOMICS?

*T*HE FINAL QUESTION that we will tackle here is how we can best approach our science. The startling success of physics and chemistry over the last three centuries in mastering matter and energy has often blinded people to the fact that this question has more than one possible answer.

But looking at some other established disciplines shows us that this is the case. For instance, I don't know of anyone who suggests that the right way to gain a deep understanding of Shakespeare is to analyze the chemical composition of the paper and ink he used to compose his plays.

We don't expect to study geometry or logic in the same way as the physical sciences, either. To determine that the three angles of a triangle add up to 180 degrees, we don't measure thousands of real triangles. In fact, the triangle of geometry is an idealized figure that we could not find in reality. Or take the following syllogism: "All men are mortal. John is a man. Therefore, John is mortal." We do not have to wait around for John to kick the bucket to see that this is true. Should we discover that John is, in fact, immortal, we would have found that one of our premises was false. But the syllogism itself would still be valid.

We can see this more clearly when we look at a syllogism that has no basis in reality, for instance: "All unicorns have a single horn. If I see a unicorn in my yard today, it will have a single horn." The syllogism is clearly true, even though no unicorns have ever existed, so that we could not possibly have any empirical facts about them.

The question of *why* we can assert that the propositions of geometry and logic are true has been the subject of much philosophical and theological debate. The principles of human action are similar in that, once we notice them, they appear self-evidently true, without it immediately being clear why that is so. But economics does not attempt to solve the riddle of why we think the way we do. To economics, this fact is an ultimate given.

All sciences have limits, determined by what may be seen from their vantage point on the world. Physics, for all its pride in having reached back to "the origins of the universe," has only succeeded in explaining one physical state of the world in terms of an earlier one. For physics, the fact that there are physical states is an ultimate given. This is not a failure of physics—it is only because a subject has limits that it is a coherent subject. The alternative is to have a single subject named, perhaps, "Everything." Human attempts to acquire knowledge in this fashion have not been highly successful.

Because the subject matter of economics is human action, and because human action proceeds by plans formulated by humans, it is the nature of our own human mind that is our chief exploratory tool. In this respect, economics has an advantage over physics and chemistry. We do not understand why matter and energy act as they do, only that they do so. (Certainly, we can explain some facts of their behavior in terms of more elementary facts. But however far back we take these explanations, we will ultimately hit a point where all we can say is, "Well, it just does behave that way.")

But economics is different. We are all human. (At least I don't think Amazon.com has any extraplanetary sales yet.) Our minds are like the minds of the economic actors (including ourselves!) whom we hope to understand. We know, in a basic, direct sense, what it is to choose, to suffer loss, to achieve happiness. Our chief tool in studying economics is our knowledge of what it is to be human, to prefer certain outcomes to others, and to act to bring about those preferred outcomes.

As an example of the centrality of the human mind to economics, let's examine a commonplace economic event: a real estate closing on a piece of land. How can we understand what has occurred?

Let us say that we choose to examine this event from the points of view of physics and chemistry. The closing might be many miles from the land itself. Nevertheless, we diligently set up our instruments on both the land and in the bank where the closing is taking place. We collect all information on every atom and every bit of energy that we are capable of gathering. We pore over the data with the aid of the fastest supercomputers available. Still, it is hard to imagine that we could find anything tying the events at the bank to the piece of land being sold.

Perhaps the seller has never been to the property, and the buyer doesn't intend to go there either. No amount of observation of the property could discover the transaction that has occurred. What has happened is real in that it is a real idea, believed in by the people involved. It is the meaning attached to the closing by those participating that makes it a transaction.

Now, let us say that this land is located in an area that undergoes rapid development. The value of the open parcel soars. The new owner now knows that he could sell his land for double the price at which he bought it. But where would our intrepid physicists and chemists discover this fact? It exists only as an idea in the mind of one or more human beings. And yet we can't explain the fact that the owner would turn down an offer for one-and-a-half times his purchase price without taking into account that idea.

The subject matter of economics is human plans and the actions resulting from those plans. We must study the various options with which the world presents to human actors, as *they themselves interpret them.* We must consider the meaning that they attach to the ends that they seek to achieve by choosing one of these options. The central concept of economics is the planned actions of real human beings, and it advances by analyzing the thinking used in making those plans.

The attempt to make economics a "real" science by basing its study on "hard, objective data," such as physical quantities

of goods, misses the essence of the subject. It is as though we
undertook a study of biology by limiting our research to the
behavior of the subatomic particles making up organic bodies. We would never even detect that we were dealing with a
living creature! All fields of study are, after all, investigating
the same world. It is only that they approach that world from
different points of view, through the use of different central
concepts, that makes them different subjects. In studying economics, we take the thoughts and plans of acting humans as
an ultimate given, and begin our investigation there.

CHAPTER 2

Alone Again, Unnaturally

ON THE ECONOMIC CIRCUMSTANCES
OF THE ISOLATED INDIVIDUAL

THOUGHT EXPERIMENTS

*W*E CLOSED THE introduction by considering the situation of Rich, from the TV show *Survivor*, stranded on a desert island. Living alone, does the subject of economics still apply to him? Furthermore, what is the point of studying the situation of an isolated human being? Isn't man a social animal? And isn't our interest in economics based on its applicability to our real situation, where we live in interaction with countless others?

While it is true that man is a social being, contemplating the situation of an isolated individual is, for economics, as necessary as isolating particles in a nuclear reactor is for physics. It is in the conditions of an isolated individual that the basics of economics emerge in their clearest outline, and it is these basics that we are after. Carl Menger said in *Principles of Economics*:

> In what follows I have endeavored to reduce the complex phenomena of human economic activity to the simplest elements that can still be subjected to accurate observation . . . [and] to investigate the manner in which the more complex phenomena

evolve from their elements according to definite principles.

Austrian School economists, basing economics on human choice, are committed to *methodological individualism*, because only individuals make choices. Whenever we analyze a situation where we would colloquially say that a group has "chosen," we see that one or more individuals made the choice. Perhaps a dictator chose for the whole nation, or the citizens of a town made a choice by majority vote. However the choice came about, it occurred first in the minds of individuals.

Indeed, when we say that an individual belongs to a group, we mean that he is *considered* to be in the group, by some individual(s). Group membership exists in human minds. Whether a group milling about outside your door is an accidental crowd or an angry mob depends on what meaning the individuals in the crowd assign to the gathering. If, in the minds of the individuals, they are there to violently protest your recent decision to fill your yard with flamingos, then they are a mob. Similarly, the group nature of a crowd in a stadium depends on why the individuals believe they are there. We can characterize such a group as fans of satanic rocker Marilyn Manson or Christian evangelicals only based on the meaning that the individuals in the group attach to the gathering. No physical survey of the scene could yield us this information. If, through a scheduling mix-up, Marilyn Manson arrived at an evangelical convention, that would not make the attendees Marilyn Manson fans, nor would it make Marilyn Manson a Christian minister.

Fair enough, you may say, but why are we merely imagining Rich's situation on the island? Couldn't we make economics a "real," empirical science by doing actual experiments like physics does, rather than thought experiments? Given the astounding success of empiricism in the physical sciences, it is tempting to at least try this approach. We must be cautious, however—simply because a sledgehammer does a good job breaking up stones does not mean that it's the right tool for slicing tomatoes. Such experimentation is not without value— indeed, economist Vernon Smith has done important work in the area—but we cannot rely on it in the same way we do experimentation in the physical sciences.

The first obstacle to trying to proceed along strongly empirical grounds in economics is that humans act differently when they know they are being watched. Now, many people are familiar with the role of "the observer" in quantum mechanics, where it seems that, at the level of subatomic particles, energy, the subject matter of physics, acts differently if it is "being observed." (Just what this "being observed" consists of is a matter of intense debate in interpreting quantum mechanics, and is quite beyond the scope of this book.) Isn't this the same problem that economics faces?

But the behavior of subatomic particles varies in predictable, mathematically describable ways depending on whether or not they are under observation. Light acts like a wave when we don't try to detect particles, and like a particle when we do try to detect them, but it does this every time. It can't choose to ignore "the observer," nor can it learn anything about the experiment and then modify its behavior accordingly. This is not true of people!

Humans, as experimental subjects, *do* attempt to learn about the experiment, and they modify their behavior based on what they learn. For one thing, if the person running the experiment is liked by the subjects, they will often try to figure out what result he wants, and act to bring it about.

Merely knowing that they are in an experimental setting modifies their behavior as well. *Survivor* was not a test of how humans act when placed in a small group with minimal resources available. Every participant knew that he or she would be fine, as far as the TV crew was able to make it so. They would not be allowed to starve to death, to go to war with each other, or to suffer a severe illness without medical assistance. Every one of them also knew that they were on camera, competing with each other for a prize, with a definite limit as to how long they would have to spend on the island together. There was no incentive to cooperate beyond the minimum necessary to avoid being tossed from the island, and there was no incentive to try to create a lasting social structure.

Survivor could be viewed as an experiment in how humans act when on a television show that places them in a "survival" contest, in conditions set up by the producers. However, even that view of the experiment is of limited usefulness, since future contestants, participating in *Survivor II*, will have learned something from the first series, and will modify their behavior accordingly. I know of no interpretation of quantum physics that contends that photons learn from having been watched. They behave in the same particulate way every time you try to detect them as particles—they don't ever try to outfox the measuring device. The fact that humans learn makes exact prediction in the social sciences impossible. It means that we will never discover constants in human behavior equivalent to the constants representing the speed of light in a vacuum or the ratio of hydrogen to oxygen in water. The effects of future learning on human behavior are by definition unknown. We can't already know what we have yet to learn, because that would mean we had already learned it.

Because humans do understand the idea of an experiment and take the fact that they are participating in one into account, we cannot test human action in the same way we do the behavior of photons. Instead, we must mentally isolate the basic components of human action. Based on the fact that we ourselves are human and employ the same logic of action as our isolated actor, we try to understand those components.

THE BIRTH OF VALUE

So, RICH IS alone on the island, and does not know if or when he will be rescued. What insights can economics bring to his situation?

First of all, Rich must choose an end for his time upon the island. OK, he's stuck there for now. Accepting that as his basic condition, what should he do? To answer this question is to choose an end. Perhaps his goal will be to survive until he is rescued. While this end seems reasonable enough, we must realize that other ends are possible. From the point of view of economics, no particular end is more or less valid. (To again stress an important point, that does *not* mean economics holds that any system of values is just as good as any other. Economics simply does not attempt to address the problem of what we *should* value.)

Let's say that Rich is a devoted follower of the religion of Jainism. It is against his religious principles to harm any living creature. While he is able to scrape up a coconut or two, he realizes that by passing up all of the island's abundant rats, which he could be roasting, he will slowly starve to death. Yet, he lives by his principles anyway. Does this mean that

Rich ignored economics, or behaved irrationally? While some schools of economics would say "yes," to an Austrian economist the answer is an emphatic "no." Rich simply pursued the end that he valued most highly, that of adhering to his religious beliefs.

Anyway, let us imagine that Rich *does* choose survival as his ultimate end. To survive, he needs water, food, shelter, and rest. Those are the means by which he hopes to achieve his end. However, he has no shelter built. Food is available, but scattered around the island, taking some effort to collect. There are springs, but with only a minimal flow of fresh water.

Since Rich must employ yet other means to acquire water, food, shelter, and rest, they become subsidiary ends. Food is a means toward the end of survival, but an end sought by employing the means of rat hunting. The same good can be a means from the vantage point of plan *A* and an end from the vantage point of plan *B*.

So, Rich finds himself in a similar situation to all other humans: He has some ends in mind, and limited means by which he might achieve those ends. He must economize his means in order to achieve the most valuable of his ends. For instance, if he spends all his time building a shelter, he will not have food or water.

Rich must economize his time. He also must conserve other resources. He cannot afford to shake all of the coconuts off of a tree in one day, only to have those he can't eat rot. Although he'd like to use water for cooking, if he only has enough for drinking, then he will have to use his supply for drinking in order to live.

How does Rich decide how he will employ his scarce means? To do so, he has to make choices. Even after he has chosen survival as his primary goal, he still has to choose how to go about achieving it. And as long as Rich's minimal needs can be met with less than his highest possible expenditure of energy, he also must choose how to expend that surplus energy. Perhaps Rich is vain, and very concerned about how he looks when he is rescued. In this case, he will spend a great deal of his surplus time tending to his appearance. If he is a person with a low tolerance for risk, he might spend his time stockpiling food. If he is a scientist, he might conduct experiments with the local flora and fauna.

Economics is unconcerned with how Rich arrives at his values. It takes as its starting point the fact that humans *do* value some things more highly than others, and that their actions are the manifestation of those values. To economics, it is an ultimate given that what is valued more is chosen, and what is valued less is forsaken. This is the very logic of human action, and thinking beings that did not follow such logic would be sorely puzzling to us.

Let's say I could have taken a vacation in Athens, but I chose Istanbul instead. It is a loose use of words to say that I "really preferred Athens," but nevertheless picked Istanbul. The fact that I really did go to Istanbul is the essence of preferring. It may have been because the airfares were cheaper to Turkey, or because my wife chose Istanbul and I didn't want to argue. In any case, I picked Istanbul and the associated cost of going there because I preferred that option to Athens and the associated costs of going there.

When we say that my picking Istanbul shows I preferred it, we do not imply that, after the fact, I might not decide I had been wrong in my initial judgment. After the trip, I might decide that Istanbul is not the place for me, and that I ought to have picked Athens. We must take care to distinguish forward-looking and backward-looking evaluations. Action implies learning, and learning implies that sometimes, in choosing A, I will discover that I really ought to have chosen B.

The notion that we always choose what we prefer may seem too extreme. You might claim, in protest: "I prefer not to go to the dentist, yet I go anyway." Such a statement is fine in common speech, but economics must be more precise. In making your choice, you weigh the benefits of not going to the dentist (e.g., no scraping) against the costs (e.g., tooth decay). The fact that you *do* go implies that you prefer the dentist to the alternative of rotten teeth, despite the pain involved. What you mean, stated more precisely, is that you wish that your teeth never decayed and the dentist was unnecessary.

Economics is not concerned with the world of wishes and idle fancy, except when these daydreams manifest themselves in action. In everyday speech, we may say, while on a long walk, "I'd prefer an iced tea when I get home." This indicates a plan of action. But to economics, it is action itself that counts, and the plan only matters so far as it influences action. Preferences, from the point of view of economics, become real at the moment of choice. You may constantly assert that you prefer losing weight to eating cake. But economics ignores such assertions. It is only interested in what you do when the dessert tray comes out.

So Rich chooses, apportioning his time. Let's say he spends the first four hours of every day gathering food, the next two hours collecting water, and the next four working on a lean-to. For the remainder of the day he relaxes.

All of the above actions have as their goal the direct removal of some dissatisfaction. The food directly satisfies Rich's hunger, the water his thirst, and the lean-to his desire to be sheltered from the wind and rain. Even his leisure time is action, with an end in mind—relaxation. As long as Rich is physically capable of continuing work, to stop and rest is a choice.

We will examine the point at which Rich makes this choice, because it illustrates the crucial insight by which Carl Menger solved the value problem that had plagued classical economics.[1] Imagine Rich tying poles together for his lean-to. He has eaten, he has water, and the lean-to is progressing nicely. What's more, he's beginning to feel a little weary.

Just when will he stop working? It will be at the point when the satisfaction that Rich expects from the next "unit" of work falls below the satisfaction that he expects from his first "unit" of rest. That fact is implied by the very existence of choice. Since, as we've seen, to choose means to prefer, Rich will work as long as he prefers the gains he expects from the next unit of work to the gains he expects from his next unit of rest.

The "unit" in question is simply whatever time intervals Rich mentally slices his work into. The next unit might be, for instance, tying the next set of poles together, or collecting one more coconut. The unit will most likely be a task that, if not finished, is not worth starting. There is no point, for instance, in Rich picking up a coconut, but then dropping it to the ground and going home before placing it in his bag. The amount of "clock time" that Rich considers to be a unit will change from one task to the next and one day to the next,

---

[1]In one of the amazing incidents of simultaneous discovery sprinkled through the history of science, Léon Walras and William Stanley Jevons, working independently of Menger, arrived at similar solutions to this problem in the early 1870s as well.

even for the same task—it is subjective. What matters is the particular task that he is contemplating as his next action at the moment he knocks off for the day.

Rich is about to start tying some poles, when he feels a twinge in his back. "Hmm," he wonders, "time to rest?" He is going to choose between the satisfaction that he believes he will receive from binding the next set of poles and the satisfaction he believes he will receive from a few extra minutes of rest. Because preference is tied to a concrete act of choice among particular means aiming at particular ends, economic choice does not pick among abstractions. Rich doesn't choose between "work" and "leisure," but between a specific amount of a specific kind of work and a specific amount of leisure, in the context of a specific set of circumstances.

That insight resolves the paradox of value that bedeviled the classical economists. "Why," they wondered, "since water is so much more valuable than diamonds, do people pay so much for diamonds and so little, perhaps even nothing, for water?" The disastrous labor theory of value, which attempted to equate value with the amount of labor that had gone into a good, was developed in an attempt to patch over this deficiency. Karl Marx based much of his economic thought on the labor theory of value. The flaws in this theory can be attested to by all those later enslaved by communism.

What the classical economists missed is that no one ever chooses between "water" and "diamonds." These are just abstract classes by which we categorize the world. Indeed, no one even chooses between "all of the water in the world" and "all of the diamonds in the world." When choosing, acting man is always faced with a choice between definite quantities of goods. He is faced with a choice between, let's say, a barrel of water and a ten-carat diamond.

"But wait," you ask, "isn't the water still more useful than the diamond?" The answer is, "It depends." It depends entirely on the valuation of the person who must choose. If a man living next to a clean mountain stream is offered a barrel of water, he may not value it at all. The stream itself provides him with more water than he can possibly use, so the value of this extra quantity to him is literally nothing. (Perhaps it is even negative—it might be a nuisance having the barrel around.) But this fellow may not have any diamonds, so the possibility of acquiring even one might be enticing. It is clear that the man will value the diamond more than the water.

But even for the same man, if we change his circumstances, then his valuation may change completely. If he is crossing the Sahara, with the diamond already in his pocket, but he has run out of water and is on the verge of dying, most likely he would trade the diamond for even a single cup of water. (Of course, if he were a miser, he might still value the diamond more highly than the water, even at the risk of dying of thirst.) The value of goods is subjective—the exact same diamond and barrel of water may be valued differently by different people, and even valued differently at different times by the same person. To quote Menger:

> Value is therefore nothing inherent in goods, no property of them, but merely the importance that we first attribute to the satisfaction of our needs . . . and in consequence carry over to economic goods as the . . . causes of the satisfaction of our needs. (*Principles of Economics*)

Many means can be employed toward more than one end. Rich might put water to any of a variety of uses. He will first direct any means with more than one use to that use he feels is most important. That is not a fact arrived at through a survey of numerous actions, but a logical necessity. We can say that the first use was most important to Rich precisely because he chose to satisfy that felt need first.

As long as Rich has set his goal as survival, he will use the first bucket of water he can collect for drinking. Only when he is confident that he has enough water to prevent death from thirst will he consider using some for cooking. Since each additional bucket of water is directed to a less important use, then for Rich, each additional bucket has a lower value than the previously acquired buckets. The *utility* to Rich of each additional bucket declines. When faced with a choice, it is always the next item to be acquired, or the first to be given up, that is relevant. Economists say that these are the *marginal units*, and refer to this principle as the *law of diminishing marginal utility*.

The margin in question is not a physical property of the event under consideration, nor can it be determined by objective calculations. The margin is the line between yes and no, between choosing and setting aside. The marginal unit is the one about which you are deciding: Will you work an extra hour today? Should you stay at a party and have one more drink? Will you sign up for that extra day at the hotel on your vacation? Those are quite different questions than: "Is working a good thing?" "Are parties fun?" "Are vacations relaxing?" What must be determined is whether the next hour of work would provide more benefit than another hour of leisure. Is the relaxation gained from an extra day's vacation worth the cost? Our choices are made at the margin, and are made in reference to the marginal unit.

When Rich begins his day, the marginal utility he expects to gain from an hour of work is far higher than what he expects from an hour of leisure. If he doesn't start working, he won't be able to eat or drink! But each successive hour of work is devoted to a purpose considered less important than the purpose achieved by the previous hour. Finally—let's say after ten hours—Rich arrives at a point where the satisfaction he expects from another hour of work has fallen below the satisfaction he expects to gain from another hour of leisure. The marginal utility of the next contemplated hour of labor has fallen below that of the next contemplated hour of leisure, and Rich rests.

The question of valuation is resolved at the moment of choice. Because all action is directed toward an uncertain future, the possibility of error is always present. Rich may feel he has collected enough food and decide to nap for a while. While he sleeps, a monkey steals half of his coconuts. In retrospect, he may regret his decision and decide that he ought to have collected more food. Perhaps the next time he has to make such a choice, his valuation will be different. He has learned.

The uncertainty of the future is implied by the very existence of action. In a world where the future is known with exacting certainty, action is not possible. If I know what is coming and there is no possibility of altering it, there is no point in attempting to do so. If I *can* act to alter the course of future events, then the future was not certain after all!

The fact that earlier actions may be regretted later does not invalidate the fact that people choose what they prefer, *at the moment the choice has to be made.* Waking up with a hangover on Sunday morning, a person may regret Saturday night's party. Still, on Saturday night that person preferred partying to being at home in bed.

It is true that a "fit of passion" may make certain actions seem much more desirable than they would in a moment of calm reflection. However, the fan at a game, so incensed by an opposing fan's taunts that he "had to fight him," will still refrain if an armed cop steps between him and his antagonist. A married man, so enamored that "he couldn't help himself," about to make a pass at a woman, will still stop should his wife suddenly appear on the scene.

Intense emotional feelings are another factor that is weighed when choosing. The fact that people *do* sometimes resist a fit of passion shows that, even under these circumstances, people choose. Only, for instance, in the final stages of inebriation before complete unconsciousness occurs, as an infant, in senility, or after severe brain damage, are people truly incapable of choice. But such people are not economic actors, and economics does not attempt to describe the activity of humans under those conditions.

Even for fully conscious humans there are moments of mere reaction. There is no plan or meaning involved when you immediately pull your hand off of a hot stove, or when you duck at a loud sound overhead. Economics is not a theory of reaction, but of purposeful behavior. It is the ongoing discovery of the implications of human action.

CHAPTER 3

As Time Goes By

O N   T H E   F A C T O R   O F   T I M E   I N   H U M A N
A C T I O N

THE DAWN OF SAVING

RICH, IN HIS effort to change what is into what ought to be, may realize that his ability to acquire food and water could be increased. Perhaps, by building a few traps, he could have six roasted rats a day instead of four. And, he thinks, if he had a barrel for collecting rainwater, he could use that water for cooking, and enjoy boiled rats as an occasional change from roasted rats. He sets about constructing those items.

In order to build them, Rich will have to sacrifice something else. Since his time is not unlimited, the construction of such items has a cost: the value Rich places on what he could have been doing instead of building traps and barrels. This is true even if he just gives up time that would have been spent relaxing. Having grasped the principle of marginal utility, we can see that, whatever activity Rich puts aside to make time for building traps and barrels, it will be the activity of which the next unit had the lowest marginal utility, for him. (To reiterate, "utility" should not be taken to mean some measurable substance. "Lowest utility" is just shorthand for "what pleases Rich the least.") And he will give up units of that activity only so long as the value of additional traps and barrels is greater, to him, than what he is giving up.

Perhaps Rich is working on traps, when he could have been relaxing. Each trap takes an hour to build. When the value to Rich of the next trap he could build is less than another hour of relaxation, Rich will stop work for the day. The marginal utility of an additional trap has fallen below the marginal utility of an additional hour of leisure.

But where does the value of goods like traps and barrels come from? Rich cannot eat a trap, or (comfortably) wear a barrel. And yet it is clear that these goods do have value to Rich, because he has decided to sacrifice other things of value in order to acquire them.

The value of the goods we examined in Chapter 2—food, water, shelter, rest—springs from their ability to immediately alleviate some dissatisfaction. Rich values food because he values life, and food helps to directly satisfy his desire to stay alive. Although less than he values life itself, he may also value comfort in that life. Therefore, food is also valued because it directly satisfies the pangs of hunger. (Again, economics does not claim that Rich *should* value his life more than anything else, or that everyone does so. It does not claim even that everyone does or should value life at all. Economics is about the *consequences* of the fact that we evaluate our world.)

Upon a little reflection, we can see that the value of goods such as traps and barrels comes from their ability to produce goods that *do* directly bring satisfaction. Rich values the trap for the rats, and the barrel for the cooking water.

Carl Menger termed goods that directly relieve some dissatisfaction, such as water or food, *goods of the first order.* They can also be called *consumer goods.* Goods whose value comes from their aid in producing goods of the first order, such as traps and barrels, are called *goods of a higher order, producer goods,* or *capital goods.* Note that this distinction does not exist in the goods themselves, but in human thought and planning. If I collect barrels as objects of art, then they are, for me, consumer goods. If I own a grocery store, then food items I stock are, for me, producer goods. As the Austrian economist Ludwig Lachmann put it in *Capital and Its Structure*:

> The generic concept of capital . . . has no measurable counterpart among material objects; it reflects the entrepreneurial appraisal of such objects. Beer barrels and blast furnaces, harbour installations and hotel-room furniture are capital not by virtue of their physical properties but by virtue of their economic functions.

When Rich decided to produce higher-order goods, he began *saving.* Saving can be defined as the decision to guide actions toward satisfactions more distant in time, even though more immediate satisfactions are known to be available.

The higher-order goods that Rich accumulates through saving comprise his *capital stock.* At some point in time, we find that he has five traps and two barrels. At this point there is no way to total Rich's capital goods other than listing the items of which it consists. We cannot add up traps and barrels. The value that Rich assigns to them is subjective. We don't have any sort of yardstick, scale, or stopwatch by which we might measure this "quantity" of satisfaction. In fact, the value of these capital goods is what Rich estimates to be their value for satisfying future, uncertain needs. Even if we could stick a "satisfaction meter" on Rich and determine how intense certain satisfactions are to him, it would not solve the problem Rich faces at the moment of choice: He must estimate how much satisfaction his choice will bring to "Future Rich," whose knowledge and tastes are unknown to "Present Rich," and who will be living in a world that, for Present Rich, is filled with uncertainty.

As his effort to build traps and barrels continues, Rich may decide that having a hammer, a saw, and some nails would be useful. He sets about making them. Now Rich is working two orders of goods removed from consumption. He will value the hammer, the saw, and the nails for the aid they will provide in constructing traps and barrels, which are valued for the food and water they help produce. All goods of higher orders derive their value from the goods of the next lower order that they help create. Ultimately, any producer good is valuable only because it finally yields one or more consumer goods.

That dependence can be illustrated by considering what happens when Rich's valuation of a consumer good changes. Perhaps Rich discovers that the rats on the island are diseased, and that eating them is harmful. Rich will no longer value the rats. So long as there is no other use Rich can make of the traps, they will lose their value as well. Rich will no longer be willing to sacrifice anything to get more traps, and he will not care about the fate of the ones he has already made. (Of course, if he has some other use for the traps—perhaps as kindling—they will retain some of their value.)

An interesting question arises when we begin to look at the valuation of goods of a higher order. Let's say that, without the aid of traps, Rich can catch four rats a day. With his traps, he hopes to catch eight a day. Given the productivity advantage that trap making has over catching rats by hand, why doesn't Rich spend 100 percent of his working time making traps?

The first answer that pops to mind is that he will starve to death with that work schedule. Certainly, any saving for the future that involves cutting back current consumption below the level needed to sustain life doesn't make sense—unless one is saving solely for one's heirs! However, we can imagine that Rich might be able to get by on only two rats a day, albeit with some discomfort. Why doesn't he postpone all consumption beyond minimal sustenance in order to save?

All around us, every day, people consume far more than they need to survive, therefore saving far less than they could. Yet, we all know that saving is the road to wealth. Why don't top Wall Street traders live in tiny shacks, eat canned beans, and ride old bicycles to the train station? Why do movie stars go on mad shopping sprees and stay at fabulous vacation resorts? Shouldn't they live as paupers in order to save every penny they can?

The questions should suggest the answer. There would be something very curious about a world in which people worked hard so that they could save for future consumption— yet never engaged in that future consumption, because when that future arrived, they were saving for consumption in an even more remote future. It would be a looking-glass world, such as the Red Queen described to Alice: jam tomorrow, and jam yesterday, but never jam today. (In fact, there wouldn't have been jam yesterday, either.)

Humans can only consume in the present. It is our present dissatisfactions that call out for relief. It is in the present that we experience pleasure and pain. Saving in the interest of infinitely postponed consumption is not saving at all—it is pure loss.

Now we are faced with explaining the other side of the saving question—given that we can only consume in the present, why does anyone ever save? The answer is that, while we cannot consume in the future, we can imagine it. We can envision that in this future, we also will feel dissatisfactions and will want to alleviate them. In addition, we can imagine that a high enough degree of satisfaction on some future day might compensate us for some additional dissatisfaction today.

The key to understanding saving is to recognize that the image of future dissatisfaction is itself a source of present unease. The notion that I might find myself starving next week is disturbing. I can alleviate the feeling by saving. However, if I am in danger of starving to death *today,* eliminating my worry about starving next week will not appear as urgent to me as getting some food right now. The satisfaction in knowing that I have made provision for eating next week is minimal compared to the dissatisfaction of knowing that I'll be dead by dinnertime. Likewise, the imagining of future satisfaction is itself a source of present satisfaction. The swimmer training to win an Olympic gold medal keeps herself going by imagining how magnificent she will feel when she touches the wall first. If we could not bring a sense of these future pains and pleasures into our present deliberations, we would have no way of orienting our actions toward that future.

The extent to which an individual will save is explained by his *time preference,* meaning the degree to which he prefers a present satisfaction to the same satisfaction in the future. The possible range of time preference runs from zero to infinity, with the extremes, zero and infinity, precluding human action.

At one extreme, we have the hypothetical individual with zero time preference. For him, neither action nor consumption

ever occurs. But no acting human will sacrifice today's satisfaction for the exact same satisfaction on some future date, all
other things being equal. Imagine getting a call from a stock-
broker, as you are about to leave for a vacation on the Riviera. "Listen," he says, "do I have a deal for you! If you postpone your vacation, and instead buy stock XYZ with the
money you would have spent, in fifty years, I'll guarantee you
. . . the exact same vacation on the Riviera." Who would
accept such an offer? Unless we estimate that the future satisfaction resulting from investment will be higher than the satisfaction we would have to sacrifice today in order to invest,
no saving will occur.

At the other extreme, we can picture a person with infinite
time preference. He is so oriented to the present that no offer
of any amount of future goods, however high, would compensate him for the slightest decrease in present consumption.
He would not sacrifice even a crumb of bread in his hand for
the promise of a hundred loaves in five minutes. Human
action would be impossible for such a person, as it requires
taking the time away from consumption to think through a
plan. He would operate by instinct alone. A human newborn,
whose wails cannot be stopped by anything but the immediate presence of milk, could be said to have a nearly infinite
time preference. To the extent that is true, a newborn does
not act, but merely reacts.

With time preference we are again dealing with a subjective factor. The degree of time preference will differ from person to person, and, for the same person, will differ from one
moment to the next. A person's time preference at thirty might
be lower than the same person's time preference at eighty. At
thirty, he may be quite willing to hold off on that trip to the
Alps in order to save for a house for his new family, whereas
at eighty he is much more likely to think, "Hey, I'd better get

over there now!" However, that does not imply that there is some "function" that "determines" time preference as one ages. The opposite progression of time preference could just as well occur: At thirty, one might think of nothing but "living for the moment," while at eighty, one's entire focus is on building up the grandchildren's trust funds.

Those are some of the psychological factors influencing time preference. But time preference itself is implied by the existence of human action, quite aside from any psychological influences. If we didn't prefer, all other things being equal, the same satisfaction sooner rather than later, we would never act. Inert existence would be sufficient for us. For any given satisfaction, we wouldn't care whether it arrived tomorrow or took all of eternity to come around. As Mises said in *Human Action*:

> We must conceive that a man who does not prefer satisfaction within a nearer period of the future to that in a remoter period would never achieve consumption and enjoyment at all.

There is no economic sense in which we can say that one degree of time preference is better than another. Therefore, from an economic point of view, there is no "correct" level of saving. Some people may want to "go for the gusto," whereas others save with the idea of starting a perpetually endowed foundation. Economics cannot say that one of them is right and the other wrong. It can, however, clarify the conditions under which an individual will choose to save, and point out some consequences of those circumstances.

We are now in a position to examine Rich's decision to save with more precision. Let's say that Rich must sacrifice one rat a day of present consumption for one week to gain the time to build one trap. In addition, we'll suppose that he expects the trap to last for one week, during which time he will catch 14 more rats than without the trap. Roughly speaking, we can say that he must sacrifice seven rats now to gain fourteen a week from now. His rate of return on this investment is 100 percent per week.

If Rich chooses to go ahead and produce the traps, we can say that he values one rat available now *less* than two available a week from now. A 100-percent weekly rate of return was sufficient to persuade him to exchange present for future consumption. If he does not make the traps, we know that he values one present rat *more* than two future rats. A 100-percent rate of return was not sufficient to persuade him to trade present for future rats. We will return to this topic in Chapter 7 and Chapter 8, when we examine the rate of interest in a market economy.

It is important to note that Rich's valuation depends on his circumstances. If he were to suddenly find a crate of canned sardines and crackers left behind by the TV crew, his decision might be altered significantly. Recall that, per the law of marginal utility, each succeeding unit of a good is considered less valuable to an individual than the previous unit. I might pay fifty dollars to buy one cat, but by the time I had 300 I'd be paying to get rid of them.

Therefore, well stocked with food for present consumption, Rich would be much more likely to forego catching a rat today in order to build capital goods that promise a greater supply of food in the future. The additional rat today would have less value to him than it had before he found the crate, since the sardines and crackers satisfy the same physical need as the rat—and probably taste better, too.

That must not be taken to indicate some universal rule such as "the rich will save more than the poor." There are no constant laws that determine what valuation a particular person will place on future satisfactions as opposed to present ones. We have all heard stories of some little old lady who has worked as a secretary her whole life, for a moderate wage, living in modest circumstances. Upon her death, her friends are shocked to discover that she had amassed a fortune in stocks and bonds. Equally familiar are the stories of the profligate rich, who squander a fortune in riotous living. We should also note that the law of marginal utility applies to savings as well as to consumption. Each additional dollar saved will have less value, to the saver, than the previous dollar did. You can easily relate that to your own circumstances. If you have $50 dollars in the bank, the chance to put away another $50 will seem much more important to you than if you have $50 million in the bank.

Another item of note is that, even in this extremely simple economy, Rich's capital goods have a structure. We imagined that he made a hammer, nails, and a saw. The hammer and nails have a noteworthy relationship—they are *complementary goods*. Without the hammer, there is nothing with which to drive the nails, and without the nails, there is nothing for the hammer to drive. Every day we deal with goods that are useless without other, complementary goods: a portable radio and batteries, an amplifier and some speakers, a lamp and a light bulb. In every one of these cases, such goods lose some or all of their value without the complementary good available. If some inventor develops a way to use shower mold as a cheap, plentiful source of lighting, and manufacturers cease to produce light bulbs, existing electric lights will have value only as nostalgia pieces.

That could be termed the horizontal structure of capital. We have already introduced the vertical structure: capital can be arranged into goods of the second order, which are used to produce consumer goods, and goods of the third order, which are used to produce goods of the second order, and so on. Rich's economy has not, so far, passed beyond producing goods of the third order, but it is easy to see how our principle extends through as many orders of goods as people employ.

The value of a capital good is related to its position in the capital structure. A good of a higher order will lose its value if all goods of lower orders that it can be used to produce lose their value. If Rich no longer had a use for traps or barrels, and he could not think of anything else to build with a hammer and nails, then the hammer and nails would also lose their value to him. As we noted above, ultimately, all capital goods only have value due to their finally yielding some consumer good.

The importance of capital structure increases tremendously as we begin to examine more complex economies. Capital structure will be crucial to our examination of socialism. But it is here, in the most primitive of economies, that we can see such basic economic concepts most clearly—which is why, as I mentioned, that we bother looking at such an economy at all. But to proceed further, we must complicate our picture— first, by adding more people to Rich's isolated world.

PART II

THE MARKET PROCESS

CHAPTER 4

Let's Stay Together

ON DIRECT EXCHANGE AND THE
SOCIAL ORDER

THE LAW OF ASSOCIATION

RICH HAS WORKED out the details of his solitary economy and has a somewhat comfortable existence. Then, one day he is walking along the beach, and who should he see approaching him but . . . Helena Bonham-Carter! (stranded, perhaps, during the filming of the latest Merchant-Ivory production)!

His solitude broken, what does Rich decide to do? More generally, what factors would lead man to choose between an isolated existence and life in society?

One possibility is that Rich might react like a bear does when another bear enters its territory. He could, through the threat of or actual use of force, attempt to drive the intruder away. Now, he might refrain from doing so due to moral constraints or benevolent feelings. But there is another reason for him not to drive Helena off—as long as there are sufficient unused resources on the island, it will materially benefit both of them to cooperate rather than fight. They can initiate the vastly enriching processes of the division of labor and voluntary exchange.

Adam Smith pointed out the enormous increases in material production that came about through the division of labor. The example with which Smith opens *The Wealth of Nations* is pin manufacturing. A lone, unskilled workman could "scarce, perhaps, with his utmost industry, make one pin in a day." But even 225 years ago, when Smith was writing, a small pin shop, dividing the manufacture into eighteen distinct tasks, allowed a ten-man shop to produce 48,000 pins in a day, or 4,800 per man.

The division of labor produces greater material output for three reasons. The first is that people live in parts of the world that differ from each other in many respects. Someone living in Florida is in much better circumstances to grow oranges than I am in New England. On the other hand, I'm in a better position to produce maple syrup.

The second benefit of the division of labor is that not everyone comes to the table with the same capabilities. A book on economics is not the place to attempt to resolve the nature/nurture debate, so we will simply say that, for whatever reasons, people enter the labor market with different aptitudes. I'm five feet nine inches tall and have trouble jumping over the Sunday *New York Times*, so I'm hardly suitable, even with "the right training," to fill in for Kobe Bryant should he need some time off from playing basketball.

Training is, however, the third benefit. The division of labor allows people to focus their efforts on building up certain skills and to ignore a vast array of other skills that are unnecessary to their jobs. The people who design personal computers usually have little knowledge of the aspects of the system for which they are not responsible. At the lowest levels of the system, chip designers employ their knowledge of quantum physics to achieve higher-speed components. Several levels above that, operating system programmers use their knowledge of the logical structure of the machine to create efficient code for writing disk files and displaying graphics. Another several levels of abstraction up, we find user-interface designers who specialize in creating a "look-and-feel" for a program that allows ease of learning and of use. None of these workers could accomplish their tasks if they also had to concern themselves with all of the other levels of the system. And lest you think that it is only an extremely complex device like a PC for which this is true, I recommend Leonard Read's famous essay, "I, Pencil," where he demonstrates that no individual in the world is capable of creating something as simple as a pencil on his own.

Some of the critics of modern industrial society bemoan just that specialization. People, they complain, become narrow-minded, mere cogs in a machine, and find their work boring and repetitive under a system of ever increasing division of labor. Economics cannot answer such complaints. As I've pointed out, it doesn't attempt to recommend one set of values over another. It can't say that those who chose a more interesting and varied life over greater material prosperity have chosen badly. However, economics *can* inform anyone who wishes to impose such a choice on all of society that without the division of labor the Earth could support only a tiny fraction of its current population. Perhaps those who survive the transition period will find their world more satisfactory than ours, but the billions who die during the transition might be forgiven for dissenting.

Smith recognized these various advantages of the division of labor, but left unsolved an interesting problem, which arose in discussions of international trade. The solution has implications far beyond that field, however, and it is worth our time to examine the problem.

Smith pointed out that it made no sense, for example, for Scotland to try to manufacture wine, although through the use of greenhouses it undoubtedly could do so. If Scotland produces wool and Spain makes wine, and the citizens of the two countries trade for the goods not available from domestic industry, both countries' inhabitants will be better off. But what of the case where one country, perhaps due to geographical disadvantage and an uneducated populace, is worse at producing everything than some other country is? Shouldn't the more backward nation erect trade barriers, allowing domestic industry to develop? How can it possibly offer the more advanced nation anything in trade?

The answer to this problem is *Ricardo's law of comparative advantage*, named after English economist David Ricardo. Although the initial application of the law was to trade, it is a universal law applying to all human cooperation. Because of the broad applicability of the law, Mises felt it was better named the *law of association.* In fact, it is easiest to understand this law at a personal level, after which its implications for trade become clear.

Let's use as an example a great athlete: Michael Jordan. Jordan's physical skills are truly extraordinary. There is little doubt that should he choose to apply them to, for instance, house painting, that he could be one of the best house painters in the world.

Yet it's doubtful that Jordan paints his own house. Although he could probably, with a little practice, do so far better than anyone he can hire, he still finds someone else to paint it for him. How can we explain that fact?

The law of comparative advantage is the answer. Although Jordan is better than his painter at both basketball and house painting, Jordan has a comparative advantage in basketball, while his painter has a comparative advantage in house painting. It's easiest to comprehend that arithmetically, by using wage rates as a basis for the comparison.

Let's say that Jordan can hire a house painter for $20 per hour. With a little practice, Jordan could be twice as efficient a painter as the man he has hired. We will imagine that he could market his own house-painting services for $40 per hour.

However, by playing basketball, we will suppose that Jordan can earn $10,000 per hour. Meanwhile, Joe, his painter, who can hardly sink a free throw, couldn't make more than $1 an hour playing basketball. (Perhaps some people will find his play amusing!) Jordan has a 2-to-1 advantage as a house painter, but a 10,000-to-1 advantage as a hoop star.

Perhaps Jordan plans on working twenty hours in a particular week. If he divides his time equally between painting his own house and playing basketball, his total output for the week can be valued at:

> 10 hours painting x $40 per hour = $400
> 10 hours basketball x $10,000 per hour = $100,000
> Total output: $100,400

If Joe divides his time the same way we could value his production as follows:

> 10 hours painting x $20 per hour = $200
> 10 hours basketball x $1 per hour = $10
> Total output: $210

Between them, Michael and Joe have produced $100,610 worth of output. Now let's examine the situation if, as we expect, Jordan hires Joe. Jordan's production can now be valued at:

> 20 hours basketball x $10,000 per hour = $200,000
> Total output: $200,000

And Joe's at:

> 20 hours painting x $20 per hour = $400
> Total output: $400

Their total output has risen to $200,400. But, more importantly for an understanding of the law of association, both of them are better off, at least in dollar terms. The painter, who was worse at both jobs, was still able to nearly double the value of his output by concentrating on painting, in which he had a comparative advantage, then exchanging with Jordan. The law of association demonstrates that, even putting aside moral considerations, it is to everyone's material advantage to cooperate through the division of labor and voluntary exchange. It is the basis of the extended social order.

The application of this law to international trade is a straightforward extension of our analysis above. Even if a country is worse at producing *everything* than is some other country, it can still net a material gain by specializing in the areas where it has a comparative advantage and trading for other goods. It is only in the obviously unrealistic scenario where everyone is exactly the "same amount" better or worse than everyone else at every job that the law of association would find no application.

This law only shows that a material gain is available through specialization. It doesn't take into account any personal preferences other than material gain. It could well be the case that Jordan simply *loves* house painting, and would not for the world consider hiring someone else to paint for him, harking back to our discussion in Chapter 1 of the person who decides to do his own roofing. If people believe they are saving money doing their own home repairs, they are often mistaken. However, if they love doing the work, perhaps finding it a nice break from their regular job, they may be getting a psychic profit that outweighs their monetary loss.

DIRECT EXCHANGE

*L*ET'S RETURN TO the beach, and the fateful meeting of Rich and Helena. Each of them realizes that his or her prospects for survival will be enhanced if they can develop a system of cooperative effort. Rather than producing for a general demand, Rich and Helena will find it best to agree in advance on a particular division of labor. Yet the basic principles of exchange will still apply to them. Following Carl Menger's directive to "reduce the complex phenomena of human economic activity to the simplest elements," we will first attempt to comprehend exchange in a simple setting, such as our little island economy.

Given that they have decided *to* cooperate, our two castaways next must decide *how* to cooperate. They come to an agreement that Rich, the more dexterous of the two, will make traps, while Helena, the more cunning, will do the hunting. Still, what is the best amount of each activity for them to perform? How can each of them be sure that he or she is getting a fair deal from the other?

Simply relying on goodwill does not work. The history of the Soviet Union illustrates the problems inherent in separating the performance of labor from the self-interest of the laborer. But even if the Soviet Union had succeeded in creating the New Socialist Man, only interested in the well-being of his fellows, there would have remained an insurmountable obstacle to efficient production. How can these altruistic fellows know exactly what should be produced, in what quantities, and employing what resources? I might spend my time creating finger paintings, in the belief that these will produce tremendous happiness for those around me. But if no one else likes them, I've not only wasted my time, I've also wasted the resources—paper, pigment, and so on—that went into the paintings. In the interest of pleasing those around me, I've actually caused them to suffer a loss in satisfaction, even compared to a situation in which I had merely loafed around. The same holds true even if folks love my paintings but are deeply unhappy that I've given up computer programming to indulge my artistic ambitions. In the balance, and given available resources, people want my programs more than they want my art. Absent a market price system, there is no way for consumers to inform producers of their relative values.

The route past that difficulty is interpersonal exchange. To ensure that they are actually benefiting each other, Rich and Helena must recognize that the other has a right to the goods he or she has acquired through his or her own efforts. As a corollary to that recognition, the exchanges they make must be voluntary. For every so many rats that Helena captures and gives to him, Rich *agrees* to trade a certain number of traps. If Helena threatens Rich with a club to get rats, we can bet the exchange is benefiting, in their own view, only one of them.

The law of diminishing marginal utility explains the exchange ratio that they will work out. Rich will trade traps for rats until the cost, as subjectively perceived by him, of producing one more trap exceeds the benefit, again as he subjectively perceives it, of the number of rats Helena will give him for that next trap. On the other side of the trade, Helena will trade rats until the subjective cost of the next rat she must give up exceeds the benefit she expects from having one more trap. The next trap that Rich considers trading and the next rat that Helena considers trading are the marginal units. It is the perceived benefits and costs of those units that determine the exchange ratio.

Let's imagine what is likely to happen in our island's rat and trap market. We begin with no rats caught and no traps made. At that point, the value to Rich of the first rat with which Helena can provide him is relatively high—after all, he may starve to death without it. Similarly, the value to Helena of the first trap is large. The first trap will increase her catch tremendously, as she can use that one on the most popular rat trail on the island.

We'll postulate that Rich is willing to give up his first trap for as few as three rats, while Helena is willing to trade as many as five rats to acquire that trap. We'll assume that they meet in the middle, and trade one trap for four rats.

The value to our traders of each succeeding unit acquired will be lower than that of the first one. As Rich's supply of rats increases, he will use each new rat in a way that is less important to him than the previous rat. Once he has had his fill for the day, he may begin to smoke the critters to preserve them for later. But he will not consider it as important that he have smoked rats as he considers it to have the rats that will keep him from starvation. And on the other side of the trade, Helena won't consider the second trap as valuable as the first—after all, she can only deploy it on the second most-frequented trail.

Each trap thereafter will be put to a use that she considers less important than the previous trap.

Similarly, each additional item given up by one of our traders will be *more* valuable to him or her than the previous unit surrendered. That is because they will first give up what are the least important uses, in their own valuation. It is not the traps or rats that are different when we consider subsequent trades: it is the fact that acting humans will first give up the least valued use of the good in question, then the next least valued, and so on. Each additional trap Rich builds requires him to sacrifice additional leisure time. With each sacrifice, his remaining amount of leisure is smaller. The initial units he gives up were nice to have, but soon he is cutting into rest he needs to stay healthy.

Therefore, after the first trade has been made and Rich has four rats, he is no longer as desperate for them. Similarly, having one trap, the next trap Helena could acquire will be less valuable to her. Let's imagine our traders' value scales for trading rats and traps are these:

Rich	**Helena**
1st trap < 3 rats	5 rats < 1st trap
2nd trap < 4 rats	4 rats < 2nd trap
3rd trap < 5 rats	3 rats < 3rd trap

We're assuming that Rich will require at least four rats for giving up a second trap (up from three for the first one), while Helena will give up at most four rats (down from five). Even though the value of the next units they can acquire has gone down for both Rich and Helena, they still have a trade from which each of them can profit. They will make the second trade, exchanging four more rats for a trap.

However, our traders' valuations do not support a third exchange. Helena is only willing to trade three rats for a third trap, while Rich will not trade the third trap unless he gets at least five more rats. Trading will cease in this market. It has reached what we will call the *plain state of rest* (examined further in Chapter 6).

It is important to note that the fact that an exchange took place does not mean that the values of the goods traded were equivalent to the two participants. It is only the fact that they valued the goods in question differently that caused them to trade at all. Helena valued the two traps more than she valued eight rats, while Rich valued eight rats more than he valued two traps.

Carl Menger pointed out that to regard an exchange as occurring at a point of equal valuation leads to absurdities. If two people exchange when they consider the value of what they are getting to be equal to the value of what they are giving up, there is no reason that they shouldn't simply reverse the trade a moment later. If you sell your house for $200,000, then you valued $200,000 more highly than you did your house. Conversely, the buyer valued your house more highly than he did $200,000. Otherwise (ignoring transaction costs), there is no reason that, as soon as the exchange is made, you wouldn't immediately take the house back and give up the $200,000. In fact, if the exchange took place at a point of equal valuation, there is no reason you and the other party shouldn't swap the house back and forth any number of times.

However, if we contemplate exchange from the point of view of human action, we see that people do not exchange simply to have the pleasure of contemplating goods changing hands. Exchange does not arise from a "propensity to trade." In order for an exchange to take place, both parties must feel that they will be better off after the exchange. That is the prerequisite for all action—the actor must feel that the action will improve his state of satisfaction when compared to not acting. He is attempting to move from what is to what ought to be.

The above sheds light on a phrase that is in common use when discussing exchange. Who hasn't heard someone say, after purchasing some item, that the price he paid for it was a "rip-off"? Let's set aside the case where the speaker was deceived as to the quality or nature of the good—that is fraud, and really is a "rip-off." We'll take the good in question to be something of known and consistent quality—say, bottled, brand name beer. At work Monday morning, your friend says, "We went to a ball game over the weekend. Paid five dollars for a beer—what a rip-off!"

What does he mean? As long he wasn't tricked or forced into buying the beer, and he really did go through with the purchase, he valued the beer more highly than the five dollars. Otherwise, why would he have gone ahead and bought it? If his five dollars meant more to him than the beer, all he had to do was put it back in his pocket and walk away. Given that your friend voluntarily gave up something he valued less than the beer, the vendor might make the exact same complaint— he was ripped-off as well! What your friend really means is, "I wish the beer had been cheaper." However, we all wish to give up less in order to gain more, in other words, to increase our profit. That is the universal basis of all human action. As we try to improve our own condition, we have no reason to expect that others, such as the vendor, are not doing the same.

THERE'S SOMETHING LACKING

As of yet, our human actors have no way to employ economic calculation in our little economy. Rich and Helena can compare specific quantities of specific goods and decide which bundle of goods they find more valuable. They can't, however, calculate how much they profited or lost in any exchange, either before or after the fact. We can say that Rich preferred eight rats to two traps, but there is no way to answer the question "How much did he prefer it?" The preference is something he feels. There is no measuring rod we can dip into his psyche to determine the "size" of that feeling. Certainly, he may perceive some satisfactions as more desirable than others. But, as we have pointed out, a phrase such as "I like that trap twice as much as the other" is simply a figure of speech. If someone tries to take it literally, we ask Rothbard's question: "Twice as much of what?"

Trying to calculate in terms of rats and traps will not work either. There is no arithmetical meaning to expressions such as "eight rats minus two traps," or "one trap plus three rats."

The attempt to use labor as the common unit of value, as did Marx and the British classical economists, doesn't succeed. The cost of Rich's labor is his subjective evaluation of what he had to give up in order to perform the work in question. The value to Helena of Rich's labor is her subjective valuation of the fruits of his efforts. To attempt to calculate profit and loss in terms of the ticking of a clock or the expenditure of energy is to miss entirely the economic aspect of what is occurring. Rich might expend just as much time and effort grinding existing traps into sawdust as building new traps, but, in our scenario, Helena certainly will not pay him to grind up traps! The fact that creating traps is valuable and destroying them isn't depends entirely on the valuation of those involved in exchanging them, and can't be determined by physical measurement. In fact, we can easily imagine a situation where the exact same physical activities have their valuations reversed. If our castaways found themselves in a situation where the rats had been hunted to extinction, but the island was littered with useless traps, building traps would have no value, while destroying them, in order to tidy up, *would* have value.

The lack of economic calculation does not hamper our little economy significantly. Only two people are trading all goods. Since a trader is the creator of his own value scale, he only has to get a sense of his partner's values in order to trade sensibly. But as an economy grows larger the absence of calculation will become a roadblock.

TWO'S COMPANY, FOUR'S A MINI-MARKET

Now, we must fast-forward the history of our island—let's christen it "Richland"—economy. We will move forward several generations. (We can imagine that Rich and Helena found yet another way to cooperate for their mutual benefit.) For some strange reason, the island has remained isolated from the global economy. But the population has grown, a village has been built, fields tilled, shops opened, and professions begun. A flourishing trade exists among the inhabitants.

The basics of exchange have not altered from our two-person economy. The addition of other people who might want to exchange complicates our picture, but does not alter it in any basic respect. It will behoove us to take a little time and study the multiperson situation, in order to be prepared for the further complications to come.

We'll imagine that goats were domesticated on the island, and that the cultivation of corn is now practiced. We have two goat herders, Kyle and Stephen, and two corn farmers, Emma and Rachel. For people living in a modern economy, there is an inherent difficulty in studying such a situation—we are not used to dealing with exchanges where goats and corn are traded directly for each other. Since we haven't yet brought money into the picture, we must think of the price of goats as their price in terms of corn, and the price of corn as its price in terms of goats. This type of exchange is called barter, or *direct exchange*. It takes some getting used to, but it is worth the effort in order to gain a better comprehension of how market prices are established.

Let us imagine that Rachel will pay up to four bushels of corn for her first goat, up to three for her second, and as many as two for her third. Emma will pay up to three bushels for her first goat, up to two for her second, and no more than one for her third.

On the other side of the market, Kyle will accept as few as two bushels of corn for his first goat, as few as three for his second, and as few as four for his third. Stephen will accept as few as three bushels of corn for his first goat, as few as four for his second, and as few as five for his third. So, we have:

Kyle	Rachel
1st goat < 2 bushels	4 bushels < 1st goat
2nd goat < 3 bushels	3 bushels < 2nd goat
3rd goat < 4 bushels	2 bushels < 3rd goat

Stephen	Emma
1st goat < 3 bushels	3 bushels < 1st goat
2nd goat < 4 bushels	2 bushels < 2nd goat
3rd goat < 5 bushels	1 bushel < 3rd goat

We can picture the market progressing as follows: First, Rachel trades three bushels of corn for Kyle's first goat offered—clearly, as Rachel prefers to surrender up to four bushels for that goat, and Kyle will accept as few as two, the trade is mutually beneficial. In this "round" of trading, another trade also takes place: Emma trades three bushels of corn for Stephen's first goat offered.

Now, the possibility of another round of trading is considered. Emma will pay at most two more bushels for another goat. But neither Kyle nor Stephen is prepared to supply a goat at that price—Kyle demands at least three bushels for the next goat, while Stephen demands four.

Similarly, Stephen will supply another goat for a minimum of four bushels, but no one in the market is willing to bid four bushels for that second goat—Rachel will bid at most three, while Emma will bid at most two.

Therefore, Emma and Stephen drop out of the market. But Rachel and Kyle have one more mutually profitable trade to make—the trade where Kyle gives up his second goat for three more bushels of corn, and Rachel gives up three more bushels for a second goat.

In this scenario, Kyle's goat-demand for corn is greater than Stephen's—perhaps Stephen really loves goat meat, and so is more reluctant to give up goats. Kyle sells a second goat for only three bushels of corn, while Stephen would have sold a second goat only if he could have gotten at least four bushels. Similarly, Rachel's demand for goats is greater than Emma's— she pays three bushels of corn for her second goat, while Emma would only pay two bushels.

In any market, it is the buyers such as Kyle and Rachel— called the *most capable buyers*—who will acquire more of the goods in question. Because, for whatever reason, those buyers are willing to pay more, they will use this willingness to outbid the less capable buyers. Similarly, the *most capable sellers*, those who are the most anxious to move the goods they are selling, will move more of their stock than the less capable sellers.

It is the very nature of human action, the desire to improve our situation as much as possible, that propels the market process. Traders will exchange as long as they feel their trades are improving their situation, and no longer.

The principles of human action only guarantee that people will *attempt* to find all profitable exchanges. There may be trades available where the cost of finding the trading partner is simply too high, and would turn what otherwise might have been a profitable trade into a losing trade. There are other cases where potential traders simply fail to discover one another. Just over the next hill, there might be a corn farmer who would pay four bushels for a goat, if only he knew that goats were available. The market process does not guarantee that all traders who might be able to make profitable exchanges will always discover one another. But the human drive to better our circumstances implies that people will always be on the lookout for such opportunities. The search for potential profit opportunities that are not being taken advantage of is the role of the *entrepreneur*, which we will discuss at length in Chapter 7.

So the goat-corn market will establish a price of three bushels of corn per goat. At that price, Emma's demand is for one goat, and Rachel's is for two. From the perspective of the corn buyers, the market price is one-third goat per bushel. At that price, Kyle demands six bushels and Stephen demands three bushels. The market process will tend to establish a price that *clears the market*: all sellers willing to sell at the market price will be able to do so, and all buyers willing to buy at that price will also be able to do so. At the market price, Stephen and Kyle between them attempt to sell three goats, while Emma and Rachel, between them, attempt to buy three goats. And Emma and Rachel will attempt to sell nine bushels of corn, while Stephen and Kyle will attempt to buy nine bushels.

If these dynamics of supply and demand change, the market process will adjust the price to the new realities. Let's say that Stephen and Kyle get sick of eating corn. What's more, a farmer down the road has started growing squash, which they can eat instead. Their demand for corn will drop, and they will not be willing to offer as much goat per bushel as before—they find it better to spend some of their goats on squash. If Emma and Rachel still want goats, they will have to bid more for them. A new market price will emerge—let's say, four bushels per goat—and the market will clear at that new price. If Emma's and Rachel's value scales have not changed, then Rachel will buy one goat for four bushels, and Emma will not buy any. No one had to decree a higher price for goats in order to bring one about.

It is this seemingly magical property of markets that led Adam Smith to speak of the "invisible hand" guiding market participants. Without any central authority directing them, their own plans and desires tend to create a situation in which all those exchanges take place that both parties believe will benefit them. (As we have mentioned, human action, directed toward an uncertain future, always contains the possibility of error. After the fact, any trader might decide that he or she had made a mistake.)

Because market exchange is voluntary, it allows every participant to express the urgency with which he demands particular goods. It allows humans to cope with the scarcity of means through cooperation, rather than through violence and plunder.

Scarcity is a necessary condition of economic goods. Air is not scarce, and, therefore, it is free, and outside the scope of economics. We must not take "scarce" in an absolute sense, but instead consider scarcity relative to demand. There are few videotapes of me rapping—only one that I'm aware of—but they are not scarce in the economic sense, as the supply of one is infinitely greater than the demand of zero. No price will be paid for such a tape, or at least no price greater than the going rate for used tapes sold for retaping.

In the above scenario, Stephen would have been happy to buy more bushels of corn, if the price were lower. If corn were so abundant that it littered the ground everywhere in Richland, Stephen might use far more than the three bushels he actually purchased. But, given that corn is scarce, the market process sends it to whoever demands it most urgently. Kyle, for whatever reason—perhaps he likes corn more than Stephen does, or he has a plan for a new food product made from corn, which he feels will be a big hit—is willing to pay more for corn than is Stephen. Because of this, he acquires six bushels while Stephen only acquires three.

The demand we are speaking of is *effective demand*. In order to take part in voluntary exchange, we must offer others something that they value—we have to bring something to the table. Demand at the point of a knife and demand that is simply a wish for some good are altogether different from demand in the market.

Although we will take up the topic of intervention in the market process in Part 3 it will be instructive now to see if the Richland town council could improve upon the market outcome. Let's say that the goat lobby persuades the council that the corn price of goats is too low and is hampering the goat industry. The council passes a law setting the price of goats at four bushels of corn. The goat lobby is thrilled—now their profits will soar! Stephen, who was only willing to sell one goat at the previous price of three bushels, now is willing to sell two for four bushels. Kyle, who was only willing to sell two goats at the previous price, now is willing to sell three.

But if we consider Emma's and Rachel's demand for goats, we see that the goat herders will be sorely disappointed, because at the new, higher price, they will only want one goat! Rachel, who in an unhampered market would have bought two goats, only values the first goat more than four bushels of corn. Emma, who would have bought one goat in the unhampered market, now will not buy any. Kyle and Stephen bring five goats to market, planning on "cleaning up," but instead go back home with four. There is now a glut of goats and a shortage of corn: gluts and shortages are the result of price-fixing.

In the regulated market, we can't even be sure whether Stephen or Kyle will get the corn. Although Kyle demands corn more urgently than does Stephen, the new regulation prevents him from outbidding Stephen. What's more, in the unhampered market there would be three exchanges, each of which both sides consider to be beneficial. In the regulated market only one exchange will take place. Although there is no way to calculate how much worse off the market participants are in our regulated market than they would have been in the unhampered market, we can use historical understanding to comprehend that they *are* worse off.

WINNERS, LOSERS, AND THE MARKET PROCESS

*P*EOPLE OFTEN USE words from the arenas of games and war to describe the market. We hear that international competition will result in some nations being "winners" and others "losers." We read a headline that some company has "crushed" its competition, or that the U.S. is at "economic war" with Japan or OPEC.

Employed as loose metaphors, such terms are useful. But the analogy does not extend very far. The key difference between a game and the market process is that, in the market, all participants gain from voluntary exchange. Kyle, Stephen, Rachel, and Emma were *all* better off after completing their trades than they had been beforehand.

Imagine that you and I open competing software companies. Over time, it becomes apparent that consumers prefer your product. I close my business down, and you wind up hiring me as your lead programmer. Now, in one sense, I lost and you won. But in a much more important sense, everyone won. I now have a role in fulfilling the needs of the consumers to which I am better suited than previously, you have a new lead programmer, and the consumers have a better software company. This stands in sharp contrast to sports, where the winner gets a "1" in the standings, the loser a "0," and everyone goes home. It is also very different from war, where the winners may do what they want with the losers, including annihilate them.

To take the metaphors of games and war too literally in describing the market process is a misapprehension of its nature. Market competition is different than sports and war in crucial ways. It doesn't exist to pick "winners" and "losers": it exists to allow everyone to find a place in the scheme of production in which they can best satisfy the wishes of consumers.

It is just as mistaken to view international markets as pitting one nation against another as it is to view the domestic market as pitting employees against employers, or producers against consumers. In a market economy, whether it is domestic or international in scope, everyone's standard of living can rise at once. America has not lost if Japan or China should become wealthier than the U.S. An increase in the standard of living anywhere benefits all people who are economically integrated with the area in question.

The discovery of the law of association was a great achievement of the classical economists. It points the way toward social harmony, showing that the powerful and the weak have a better way to relate to each other than through exploitation. The nature of the market as a network of voluntary exchanges means that each participant must feel he is benefiting from a trade, or he would not enter into it.

With the basics of multiperson exchange under our belts, we can move on to economic calculation, and the tool that made it possible—money.

CHAPTER 5

Money Changes Everything

ON INDIRECT EXCHANGE AND
ECONOMIC CALCULATION

INDIRECT EXCHANGE

ALTHOUGH THE RICHLAND economy includes markets with several buyers and several sellers of the same good, it is hampered in two important ways. As we saw in the previous chapter, anyone who wants goats and grows corn must find someone who wants corn and has goats. But it will not always be easy to find someone who has the good you want and wants the good you have. A great deal of time will be spent looking for someone with whom to trade. And during that time you need to keep feeding the goat, or keep the corn from spoiling.

Second, although there are now a couple of hundred Richlanders, and their economy is growing more complex, they still have no means of economic calculation. A tradesman, let's call him Marco, who is making fishing equipment, cannot use a set of books to see whether his business is profitable or not. All his books could record would be various quantities of incommensurable goods. He might have, on the expense side of his ledger, 1000 fishhooks, 4 nets, and 20 fishing poles. On the income side, he might have 4 hammers, 20 pounds of iron,

2 chairs, and 10 cords of wood. He has no way of determining whether the net of these transactions yielded a profit. Is he doing well enough that his operation will sustain itself and keep him supplied, not only with a livelihood, but also with the capital goods he needs to continue in business? What's more, he can't say whether there was some other combination of capital goods he should have purchased instead. Is he better or worse off than if he had eight hammers, ten pounds of iron, three chairs, and fourteen cords of wood? In order to engage in accounting, as we know it, Marco needs a common unit in which to enter these items in his books. In the Richland barter economy, the best he can do is to use his intuition as to whether he's "doing OK" or not.

But humans are ingenious in their attempts to improve their condition. In a barter market, some perceptive trader will notice that certain goods are more marketable than others. Let's imagine that Richland has plenty of good grazing areas for goats and that most residents keep a small herd. Marco has fishhooks and wants corn. While he cannot find a corn farmer who wants his fishhooks, he is able to locate a fisherman who will trade him goats for fishhooks. Now, goats in tow, he is able to find a corn farmer who is happy to acquire a few extra goats. Marco has been able to exploit a profitable opportunity that was not open to him through direct exchange. Employing *indirect exchange*, he acquired a good more marketable than the one he originally had to sell, and used that good to acquire the good he really wanted.

In a society unfamiliar with this practice, we can expect that it will be adopted only gradually. At first, only the cleverest traders will employ it. But others will notice their success and begin to employ the same technique. Over time the most marketable commodity comes to be used as a *medium of exchange* and will be accepted as payment in almost all transactions. This is the origin of money, the missing ingredient that we mentioned in the previous chapter.

Historically, a great variety of goods has been used as a medium of exchange: cows, salt, cowry shells, large stones, exotic feathers, cocoa beans, tobacco, iron, copper, silver, gold, and more. Economist Milton Friedman notes that cigarettes were used as money in post-World War II Europe.

However, not every good is equally suitable as money. There are certain characteristics that favor the use of a good for indirect exchange:

The good is widely marketable.

This is the chief prerequisite for a good to become money. There is no point in trading a good you want to sell for one less marketable, unless you have a specific use for the less-marketable good. The rest of these factors are important in that they contribute to a good being widely marketable.

The good transports easily.

If someone wants to trade using a commodity, it helps to be able to get the commodity to the trading site. Early instances of indirect exchange often employed livestock, especially cattle. That was money that not only talked but walked as well. Land is a poor medium of exchange because you can't ever bring it anywhere.

The good is relatively scarce.

This criterion is closely tied to the one above. If the good used as money is plentiful, you'll tend to need a lot of it to make your purchases, making it hard to move around. For instance, if we used topsoil as money, we would all need a dump truck to go grocery shopping.

The good is relatively imperishable.

You don't want your money "going bad" a couple of hours or days after you get it. The longer you can hold your money, the more opportunity you have to wait for a good deal to come around. This is why items like milk, eggs, meat, and so on are not suitable as money. Livestock can, of course, die, but you can check when you're trading to ensure that you're not being given money that's on its last legs. The precious metals and gems clearly stand out in this regard.

The good is easy to store.

Not only should your money last, you don't want to have to go through a lot of rigmarole to get it to last. A chemical compound that is only stable below -300 degrees Fahrenheit will not come to be used as money. Carl Menger mentions that cattle were a popular medium of exchange among people in societies that were primarily agricultural and had plenty of open land nearby. The rise of cities made cattle much less useful as money. Most co-ops have strict rules against keeping livestock in an apartment, and the practice makes it very hard to keep the shag carpet clean. The precious metals and gems are again winners here.

The good is easily divisible.

Not every exchange ratio will result in whole numbers of each good being exchanged. If your money is easily divisible, you can make change. Livestock clearly falls short in this regard, as once you divide it up, it's not going to walk anywhere for you, and it becomes much more perishable. Gems are weak here also, given the difficulty in dividing them without destroying much of their value.

Each unit of the good is very similar to every other unit.

You don't want to keep fussing around checking out the quality of your money and adjusting the exchange ratio based on this quality. For one thing, someone else might judge this quality differently than you do. Diamonds, while in many ways suitable as money, are problematic in this regard—it takes an expert to judge the value of any particular diamond. The divisibility problem with diamonds is related to this. You can't get the price of a whole diamond by adding up the prices of its pieces once it is cut.

The only goods that stand out in all of the above criteria are the precious metals, and most societies eventually came to use silver and/or gold as money. As international trade increased, gold gradually displaced silver in most places. (The amount of gold that needs to be shipped for any particular payment is only a small fraction of the amount of silver needed for the same payment.) This process finally led to the international gold standard of the nineteenth century.

There is nothing mystical about the choice of gold as money. It is merely the commodity that best fit the above criteria. Another commodity, such as platinum, could easily prove superior at some point in the future.

The value of a good used as money originates from its value as a good employed in direct exchange. However, in the process of becoming money, the good gains additional value as a medium of exchange. Still, the value of money is determined in the same way as that of any other good—by the subjective evaluations of those trading it. We could substitute "ounces of gold" for "goats" in our analysis in the previous chapter, and it would proceed in the same fashion. We would find that Kyle would pay two ounces of gold for six bushels of corn and so forth. We would say that the gold price of corn is one-third of an ounce per bushel.

All of the above discussion of gold and other commodities may seem puzzling, as today we employ pieces of paper as money. The value of this paper clearly does not arise from its value as pieces of paper. The government has decreed that it is money. The fact that the government can demand that taxes be paid in "its" money helps to give its decree force. Such a currency is called *fiat money*. The original value of fiat money comes from an earlier time when it *was* a commodity money (e.g., the U.S. dollar once represented a claim on a fixed amount of gold). When the government removes the link between the commodity and the paper currency, people understand how to value the paper because of its former tie to the commodity. We will look at fiat money in more depth in Chapter 9.

ECONOMIC CALCULATION

BESIDES THE EASE of trade, there is another major difference between a barter economy and an economy employing money: the use of money enables economic calculation. Money provides us with a common unit in which to express different quantities of different goods. Since, in a well-developed system of indirect exchange, all economic goods will trade against money, we can express any amount of any good in terms of the amount of money necessary to acquire it, or, alternately, the amount of money for which it will sell.

If we place Marco in a money-based economy we can appreciate this difference better. He is now able to set up his ledger with a definite numerical value assigned to each item— let's say, the amount of gold for which the item would sell. Let's look at two consecutive months' balance sheets. In the liability column, there is both gold that Marco has borrowed to set up shop, as well as some items he has sold forward—when, for example, he accepted payment today for an order to be delivered next month.

Assets	Liabilities
1 hammer @ .25 oz. gold = .25	80 fishhooks @ .01 oz. gold = .80
2 chairs @ 1 oz. gold = 2.00	9 oz. gold = 9.00
20 cords wood @ .5 oz. gold = 10.00	1 net @ 1 oz. gold = 1.00
10 pounds iron @ .1 oz. gold = 1.00	3 poles @ .25 oz. gold = .75
100 fishhooks @ .01 oz. gold = 1.00	
1 pole @ .25 oz. gold = .25	
Total: 14.50 oz. gold	**Total:** 11.55 oz. gold

One month later, we find:

Assets	Liabilities
2 hammers @ .25 oz. gold = .50	120 fishhooks @ .01 oz. gold = 1.20
3 chairs @ 1 oz. gold = 3.00	7 oz. gold = 7.00
18 cords wood @ .5 oz. gold = 9.00	5 poles @ .30 oz. gold = 1.50
8 pounds iron @ .05 oz. gold = .40	
1 net @ 1.2 oz. gold = 1.20	
200 fishhooks @ .01 oz. gold = 2.00	
Total: 16.10 oz. gold	**Total:** 9.70 oz. gold

Marco's assets over the month have increased by 1.6 ounces of gold, while his liabilities have diminished by 1.85 ounces. Adding these changes together, we see that he increased his capital during the month by 3.45 ounces of gold. The fact that his capital increased shows Marco that he has not withdrawn so much from his business, for current consumption, that he will not be able to continue operations. In fact, he has a margin within which he could have withdrawn more. Marco has been engaged in *capital accumulation*. If we had totaled up Marco's books and found a negative number, Marco would have been engaged in *capital consumption*. It is crucial for a business to be able to determine whether it is accumulating or consuming capital, as one that is consuming capital is not viable in the long run.

Without money prices, Marco could not have arrived at these figures. His books would have consisted of columns of goods, with no way of summing them. Beyond being able to gauge the overall state of his business, the existence of money prices aids Marco in evaluating individual decisions as well. The price of iron fell during the month in question. If Marco expects the trend to continue, he might be better off keeping less iron in stock, perhaps finding a way to purchase it just before he needs it. And since iron is less expensive, Marco might alter some production process to use more iron and less wood. Meanwhile, the price of poles has risen. If Marco thinks *that* trend will continue, he will not want to sell forward as many poles. Instead, he will wait to sell them until they are made, in anticipation of a higher price.

The ability to calculate in terms of money prices opens a tremendous new vista to human planning, extending the capabilities of human thought. As Mises says in *Human Action*, "Goethe was right in calling bookkeeping by double entry 'one of the finest inventions of the human mind.'" The

enormous significance of this advance will be examined further in Chapters 8, 10, and 11.

THE VALUE OF MONEY

*I*T IS IMPORTANT to realize that money is like all other goods
in that its value is determined subjectively, and in that it,
too, is subject to the law of supply and demand. The key
difference between money and other goods is that money is
acquired neither for direct consumption nor for use in manufacturing goods for direct consumption. Money is acquired to
trade later for consumer or producer goods. Its value consists
in being available for such use.

The demand for money is the demand for *cash holdings.*
All human action takes place in the face of an uncertain
future. Because of that uncertainty, people desire a cushion
against shocks, "something for a rainy day." In the market
economy, this desire expresses itself first and foremost in the
desire to keep a supply of cash around. Although a reserve of
other items can help as well—grains, canned goods, fuel, and
so on—it is the tremendous flexibility of money in meeting
our needs that makes it the most desirable good to have in
reserve. The very nature of any event that is a shock is that
we don't now know exactly what we'll need when the surprise arrives. The baby may get sick and we'll need medicine.
The car breaks down, or the roof springs a leak, and we need
some repairs done. Or perhaps a great job opportunity comes
up, but we need to make a long, expensive flight to look into
it. A cash reserve can help in any of those situations, while a
big bag of rice in the basement is very difficult to use for
booking a cross-country flight.

People's demand for cash holdings fluctuates. In times of crisis, it may rise dramatically. Often, this leads to government propaganda and perhaps even laws against "hoarding." But this so-called hoarding is only an expression of individuals' desire for a sense of security. There is no economic basis for deciding what is a reasonable level of cash holdings and what constitutes hoarding. Government attacks on hoarding are especially ironic in that the state often created the very crisis that led to the increased demand for cash, often through war.

Once we understand the subjective nature of the demand for cash balances, we can see through another common economic fallacy—the idea that we should have stable money. By the very nature of being an economic good, subject to human valuation, money cannot be stable, as valuation implies the possibility of change. In an economy where nothing changes, there would be no valuation, as there is nothing to choose. Goods would circulate in a purely mechanical fashion, driven by who knows what impetus.

The idea of a stable money has spawned the idea of price indices, designed to measure the value of money. We will examine the changing valuation of money as well as price indices in Chapter 9, where we take up the topics of inflation and deflation.

THE DETERMINATION OF MONEY PRICES

*T*HE FAMED ENGLISH economist Alfred Marshall criticized Carl Menger's concept of consumer utility as the sole source of value. Surely, he claimed, market prices are determined by both the utility of the good in question to consumers *and* the objective, monetary cost of producing it. His famous metaphor was that utility and cost were like the blades of scissors, and that it was foolish to debate which blade did the cutting.

But we must conclude that Marshall hadn't understood or fully grasped Menger's vision. As Israel Kirzner emphasizes, Menger was after the essential cause of economic phenomena, not incidental factors determining their magnitude. A price is paid for a good because someone values it. The price will not exceed that value, whatever the cost of producing it may have been.

Perhaps I want to sell illuminated manuscripts of *The Life and Times of Gene Callahan.* I contract with a monk in the Carpathian Mountains to produce the book, at $10,000 per copy. After the first copy is made, I start trying to sell it. Due to consumers' lack of interest in the finer things in life, I find that I am unable to sell even my sole copy at that price. Since I've already paid for the darned thing, I finally sell it for $9.95 and cut my losses. Even though my costs were over $10,000 per copy, I was not able to sell this book at a price anywhere near that.

It would have been useless for me to attempt to drive up the price by adding more cost. If no one was willing to pay more than $9.95 for such a book, doubling the amount of time the monk spent producing it, and therefore doubling my cost, wouldn't have budged the price a penny.

It is true, as Mises's student F.A. Hayek pointed out, that in the long run the sale price of a good will tend toward the cost of producing it. But this is not because costs *cause* prices to be paid. Rather, if the price fetched for the good is below the cost, the good won't be produced anymore! After suffering a $9,990.05 loss on the first sale of my book, I'll be very unlikely to want to continue production. And if the price fetched is above the cost, the market will attract other sellers who hope to take advantage of this profit opportunity, driving the price down toward the cost of production. In the meantime, valuations will change, new data will appear, and new profit opportunities, where prices paid will exceed costs, will emerge. Although in the long run, prices will equal costs, we will never arrive at that long run. The notion that prices equal costs must be taken as the expression of a tendency in the market, not as a description of a state that the market ever achieves.

Taking this long-run view, we might say Marshall was right after all. Don't "objective costs" eventually help determine price? However, Menger's deeper point is that the costs of producing a good are simply what the producer estimates the demand for the necessary factors of production would be in an alternate use. The cost of the monk's time for me arises from the subjective demand of others for alternate uses of his time. Costs are not objective. Both blades of Marshall's scissors are honed by subjective valuation.

Menger's insight is relevant to some policy debates, where we might see critics of an industry contending that its prices are "too high" and are not justified by the industry's costs. Whether or not they realize it, such critics are using a Marshallian notion of objective costs to make their case. The fact that costs are subjective derails such arguments.

How could we quantify the costs that equal Michael Jordan's salary when he played for the Bulls? Did it "cost" him $34 million a year to produce his basketball output, justifying his salary? For some economists, the answer is "yes"—his costs justify his salary, once we realize that Jordan's cost in playing for the Bulls is what he could make instead of playing for the Lakers (or some other team).

To answer that question, we must look at Jordan's *opportunity cost*. That concept was introduced by Friedrich von Wieser, who was a follower of Menger and teacher of Hayek. We touched on opportunity costs, without naming them, in Chapter 2, when we saw that the cost to Rich of continuing work was the value to him of the relaxation he was giving up. The cost to me of marrying Sue is that I can't marry Betty. To be more precise, the cost of End A is the cost of the most valuable, alternate end given up in order to achieve End A. My cost in marrying Sue is how much I value the next-best marriage prospect (or, perhaps, remaining a bachelor).

Let's look at opportunity costs more closely. Unless we can arrive at an objective statement of what someone's opportunity costs are, we cannot judge that a market price is "too high" relative to costs. If we try to arrive at an objective accounting of Michael Jordan's opportunity costs in playing for the Bulls, we encounter the following difficulties:

(1) Jordan may never have received any offers from any other team (a quite realistic scenario) before signing his contract. In that case, no one has any idea what the Lakers would pay him. And opportunity costs are never realized: Even if he had received an offer, the alternate deal might have fallen through, if he had chosen to act on it.

(2) Jordan may love living in a cold, windy city, in the proximity of meat-packing plants, near a large Polish population. While each of these could come into play in his decision, raising his opportunity cost for moving, even Jordan himself could not quantify them. His preferences represent an ordering, but they cannot be measured. As

Mises says: "Profit and loss in this original sense are psychic phenomena and as such not open to measurement and a mode of expression which could convey to other people precise information regarding their intensity."

(3) He might also be considering an acting career, in which he thinks he *might* be able to make $40 million a year, without sweating as much. Then again, he might fail miserably. That is often the real situation of entrepreneurs considering a speculative venture, for instance, of a bank considering placing an automatic teller machine (ATM) at an area hotel. How will the profits from the ATM compare to those the bank might garner from a new advertising campaign? At best, the bank's managers have an educated guess as to the answer. Far from being amenable to objective calculation, real business estimates of opportunity costs are often based on vaguely sensed premonitions of future market states. (For example, "Joe, I think we're gonna sell a lot of this stuff.")

(4) Even if we knew precisely what someone's opportunity costs were, pricing based on such figures does not account for the possibility of entrepreneurial profit. By correctly adjusting the factors of production to anticipate consumers' future desires, the entrepreneur hopes to achieve returns well beyond what he might have made in some other venture. (We will discuss entrepreneurial profits further in Chapter 7.)

Formal models that attempt to quantify entrepreneurship are sterile. They are akin to predicting the future batting average of major league ballplayers with a model that abstracts out the human batter and formulates its equations with the bat and the ball as the only variables.

CHAPTER 6

A Place Where Nothing Ever Happens

ON THE EMPLOYMENT OF IMAGINARY
CONSTRUCTS IN ECONOMICS

SOME STATES OF REST

*W*E WILL NOW consider several situations in which the market has, in some sense, "come to rest." While some of the market states we will examine are not possible states of the real world, they are nevertheless important to our understanding of economics. In order to conceive of the impact of changes in the economy, we must first imagine an economy where change has stopped. We can then introduce a single change and ponder what its impact will be. Gradually introducing change into our mental models, we build up an inkling of the market process in its full complexity.

The first of these states is the *plain state of rest*. The plain state of rest is not an imaginary state, but actually occurs in the market. It comes about whenever all buyers and sellers who wish to exchange at the market price, and who know that the option is available to them, have been able to do so. We saw the plain state of rest in Chapter 4, where our goat and corn traders made all of the trades from which they expected to profit, then stopped trading.

In the real market economy, this state occurs again and again. Anyone who watches a stock market ticker can observe the plain state of rest many times a day. Sometimes for seconds, sometimes for minutes, sometimes, with lightly traded securities, for hours, no market activity will take place. All buyers who wish to buy at the current price and all sellers who wish to sell at the current price have done so.

The plain state of rest never lasts. A change in the market data prompts market participants into activity. In our example of the goat-corn market, we imagined that Kyle and Stephen grew tired of eating corn and found a source of squash down the road. That change starts the market process anew, as the buyers and sellers search for a new price, which will again result in the plain state of rest.

Similarly, in the securities market, a given price lasts as long as there is no change in data that are seen as relating to that price. Even an investor's view of the prospects of a company could be an item of market data. A price may last only while some investor is recalculating a spreadsheet evaluating the stock at the current price. If the investor decides to buy as the result of that evaluation, that increases the quantity demanded, introducing new data into the market.

The plain state of rest may not take into account future plans of market participants. Perhaps Emma has planted a new strain of corn that she will have on the market next season. Today's goat-corn market may have reached the plain state of rest, but looking ahead we can see that there is new data coming that will alter this state. However, we can imagine a situation where all changes in the data relevant to this market have stopped. Such a market will approach the *final price*, or the *final state of rest*. It is an imaginary state, which can never come about in the real economy. The essence of human action is the attempt to replace what is with what ought to be, in the eyes of the actor. As long as humans and not robots populate the economy, we will never see the final state of rest emerge.

Now, we can take our imaginings one step further, and picture an economy where for all goods, the final state of rest has been reached. Such an "economy" is an endless cycle of the same events being repeated. The same number of babies is born each year, and that number exactly equals the number of people dying. The same goods are manufactured each year and demanded in the exact same quantities. No harvest ever fails, no business ever goes bankrupt, no new products are ever introduced, and no person's tastes ever change.

If you have seen the movie *Groundhog Day*, you can begin to envision what such a world would be like. The star of that film, Bill Murray, awakens each morning to find that it is the *same day* as the previous one, with all of the same events occurring again and again. The difference between the movie and our imaginary world is that, in the movie, Bill Murray's character continues to learn and change. If we eliminate that difference, *Groundhog Day* is a perfect image of the world we are envisioning.[1]

Such an economy is sometimes described as being in equilibrium. However, because it does not lack economic activity, but rather consists of a situation where every economic activity is repeated at the same time interval, over and over, Ludwig von Mises christened it the *evenly rotating economy*.

---

[1]Thanks to Sanford Ikeda of SUNY Purchase for pointing out this analogy.

Such a world could not possibly exist, but it is helpful for us to create the image of such a world for use as a mental tool. By introducing a single change into our mental construction, we can isolate what the effects of that particular change would be, apart from the welter of complicating data that exists in our real world. We will see applications of the evenly rotating economy in chapters to come.

Regarding such a mental construct, we face danger from two sides. As Mises commented in *Human Action*:

> The method of imaginary constructions is indispensable for praxeology; it is the only method of praxeological and economic inquiry. It is, to be sure, a method difficult to handle because it can easily result in fallacious syllogisms. It leads along a sharp edge; on both sides yawns the chasm of absurdity and nonsense. Only merciless self-criticism can prevent a man from falling headlong into these abysmal depths.

On one side of the razor's edge is the danger of failing to employ imaginary constructions at all, because they are not realistic. However, we employ such mental tools *precisely because they are not realistic*—they allow us to abstract from reality just those factors relevant to any given analysis. We should not for a moment mistake our models for images of the real world, nor should we judge the real world by how closely it approximates the models.

On the other side of the blade lies the danger of taking our fancies too seriously, as in too much of modern economics. Reams of paper have been filled with mathematical equations describing "equilibrium conditions," as if the real economy were being discussed. But equilibrium is a mental tool for studying human action isolated from all changes but one, and not a potential state of the economy. As Mises says, "What they are doing is vain playing with mathematical symbols, a pastime not suited to convey any knowledge."

CHAPTER 7

Butcher, Baker, Candlestick Maker

ON ECONOMIC ROLES AND THE
THEORY OF DISTRIBUTION

ECONOMIC ROLES AND HISTORICAL TYPES

> The entrepreneurs, capitalists, landowners, workers, and consumers of economic theory are not living men as one meets them in the reality of life and history. They are the embodiment of distinct functions in the market operations.
>
> LUDWIG VON MISES, *HUMAN ACTION*

*W*E HAVE BUILT up an economy with a capital structure, interpersonal exchange, and money, and have examined the states of rest that are the still points toward which human action gravitates. Now, we are ready to ask what is perhaps the most common economic question: "Who gets the money?" (Or perhaps the second most common, behind, "How do I get more of it?") When a good is sold, to whom do the proceeds flow? And how can we account for the fact that they got to put their hand in the till? What is the *distribution* of the wealth produced in an economy?

Karl Marx offered an explanation for distribution: He contended that all of the value of a good comes from the labor that went into it. The fact that the workers do not get all of the proceeds from a sale is due to exploitation, according to Marx. The capitalists and landowners, having control of the political system, are able to siphon off a portion of the wealth that should flow to the workers.

However, we previously saw that Helena would not pay Rich to grind up traps, even though he might have to work just as hard at doing that as he did at making them. We cannot account for the value of goods through "totaling" the labor that went into them. People do not value labor *per se*; they value things that they think will improve their life. Even Marx recognized that totaling hours worked or calories expended would not give any sort of account of value: Consumers are unlikely to value the large number of calories I would burn if I spent my days doing jumping jacks in my living room. Marx attempted to dodge the problem by basing value on "socially useful" labor. But we can only gauge what labor people consider useful by seeing what they are willing to pay for that labor! We call that amount a wage. Marx unwittingly had made the case for the market economy.

Marx's theory further leaves unexplained all of the machines the workers are using. Forget how they were created and who owns them in the market before socialism is adopted—how will they be maintained? It takes resources to do that. In a market economy, capitalists supply those resources. Far from being able to return the wages that were being "stolen" from the workers by the capitalists, communist governments simply had to steal that portion themselves. In fact, they had to "steal" *more* than the capitalists did, due to the inefficiency of resource use under socialism.

Besides the "normal" returns to capital, we also should explain from whence enormous "windfall" profits arise. Even for many people who believe that capitalists deserve a "decent return" on their investment in machines, buildings, research, and so on, the sight of someone earning several billion dollars in a few years is disturbing. What did that person do to "deserve" so much money?

Economics cannot tell us which people deserve which earthly goods. But it can explain how consumers' valuation of first-order goods flows back to the various factors that helped to produce them. To understand that flow, we abstract out several distinct economic functions from the totality of human action: entrepreneurs, capitalists/landowners, workers, and consumers.

The market is a process of bewildering complexity, where all economic events are intertwined with all others. It is beyond human capability to grasp the web of relationships that makes up the market in its entirety. We comprehend the market by isolating key abstractions, such as the productive functions we study in this chapter. In essence, such a procedure is not different than the use by physics of terms like matter and energy, two abstractions that aid in the comprehension of the stunning multiplicity of forms of physical existence. The basic difference between the two sciences is that physics searches for the abstractions that help explain the world of "stuff out there," while economics searches for the abstractions that will help explain the world of human plans and actions.

Each of the functions that Mises mentions in the quote at the start of the chapter—entrepreneurs, capitalists/landowners, workers, and consumers—besides being an economic function, is also used as the name for a *historical type*. When history speaks of "the plight of the workers in nineteenth-century factories," it is using the term "workers" to designate a category of people in the real world. Depending on the context, *workers* in this sense means something like "manual laborers" or "wage earners." But economics uses the terms to designate, not categories of people, but functional roles. When it speaks of the role *worker*, it means that aspect of action that involves employing human labor. From the economic point of view, *all* people who are not purely supported by others (e.g., infants) take on the role of worker. When the wealthy landowner opens the mail containing his rent checks, he is, at that moment, acting as a worker. Even during consumption, the role of worker is present—you must expend some labor to flip the pop-top on your beer.

As a historical type, *entrepreneur* means the class of men who start great enterprises and take bold risks in the financial markets. History may discuss, for instance, "the entrepreneur as social icon in the 1990s," meaning Bill Gates (Microsoft), Larry Ellison (Oracle), Steve Case (America Online), Jeff Bezos (Amazon.com), Jim Clark (Netscape), and so on. But when economics uses *entrepreneur* as a category of action, it means that aspect of action that attempts to cope with uncertain future conditions. Entrepreneurship as a function is something that everyone employs: We all must risk acting in the face of an uncertain future.

Mises defines our functions as follows:

> In the context of economic theory the meaning of the terms concerned is this: Entrepreneur means acting man in regard to the changes occurring in the data of the market. Capitalist and landowner mean acting man in regard to the changes in value and price which, even with all the market data remaining equal, are brought about by the mere passing of time as a consequence of the different valuation of present goods and of future goods. Worker means man in regard to the employment of the factor of production human labor. (*Human Action*)

Each category earns a different type of return in the market: entrepreneurs, through creative judgment, earn *profits*; capitalists, by planning for the future, earn *interest*; and workers, through their labor, earn wages.

We will now examine each of Mises's definitions in more detail.

THE ENTREPRENEURS

*T*O UNDERSTAND "ENTREPRENEUR" as an economic category, we will look at the role of the entrepreneur in the evenly rotating economy, or rather, the complete lack of role! The main characteristic of the evenly rotating economy is that there is no uncertainty as to the future. Under that special condition, the function of the entrepreneur does not exist—there is no uncertain future with which to cope.

We comprehend the effect of a change in the market by imagining a situation where no change is occurring, then introducing the change in question. Let us say that we have an evenly rotating economy "up and running" in a land we will call Nirvana. (Remember, though, that the evenly rotating economy is an *imaginary construction.* Thought of as a possible state of the real world, it is nonsensical.) From somewhere, a change comes in and disturbs the unreal smoothness of the operation of that economy. Let us say that the current generation of Nirvanians has a few more babies than the previous generation did. Suddenly, the perfect adjustment of all elements of their economy is out of whack. There will be a little more food demanded in the current year than was demanded in the previous one. Nirvana will need more baby clothes and cribs. In many other ways, the structure of the economy will no longer correspond to the needs of the citizens of Nirvana.

It is entrepreneurs who make the necessary adjustments. Some factory owner must judge that he can bid more for the items that go into baby carriages than the prevailing price. He will bid them away from other uses. If his judgment is correct he will profit because of the new demand for carriages. But suppose Nirvanians decide to just plop two kids in some carriages, so that demand remains unchanged? Then the factory owner will suffer a loss. Loss by those who misjudge the changing desires of the consumers is as much a part of the market process as is profit by those who judge correctly. The factory owner must risk acting on his personal interpretation of events even though that interpretation is necessarily contrary to the prevailing market interpretation. (If "Mr. Market" has already adjusted his bids and asks based on the entrepreneur's interpretation, then there is no more profit to be had.)

Similarly, some landowners must see that it now will be to their advantage to shift some land to raising crops from some other use. Some workers must perceive that they will be better off becoming nannies than continuing at whatever they were doing before. In making those adjustments, all of those people are acting in the role of entrepreneur. As Mises says in "Profit and Loss":

> The activities of the entrepreneur consist in making decisions. He determines for what purpose the factors of production should be employed. Any other acts which an entrepreneur may perform are merely accidental to his entrepreneurial function. (*Planning for Freedom*)

It is the correct perception of the possibility for improvement, for turning what is into what ought to be, that creates profits in the economy, and the incorrect perception that creates losses. We can see that in the evenly rotating economy there is no profit or loss in the economic sense. (The capitalists will earn the market rate of interest on their investments. Accountants and tax collectors may consider such returns profit, but economics considers profits to be returns *above* that rate.) All elements of the evenly rotating economy are perfectly adjusted to meet the unchanging demands of the consumers. For the opportunity for profit to arise, there must be a change in the data of the market. Furthermore, the change must be one that introduces an element of uncertainty into the future plans of acting humans.

It is risk and uncertainty that create the need for the entrepreneurial role. If Nirvanians have more children, will they consume proportionally more food? Will the new rate of childbirth continue, or is it an isolated event, or even the first in a series of increases in the birthrate?

Human choice both presupposes and creates uncertainty. Choice is absent in the evenly rotating economy, since all relevant data is already known. Such perfect knowledge is incompatible with true choice. Real choice implies that the person who is choosing might pick a steak or might pick a lobster. Until the choice is made, even he doesn't know which he will select—if he already knows, there is nothing to weigh and no decision to make. If he chooses a steak instead of a lobster, there is no guarantee that he will not choose a lobster tomorrow. If he picks a steak over a lobster, that does not mean he would pick two steaks over two lobsters. (The marginal utility of steak might decline faster than that of lobster.) If he picks a steak over a lobster today, and a lobster over a pheasant tomorrow, that does not mean that the next day he might not choose a pheasant over a steak. Mises described the importance of true human choice in differentiating economics from the physical sciences as follows:

> As there exist constant relations between various
> mechanical elements and as these relations can be
> ascertained by experiments, it becomes possible to
> use equations for the solution of definite technolog-
> ical problems. Our modern industrial civilization is
> mainly an accomplishment of this utilization of the
> differential equations of physics. No such constant
> relations exist, however, between economic ele-
> ments. (Mises, *Human Action*)

We cope with the uncertain future of human action by
using our understanding. To employ human understanding is
to "walk a mile in the other fellow's shoes." We try to place
ourselves in another person's mind, to imagine how they are
evaluating a situation, to guess their desires and plans. When
a waiter walks up to us at our restaurant table, we don't need
to gather reams of information on the entirety of his physical
existence to surmise that he wants to take our order and not
to assault us. Now, at times human understanding goes astray:
People have been attacked by waiters! But the plain fact is
that in the vast majority of cases it works pretty well. We *do*
treat other people as acting, thinking beings, like ourselves,
and attempt to grasp the purpose of their actions. (Kurt Vonnegut wrote a novel, *Breakfast of Champions,* in which one of
the protagonists, Dwayne Hoover, abandons that view and
begins to treat others like automatons in a play that God is
putting on for him. The results are not pretty.)

The entrepreneur relies on his understanding of humans,
his "gut feeling" about what choices other people will make
in response to change, in order to comprehend the effects of
that change. That skill, like all others, appears to be unevenly
distributed among humans. Those who are good at it are able
to gain entrepreneurial profit. Using their superior understanding, they adjust production to meet new needs faster

than their competitors can. They recognize that a change will eventually be reflected in market prices, but that it will take time for all actors in the market to fully digest the meaning of the change. Until that happens, prices are out of alignment. There are some factors of production—workers, land, raw materials, machines, and so on—that best can be used to meet new needs. At the moment of the change, however, they are in less important uses. Eventually, the prices of those items will be bid up so that their usefulness in meeting the new needs is fully reflected in their price, but at the moment the change occurs, their prices are too low, while the relative prices of some other factors are too high.

Let's imagine that word reaches the evenly rotating economy of Nirvana that a new animal has been discovered in Freedonia: the Freedonian foozle. The foozle is sort of a combined kitten, teddy bear, and monkey, and Nirvanians are smitten with it. It is the job of the entrepreneur to understand what adjustments in the market that new infatuation may call for. Perhaps consumers will want a line of foozle dolls available by Christmas. But the available resources in the economy are employed making other things. In order to rush out a line of foozle dolls, an entrepreneur will have to bid some of those resources away from their previous employment. That will raise the price of those factors—but by how much? Will it be worthwhile to manufacture foozles at that cost? How many dolls will consumers demand? How much will they pay for them?

All human actions have an entrepreneurial aspect to them, not just those of the people who run businesses. Workers who make teddy bears will have to decide whether the higher wage offered at the foozle factory makes it worthwhile to switch jobs. Landowners have to decide how the location of the new foozle store will affect their property values. Capitalists must decide whether to lend the foozle entrepreneur the money to start his company. Austrian School economist W.H. Hutt pointed out that entrepreneurship is present even in acts of consumption. Personal-computer buyers speculate on how large the Christmas price cuts will be—should they buy a computer now, or wait until after Christmas for the drop in price? Entrepreneurship is the attempt to deal with the uncertainty of the future when planning one's actions.

Let's say that the foozle entrepreneur judged the situation correctly, went ahead with his project, and made a bundle. Those profits will attract the attention of other businessmen, who will enter the business as well. But they must bid for the same scarce resources as the first foozle maker. Let us further imagine that the event was an isolated occurrence in Nirvana, and that the evenly rotating economy is gradually being reestablished there by the market process. In that case, competing businessmen will bid up the cost of foozle-making resources until profits in the foozle-doll business disappear completely, and the evenly rotating economy comes back into existence. The entrepreneurial profits available as a result of any change are always temporary, as are the entrepreneurial losses.

Of course, in the real world, new changes in the market data *will* occur. Uncertainty, in our world, is always present. No entrepreneur can rest on his laurels. Since the profits available from any single change will disappear over time, the entrepreneur, if he wants to continue profiting, must continue to search for the significance of further changes. Those who continue at that task with the most skill and energy, over time, will accumulate more and more capital. Those who are the very best at it become the "titans of industry," the "superrich." Their wealth is mostly in the means of production. In the unhampered market, if they want to remain wealthy, they must never stop evaluating how to best use their resources in order to satisfy the demands of the consumers.

We must also realize that it is *only* entrepreneurial effort to profit from price discrepancies that eliminates those discrepancies. A major focus of the work of Israel Kirzner has been to demonstrate that the idea of equilibrium prices without the entrepreneurial process is nonsensical. When mechanistic economists draw supply and demand curves and write equations describing the equilibrium state (the evenly rotating economy), they offer no explanation of how the economy arrives at that state. It is as though a mystical power (Federal Reserve Chairman Alan Greenspan?) simply transmits the equilibrium price into the minds of buyers and sellers. But our economics is the economics of real people. We recognize that it is the desire to profit, to improve one's condition, that is the driving force of the market. It is that force that alters prices to bring supply and demand into balance.

THE CAPITALISTS AND LANDOWNERS

*T*HE CAPITALISTS AND landowners are the suppliers of the nonhuman factors of production. The classical economists, having failed to arrive at the subjective theory of value, had to develop specialized theories of land and capital to account for the value of each. But the subjective theory of value unites those elements under the category of factors of production, or higher-order goods. The factors of production are valued by estimating their contribution to the value of the consumer goods they can produce: All economic value originates with someone's judgment as to the role a good or service can play in improving his or her life.

However, we have a puzzle to solve. In the evenly rotating economy, if we total up the price of all of the factors of production that help create a consumer good, we would find that total was somewhat less than the price the manufacturer received for the good itself. What is the source of that "surplus value"?

Let's consider, in the evenly rotating economy, a machine that we *know* will be rented for $1,000 for the next ten years and then fail, having produced a $10,000 return. (By definition, we have absolute certainty as to future prices in the evenly rotating economy—they will be the same as today's prices.) The price paid for such a machine will be less than $10,000. How do we know that? No one will give up a good today in order to receive the same good back in the future, all other things being equal. (And in the evenly rotating economy, all other things are, of course, equal!) So no one will pay $10,000 today for a machine that will give him $10,000 over the next ten years.

Let's say the machine sells for roughly $6,144. The capitalist who buys it can rent it out for $1,000 per year, so he earns a 10 percent annual return. Where does that 10 percent return come from?

The answer is apparent from our discussion above: it is a return for the capitalist's time, for the patience to forego current consumption and allow one's resources to be devoted to future production. If the return on capital is 10 percent in the evenly rotating economy, that means that 10 percent is the marginal time preference of the buyers and sellers of future goods against present goods.

The concept we are discussing is sometimes called the *normal rate of profit*. In the evenly rotating economy there are no entrepreneurial profits, as they arise through adjusting production to changing conditions, but there will still be "normal profits." Since the source of the return to capital is significantly different than the source of entrepreneurial profits, it is better to use a different term for it. We will call that return *interest*.

The capitalists and landowners refrain from the current consumption of part of the goods available to them and permit those goods to be used in order to satisfy future needs. (They may either use those goods for production themselves, or rent, lease, or lend them to others to use.) The return they receive for the use of their goods is interest. The magnitude of the return (the interest rate) is determined by the marginal time preferences of all actors in the economy in the same way that all other prices are determined: Buyers and sellers of future versus present goods attempt to discover all possible trades where they can exchange a good they value less for one they value more.

Recall Rich, alone on his island: The degree to which he preferred current consumption over future consumption determined how much effort he would devote to accumulating capital goods. In addition, we concluded that time preference in human action will never be zero or infinite. If a person's time preference is zero, he will never consume anything, as he has no reason to bestir himself from an inert state. A society-wide time preference of zero would result in an interest rate of zero: People would lend out money for no interest, and never care when they got it back. If a person's time preference is infinite, he will be reduced to instinctual behavior. A society-wide infinite time preference would result in an "infinite interest rate": no one would ever make loans, as they would prefer to consume everything they have immediately.

We generally think of interest as the rate of payment for money loans, which is true, as far as it goes. But, more fundamentally, interest is the market's discount of future goods to present goods, an expression of the time preference of market participants. Let us say that an entrepreneur buys the rights to next year's grape harvest from some vineyard for $1,000. If the risk-free rate of interest is 5 percent, the entrepreneur will not consider that he has made a profit unless he can sell the grapes for *more than* $1,050. This is because he could, with less effort and risk, simply lend the money out at 5 percent and have $1,050 at the end of the year. The distinction between interest and true entrepreneurial profit is well established in modern finance. No investor is happy with an investment in a risky high-tech venture that yields him 2 percent a year when U.S. Treasury bonds (which are generally considered the least risky investment) are yielding 5 percent. He realizes that the high-tech firm is suffering entrepreneurial losses. If it cannot turn things around, both the investors and the economy as a whole would be better off if the funds tied up in it are freed to be invested elsewhere.

The return to the capitalist arises because he exchanges a present good for a future good, and therefore earns the price differential between them. The capitalist always has the option of consuming his capital now. The landowner who rents to a farmer could instead throw lavish hunting parties on his land. The person who lends out money at interest could have used it for a world tour. Someone who buys a cattle futures contract on an exchange could instead have bought a new Lamborghini.

Arbitrage—simultaneously buying and selling goods to take advantage of price discrepancies between different markets—will tend to establish a single interest rate for the economy as a whole. Let's say that the interest rate on money loans is currently 5 percent per year. Meanwhile, cattle futures maturing in one year are selling at a discount to spot (current) prices, so that for $90.90, an investor can contract for the delivery of $100 of cattle a year from now. For simplicity's sake, we will assume there are no transaction costs, no carrying costs for the cattle, and no possibility of demand or supply changes in the spot cattle market. Given those assumptions, there is a pure arbitrage opportunity available. Investors can borrow money at 5 percent. They can buy cattle futures that will return 10 percent. (We have taken as a given that spot cattle will still be $100 next year, and the $9.10 they will earn is 10 percent of $90.90.) Investors net the 5-percent difference. Since they are borrowing the money and making no capital investment themselves, such arbitrageurs are essentially picking up money that has been left on the sidewalk. Once that opportunity has been noticed, investors will rush to take advantage of it.

The effect of their actions will be twofold. Their demand to borrow money *now* to buy the cattle futures will drive the price of present money higher against future money: the money interest rate will rise. Conversely, their demand for future cattle will drive the price of future cattle up against that of present cattle. Soon enough, the money interest rate will rise to, say, 6 percent, and the price of the cattle futures to $94.34. ($94.34 + $5.66 [6 percent of $94.34] = $100.) The arbitrage opportunity will vanish.

A similar story will be played out in any market with a unique interest rate, so that all rates will tend to be arbitraged toward a single rate. Of course, we are not in the evenly rotating economy, so there will be changes in supply and demand. The opportunity for arbitrage arises again and again in the market, but entrepreneurial judgment is necessary to recognize it. Is it really an arbitrage opportunity? Or is the cattle future priced below the money interest rate because traders suspect an increase in the number of cattle coming to market next year?

THE WORKERS

*H*UMANS EMPLOYING THEIR own labor to achieve their ends are acting in the role of *worker*. All people labor except those completely supported by others, such as infants and invalids. As Hans Sennholz says in *The Politics of Unemployment*:

> To sustain his life, man must labor. No abilities, however great, can command success without labor. To improve his condition, man must expend vital effort in some form.

The return to workers is in the form of *wages*. Now these wages may be explicit, as when someone takes on a job for $50,000 a year or for $12.00 an hour. On the other hand, one's wages may be mixed in with other returns, and take some effort to separate out for the purposes of gauging the result of one's efforts. That is often the case with the proprietor of a small business. His books may show he made a profit of $40,000 last year. But usually such a figure represents a mix of interest on his capital invested, wages for his otherwise unpaid labor, and true profit. In fact, many small business owners, if they fully accounted for their own efforts at a wage they could draw working for someone else, would find that their business loses money every year, and they are only able to stay open because they don't pay themselves the higher wage rate they could earn working for someone else. (Having made that discovery, it is quite possible they would still keep the business running for nonpecuniary reasons, perhaps because they like being their own boss. Still, it is worthwhile for them to have an idea of how much money they are giving up for that benefit.)

A feature of work is what Mises called the *disutility of labor*. The phrase signifies the fact that, in our world, people prefer leisure to work. As Mises says: "The spontaneous and carefree discharge of one's own energies and vital functions in aimless freedom suits everybody better than the stern restraint of purposive effort" (*Human Action*).

The disutility of labor does not come about from some aspect of "the system." No changes in social structure—communal living, the dictatorship of the proletariat, or a return to guild labor—can do away with that fact. A CEO making $5 million a year is as much subject to the disutility of labor as a "burger flipper" making $10,000 a year.

The price of labor is an outcome of the same process as all other prices. The buyer (an employer) and the seller (an employee) must try to agree on a price for the labor offered. The wage will fall within a range. The endpoints of the range are determined by the value judgments of the employer and the employee. At one end of the range is the lowest wage rate that will interest the potential employee. He may have another employer offering to pay $11.95 an hour. This might mean that the lowest bid he will take is $12.00 per hour. Or, if he has some other means of support, he might consider that, for any rate under $12.00 per hour, it is not worth leaving home. At the other end of the range the employer has a certain amount of revenue he expects to gain from adding one more employee, let's say, $13.00 per hour. He may not be willing to bid above $12.95 for the employee's services. If they agree on a wage, it will be between $12.00 and $12.95 per hour.

As we mentally approach the condition of the evenly rotating economy, the range will narrow until the difference between what the marginal employee receives and what the marginal employer pays becomes vanishingly small. Competition among employers for labor will tend to move the level of wages toward the *marginal productivity* of labor. An employer will attempt to hire workers until the revenue he expects from the last worker hired—the marginal unit—just exceeds the wage he must pay to attract the worker. The revenue he would expect from the next worker he might hire will fall below the wage he would have to pay. The bidding among employers for labor constantly reshuffles the labor supply, aligning worker and job with the entrepreneurs' best estimates of the wishes of the consumers.

If an employer and employee reach a deal, it should be recognized that both of them feel they are better off than if they hadn't done so. The employer has not done the employee a favor by hiring him. He has hired him because he expects to profit by doing so. It is only because of the expected difference between wages and revenues that anybody hires anyone else at all! At the same time, the employee is not being exploited by the wage he agrees to—if he knew of any better opportunities, he surely would have taken advantage of one of them.

The capitalist *does* add something to the production of consumer goods—he adds his capital. Without the capital goods he makes available, the workers would be far less productive. A Marxist would counter by saying that it is only due to exploitation that the capitalist owns capital. But such a contention is unfounded. Capital arises from acts of saving and investment. Without the efforts of a farsighted few, the bulk of humanity would still be struggling for survival with rudimentary tools.

Now it is true, of course, that there are many people in the world today who possess capital as the result of some past act of theft. How we could sort through history and set all wrongs aright is a bit of a puzzle, since there have been so many of them. Nevertheless, for our purposes it is enough to understand that the ultimate source of capital is saving. Theft is a violation of, not a part of, the market economy, and capital does not rely on theft for its existence.

THE CONSUMERS

*O*UR FINAL FUNCTION, the consumer, also involves all human actors. Whenever we stop to enjoy the fruits of our labor, when we rest, when we vacation, when we eat, we are consumers. In the popular press this term is sometimes used in a limited and derogatory sense to refer to those obsessed with acquiring material things for their pleasure. But from the economic point of view, someone enjoying a symphony or taking a year off of work to meditate in a monastery is no more or less a consumer than someone shopping at Tiffany's.

That does not mean that economics considers a religious retreat to be *no better than* a shopping spree. As we've seen, economics does not attempt to intrude into the ethical sphere of value judgments. All we mean is that such activities play the same part in the economic system—consumption. None of them produce (as their goal, anyway) consumer goods, and all of them require the use of such goods to achieve their ends. Even the ascetic retreating to the forest requires his bowl of rice and loin cloth.

The first three functions we examined—the entrepreneurs, the capitalists/landowners, and the workers—make up the productive forces of the economy. The goal of all production is ultimately consumption. It makes no sense to condemn consumption while praising production. All production represents a demand for consumption, either now or in the future.

Insofar as any of the producers wish to maximize their return, they must ultimately fulfill the desires of the consumers. Aside from fraud, theft, and the granting of special favors by the government, there are no other means to wealth than to produce some good or service. The production of a good or service yields a return because someone wants to consume it, or because it can be used to produce another good that someone wants to consume. (In fact, an artifact that ultimately cannot be used to produce a valued consumer good is not a good at all, and the manufacture of it was not production in the economic sense.)

We have seen that, with the exception of those completely dependent on others for their sustenance, all people are both producers and consumers. That casts a curious light on government efforts to aid consumers—for instance, price ceilings and mandatory safety features—and similar efforts to aid producers—for instance, production subsidies and tariffs. Any measure that favors consumers at the expense of producers helps a person in his role as a consumer and hurts him in his role as a producer. The reverse is true of measures to help producers. People advocating such measures are, to borrow a phrase from P.J. O'Rourke, having a leg-wrestling contest with themselves.

CHAPTER 8

Make a New Plan, Stan

ON THE PLACE OF CAPITAL IN THE ECONOMY

WHAT IS CAPITAL?

*T*HERE HAS BEEN an astounding variety of definitions of capital advanced in the history of economics. Capital has been called an abstract fund that creates a permanent flow, it has been referred to as "congealed waiting," defined as "the produced means of production," or characterized as a source of future service flows.

We look to the choices of individuals as the basis for our economic theories. In *Human Action*, Mises says: "[Capital] is a product of reasoning, and its place is in the human mind. It is a mode of looking at the problems of acting, a method of appraising them from the point of view of a definite plan." Israel Kirzner, in *An Essay on Capital*, defines capital goods as way stations in someone's plan to produce consumer goods. What distinguishes capital goods are not any physical characteristics or special circumstances under which they came into being, but the fact that they are, today, a part of someone's plan to produce a consumer good. And capital is an accounting convention for summing up those goods on a firm's balance sheet, in order to gain an overall view of the firm's health.

In a complex economy with many stages of production, it is not necessary for each producer to envision exactly how his product will aid in the manufacture of a consumer good. It is enough for him to believe that *someone* wants this product. That buyer can determine which lower-order good(s) will be produced using his higher-order good. A computer manufacturer tries to gauge next year's demand for computers. He is not concerned with whether his computers will be used to help produce cars or futons. However, we have seen that every producer good must be part of a plan to produce a consumer good, or it will cease to be an economic good at all.

That definition, as Mises and Kirzner illustrate, clears up many of the confusions in capital theory. For instance, Merton Miller and Charles Upton, in *Macroeconomics: A Neoclassical Introduction*, say that the productivity of capital is something assumed but left unexplained by economics. However, viewing capital as partially completed plans makes the explanation clear: Of course, if we have completed part of our plan for producing a good, we can produce it more readily than if we have completed none of our plan. (Given, of course, that our plan is sound.) And we will only choose a route to our goal because we think it is superior to alternative routes, based on our estimates of the cost of the various paths we might take. As Mises says:

> Capital goods are intermediary stations on the way leading from the very beginning of production to its final goal, the turning out of consumers' goods. He who produces with the aid of capital goods enjoys one great advantage over the man who starts without capital goods; he is nearer in time to the ultimate goal of his endeavors. (*Human Action*)

SOCIAL CAPITAL

*T*HE EFFORT TO stretch the idea of capital as an accounting item for a firm to yield a measure of "social capital" is confounded by absurdities. A "firm's capital" as a concept in bookkeeping was an essential advance in man's ability to plan for the future. By totaling the productive resources available to a firm at any point in time, accountancy enabled firms to determine how much of their income could be devoted to current consumption without diminishing their ability to produce in the future.

Such a summing up can only be done with the aid of market prices. By totaling the market price of all its productive resources, a firm can approximate its financial health. Taking the same sum at a later date allows the firm to see if it has been advancing (or declining) in its ability to produce in the future. If it found it had a million dollars of capital on hand last year, and only half a million on hand this year, it has been engaged in capital consumption. It could be the case that the owners have been taking out money that was not actually profits, that the firm has been paying its workers too much, has been undercharging for its products, or that it is simply not a viable business. In any case, capital accounting informs the firm that something must change or it will go broke.

The prices that are used to sum up a firm's capital are estimates. When pricing a particular capital good for the purposes of capital accounting, it is a mistake to look back to the price that was paid for the good. Rather, the firm must look forward to the various streams of revenue it expects would result from different possible uses of the good.

Consider the position of a horse-drawn-carriage manufacturer in 1900. Looking back to the prices originally paid for its

capital equipment might have left the firm with the impression
that it was doing fine. However, as the automobile began to
replace the carriage, the future yields the carriage manufacturer could reasonably expect on its equipment were probably declining drastically. It was only forward-looking prices
that would have informed the business owners that a change
in operations was necessary.

While one business can evaluate its capital in terms of its
estimated contribution to its various plans, what could it mean
to evaluate "society's capital" in terms of all the different plans
being pursued at once? Many of the plans will turn out to con-
tradict each other. Two computer manufacturers may each be
planning to win the computer contract for a new automated
factory. One of them may succeed, but there is no way that
both of them can!

And what is the meaning of the total we would arrive at by
summing the capital of all firms? If we say that FooSoft has $2
billion in capital, we imply that the owners could realize
roughly $2 billion if they decided to liquidate the firm, selling
off that capital. But what would it mean if we said "society"
has $8 trillion in capital? To whom would society sell all of its
capital? Society can't sell $8 trillion worth of goods without
someone else buying $8 trillion worth of goods.

Nor can "society's capital" be said to be permanent unless
individuals correctly plan for its replacement. Capital goods
do not automatically spawn substitutes just as they are about
to wear out. Indeed, for long stretches of history, such as the
period of the decline of the Roman Empire and for several
centuries following its fall, we can find societies consuming
their previously built-up capital, leading to declining living
standards and falling population figures.

A striking contemporary example of the fact that capital does not represent an automatic flow is the destruction of Kuwaiti oil wells by Iraq toward the end of the Gulf War. Saddam Hussein, upon occupying Kuwait, no doubt regarded the wells as valuable capital goods from which he could expect a future stream of revenue. However, the Gulf War led him to a radical reformulation of his plans. His troops detonated explosives at 700 wells, leading to the destruction of the wells and a large amount of oil. No stream of revenue flowed automatically from them.

Such considerations lead us to the Austrian insight that the most important feature of a society's capital goods is not a vague notion of their "total amount," but is, instead, that the goods are parts in an interlocking structure of individual plans.

THE STRUCTURE OF CAPITAL

AUSTRIAN THEORY DIFFERS markedly from the mainstream in the importance it places on the *structure of capital.* The Neoclassical and Keynesian theories tend to treat capital as a homogeneous lump or pool. That allows them to sum up the amount of capital and treat the total capital of an economy as a single number to be fed into mathematical equations.

Austrians consider that approach to be misguided, as it simply eliminates from consideration the most important features of capital. Capital goods, seen as the myriad elements of different individuals' plans, are not most usefully viewed as a single lump. The plans change over time, creating new capital goods, shifting existing capital goods to unforeseen uses, and leaving other items that once were capital goods useless. The plans interact with each other, some of them comple- menting each other and mutually aiding in their fulfillment, others contradicting each other and resulting in one or another plan being thwarted. Even in a socialist economy, where one central planner directs all production, the concept of the economy's total capital does not make sense; in the socialist commonwealth there is no market for capital goods, and therefore no prices with which to sum them up.

The capital structure of the economy might be likened to a coral reef. Each coral is connected to several others. The corals below any particular animal are the higher-order goods that went into its production. Those alongside it are comple- mentary goods that help it to create the next layer of goods. And the corals above it are that next layer of goods it helps to produce.

The entire structure rests on the sandy sea bottom—land. Land, taken in the economic sense to include all of the nature- given factors of production, is the foundation of economic life. At the very least, we need a place to stand or sit—and our bodies—in order to produce something. The natural world is the soil from which our reef grows, and it is built up from that soil by human action. At the very top of the reef, waving in the currents of human desire, are the consumer goods.

The "capital reef" is the basis for civilization. All of the things that enrich our lives—*Hamlet* and HBO, the libraries and the Internet, great paintings and comic books, symphony orchestras and rock bands, synthetic carpeting and Oriental rugs, tomatoes in the winter and ice in the summer, cathedrals and shopping malls—are possible only because of the painstaking building of the reef by previous generations, going back to man's earliest ancestors. If humans still relied on hunting and gathering to eke out their existence, none of those other things would exist.

The pattern of the reef is the web of interactions formed by the entrepreneurs' plans. That interaction will at times render portions of the reef superfluous. The business plan created in the hopes of raising funds may represent a major capital investment for the creator of the plan. But if his company folds while awaiting funding, there is no physical trace of that former capital other than some stacks of paper and some data on a hard disk. Furthermore, the change in those plans will affect the disposition of physical capital. The price of an unshipped, custom-built machine sitting at a supplier's warehouse suddenly sinks to its scrap value and drops out of the reef's structure altogether. Other physical goods may be shifted into other arms of the reef, to play their part in other plans.

Taking our metaphor one more step, we could say that the intensity of the changes in the currents determines how deeply they will affect the reef. As consumer preferences shift, plans are abandoned, altered, and connected to new sequences of plans, restructuring the reef. Minor changes, such as consumers shifting from buying one doll one Christmas to buying another the next, mostly affect the top layers. The doll factory may have to retool to produce the new design, but they will still need plastic, cardboard boxes, metal for their molds, assembly-line workers, and so on. Major changes in the currents will cause changes deep in the structure of the reef.

When consumers shifted their preference for personal transportation from horses to cars, capital structures throughout the economy were destroyed, created, and reconfigured. The need for hay production dropped while that for

oil production rose. Blacksmiths lost jobs while factory workers were hired. Wealth changed hands from those who continued production of goods now in less demand to those who
correctly anticipated the now higher demand for other goods.

In the long run, it is the currents of consumer desire that
determine the overall shape of the reef of plan interactions—
what Hutt and Mises refer to as *consumer sovereignty*. Entrepreneurs realign the structure of the reef in their ceaseless quest for
profits. They succeed only in that the new alignment better
matches the desires of the consumers than did the previous one.

You might object to the notion of consumer sovereignty:
The producers, you say, are sovereign every bit as much as
the consumers. But simply because someone is, for example,
a business owner does not mean he is always acting as a producer. Certainly, a business owner is free to use his business
for personal satisfaction instead of the satisfaction of the consumers. He might decide to convert his factory into a huge
party space for himself and his friends. However, in doing so,
he is acting as a consumer.

Some economists, such as Alfred Marshall, criticized
Menger's conception of goods arrayed in various orders as
vague and unhelpful, since one good can be in several different orders at once. Measured along different paths, a single
coral may be one, two, three, and four layers away from the
top. (Marshall's example was that a train carrying passengers
and various producer goods could belong to four orders at
once.)

The apparent difficulty melts away when it is remembered
that something is a capital good not because of its intrinsic
properties but because of its role in someone's plan to create
a consumer good. Consider oil. Since the dawn of man, vast
pools of it had been sitting right where we drill it from today.

However, nobody considered that oil a capital good, or, indeed, a good at all. The physical properties of the oil did not change, but one day it became valuable. It became a part of people's plans for improving human satisfaction.

If we view capital goods as elements of a plan, we can see that the same good may play a different role in the plans of different people. If I use my car to take Sunday drives, it is a consumer good for me. To a traveling salesman, using the same make of car for sales calls at people's homes, the car is a second-order good. The same model car, used to ferry plans for the construction of a factory back and forth across town, may be many orders of goods away from a final consumer good. There is no reason why a good, like the train mentioned above, should not be a part of different levels of different plans at the same time. My train ticket might represent the purchase of a consumer good while yours represents the purchase of a fourth-order good. The capital nature of a good is not something in the good itself but is the role the good plays in the plans of acting man.

That is not to say that the physical properties of a good are unimportant to its economic character. If oil didn't have the right chemical properties to be used as a fuel, it would not have become a part of anyone's plans for heating his home, except, perhaps, by mistake. But the determining factor in whether something is a capital good or not is a plan. For instance, some people believe rhinoceros horns have medicinal properties. We might doubt that, and study might show that we have good reason for our doubts. But as long as people believe the horns are useful, the tools used to process the horns will be capital goods. The tools will fetch a market price that depends on the value assigned to the horns. The moment the last person stops believing the horns have beneficial properties, the tools will cease being capital goods and will lose all their value, unless they have alternative uses.

The Austrian theory of capital debunks the notion that the market economy is wasteful because it doesn't make use of "idle capital goods." The items in question are, in fact, things that have ceased, at least for the moment, to be capital goods! (Circumstances may change so that it again becomes profitable to employ them, and they will again be capital goods.) The cost of maintaining and employing such goods has come to exceed the return they offer, so they are no longer a part of anyone's plan to produce a consumer good. To put them back into production would waste resources, as they require complementary goods that would be better used elsewhere. For instance, a steel company may have some plants sitting idle because they have become, in the owner's judgment, obsolete. In order to bring those plants back on line, workers would have to be hired, iron and coke purchased, buildings and driveways maintained, electricity and water used, and so on.

Something can only be an economic good if it is scarce. For many of the scarce factors of production, there are several alternative uses. By bidding various prices for consumer goods, consumers indicate the importance of the various uses in satisfying their unmet demands.

If the expected revenues from the output of the closed steel plant do not exceed the cost of the complementary goods needed to operate it, then consumers do not value that use of those resources as much as they do an alternative use. That fact is indicated to the owner of the steel company by the fact that others are willing to bid more than he is for the use of those resources.

Another complaint leveled against the market is that it does not abandon older, technologically less efficient methods of production fast enough. (The foes of the market economy have seldom worried about the consistency of their attacks.) But technological efficiency is not the same thing as economic efficiency. A new plant is more economically efficient than an older one only if the returns it offers on invested capital are higher than those of the older plant. That is precisely the point when a profit-seeking entrepreneur will abandon his old plant and build a new one. It is not the historical costs involved in building and maintaining the old plant that restrain him. Those are *sunk costs*, and, as we know, bygones are bygones. Rather, it is the demand in other uses for the resources needed to build the new plant that restrains the entrepreneur from proceeding. To build new equipment, the necessary resources must be bid away from other productive activities. The entrepreneur determines if it is worthwhile to do so by estimating whether he will make a profit despite bidding more for those resources than their current users are bidding.

ROUNDABOUT METHODS OF PRODUCTION

ONE OF THE frequent sources of puzzlement about the Austrian School's theory of capital has been the notion of *roundabout methods of production*. Carl Menger's student, Eugen von Böhm-Bawerk, in his masterwork *Capital and Interest*, attributed the bulk of increases in productivity to the adoption of more time-consuming, or roundabout, methods of production.

Various writers have found themselves dumbfounded by Böhm-Bawerk's contention. How, they ask, could taking longer to do something make one more productive? Why don't shorter processes mean increased productivity?

The bewilderment is understandable, but it can be cleared up. Mises, Kirzner, Lachmann, Rothbard, and other writers have refined Böhm-Bawerk's theory and explained the apparent paradox. There is nothing intrinsically more productive about taking a long time to do something. Otherwise, we could increase productivity by working very slowly!

However, if a longer process of production is adopted, it can only be because the entrepreneur who adopts it suspects that the new process will be more productive than the old one. Let us imagine a software company, FooSoft, that has been producing programs without the use of any specialized software for creating graphics, windows, and the other items of the program's user interface. The owner of FooSoft decides that he should buy a program to help the company with interface building. This new tool will take time to install, configure, and learn to use. Instead of directly producing programs for the customers, the software engineers will be spending some time working on a higher-order capital good, only then to return to direct production of their final good.

Furthermore, the software tool itself will cost FooSoft something. FooSoft could have used the money spent on this tool, instead, to hire another engineer to directly produce more of its final program.

It should be clear that FooSoft's owner will only undertake such a project if he believes that the higher productivity offered by the more roundabout method will more than make up for the costs of adopting it. Earlier, we saw that Rich will only build rat traps as long as the benefit of another trap exceeds the cost of what he gives up to build that trap. Similarly, for an entrepreneur to invest in a new process, he must believe that it will yield more than the risk-free rate of interest and more than any other project he can conceive of investing in instead. The expected return must exceed his opportunity cost.

The economy generally advances through increasing the "roundaboutness" of production because the shorter methods have been tried already. Acting man attempts to move toward his goals by the most direct route available to him. It is only when he expects that what he can achieve on a direct route will be less valuable than what he can achieve on an indirect route that he will search out alternative methods.

Imagine that you are a coin collector with the goal of owning one coin of every denomination from every date and mint issued by the U.S. government. You can easily begin your collection by pulling coins out of your pocket change. You will rapidly assemble a collection of the most recent dates of the currently circulating denominations. But gradually you will find that the marginal benefit of your efforts is declining. Each hour spent going through change yields fewer new coins for your collection.

At some point you will come to contemplate a more roundabout method of acquiring coins. Perhaps you will drive to a local trade show and see what is on display. To do so, you will have to get in your car, drive it to the show, spend time at the show, and drive home. You will wear out your car and consume gasoline. You will only undertake those costs if you expect that the reward, in terms of coins found, will exceed the costs. (And note that you are also increasingly relying on the roundabout production of others, who have produced your car, refined the gasoline, set up the trade show, and so on.)

Gradually, as your collection advances, you will find yourself going to greater lengths to complete it—perhaps traveling to shows in distant cities or joining a society devoted to exchanging information on rare coins. You have exhausted the gains you can achieve with shorter methods of production and must turn to those that are more roundabout.

It is always true that an entrepreneur will choose a more roundabout method of production only if he estimates that the higher returns from that method exceed the cost of the longer waiting time before the final product emerges. It is not always true that the only available method of increasing production is to adopt more roundabout methods. Perhaps a shorter route to some goal just has not been imagined yet. In that case, a conceptual breakthrough, rather than an adoption of more roundabout methods, will lead most directly to increased productivity. In our example above, you might suddenly discover that your neighbor is also a U.S. coin collector, and that you can complete more of your collection by walking next door and buying from him than by driving to trade shows. But historically, the constant agitation of humans to improve their circumstances is such that *most* of the opportunities to increase productivity lie in the adoption of more roundabout processes. Humans are adept at spotting the direct route to a goal in the first place.

In a remarkable passage from *Language and Myth*, the German philosopher Ernst Cassirer contended that the adoption of more roundabout processes is the means by which the human intellect itself advances:

> All cultural work, be it technical or purely intellectual, proceeds by the gradual shift from the direct relation between man and his environment to an indirect relation. In the beginning, sensual impulse is followed immediately by its gratification; but gradually more and more mediating terms intervene between the will and its object. It is as though the will, in order to gain its end, had to move away

from the goal instead of toward it; instead of a simple reaction, almost in the nature of a reflex, to
bring the object into reach, it requires a differentia-
tion of behavior, covering a wider class of objects,
so that finally the sum total of all these acts, by the
use of various "means," may realize the desired end.

CHAPTER 9

What Goes Up, Must Come Down

ON THE EFFECT OF FLUCTUATIONS
IN THE MONEY SUPPLY

MONEY SUBSTITUTES

*W*E SAW THAT money arose because people were willing to exchange a less marketable good for a more marketable one, even if it was not the good that they ultimately desired. Gradually, one commodity, often gold, emerged as the most marketable good of all. As participants in the economy came to recognize that fact, the commodity would take on the role of a universal medium of exchange: money.

There are disadvantages to lugging around gold, however. One is that although it has a high value per unit of weight compared to many other commodities (one of the reasons that it often was chosen as money), its weight is not insignificant. Another downside to gold is that, while it is divisible, it is not easy to divide precisely, in the midst of a transaction. And gold coins clinking around in your pocket alert potential thieves to a target.

Because of these disadvantages, the practice of using *money certificates* came into being. People could take their gold to a bank, which might be a purely private business, an official government bank, or, as in the U.S. today, a mix of the two. The bank would hold their gold in a secure facility and issue the depositor a piece of paper. Such an instrument is called a *banknote*, and it allows the depositor to reclaim the gold at any time by turning in the note to the bank. The paper is lighter than gold and therefore easier to carry. The bank could also issue, for instance, four quarter-ounce banknotes for a single one-ounce gold coin, easing the process of making change and allowing for finer-grained prices. *Token coins* minted with metals less valuable than gold (e.g., silver, nickel, and copper) can serve the same purpose, as well as possessing some residual value as a metal.

So long as others are confident that the bank will honor its money certificates and coins, they will accept the notes and coins as substitutes for money itself. The use of money substitutes lowers transaction costs.

The use of money substitutes does not change the amount of money in circulation. For every note issued, a corresponding amount of money proper (e.g., gold) has been stowed away in a vault. But banks may notice that they have a potential source of profit beyond whatever fees they charge for storing gold. Since not all of the claims for gold are redeemed at any one time, the bank may conclude that it can issue more gold-redeemable banknotes than the amount of gold it is holding. The bank can then lend those notes and earn interest on them. As long as every depositor doesn't show up on the same day to claim his or her gold, the bank will remain viable. Such notes, issued in excess of the amount of money proper that a bank holds in reserve, are called *fiduciary media*.

If a bank miscalculates its need for gold reserves, and is met with more demands for redemption than it can meet, it is faced with a liquidity crisis. As soon as it is discovered that the bank has failed to meet any of its obligations, all depositors will attempt to withdraw their funds. There will be a *run on the bank*. Hollywood produced a famous example of a bank run when, in *Mary Poppins*, Michael demanded his tuppence back. Customers, hearing what they thought was a depositor being denied his funds, immediately began trying to withdraw their own money. The bank shut down to avoid collapse.

There is spirited debate in the Austrian School as to whether the issuance of fiduciary media, in a pure market economy, is an acceptable practice. On the one side there are those who argue that market forces will generally constrain banks from issuing more fiduciary media than prudence permits. Those that are overzealous in note issuance will fail, and will serve as a notice to consumers to monitor the bank with which they deposit their money. Many of those economists contend that the issue of fiduciary media increases the ability of the economy to adjust to changes in the demand for money. They argue for a system of *free banking*.

On the other side of the issue are those who argue that the issuance of fiduciary media is inherently fraudulent, as the bank is not backing up each claim to gold with actual gold. They contend that the practice will inevitably lead to banking crises. The economists on that side of the debate argue for a system of *one-hundred-percent-reserve banking*, where all notes are fully backed by gold. There is an extensive literature on each side of the issue, some of which I will mention in the bibliography, but we won't attempt to resolve the dispute here.

Both sides agree that what happens next is the cause of enormous troubles. Banks, whether owned privately or by the government, tend to be politically well connected. Historically,

when a bank has gotten into trouble by issuing more fiduciary media than the market would support, it has gone to the
government for protection against the inevitable run. Insolvent banks, instead of being forced to liquidate, have been
given government relief. They have been allowed to suspend
payments or been given special loans from the Treasury or
central bank.

The special status given to banks has allowed them to
operate in an almost risk-free environment. They may make
loans far beyond what prudence would counsel. If their bets
pay off, they profit. If they don't, the government bails them
out. That leads to what is called *moral hazard*, where banks
are constantly tempted to take on more risk than if they were
forced to suffer the consequences on their own. The law
makes banks privileged players in the economy, with everyone else left holding the bag for their mistakes. Both the free
bankers and the one-hundred-percent reservists agree that is
unjust and inefficient.

One of the chief means by which governments prop up
insolvent banks is through the creation of a central bank with
the power to act as a lender of last resort. (In the U.S., the central bank is called the Federal Reserve.) Since every time the
banking system runs into trouble, the central bank is required
to supply it with reserves, the strain on its resources is often
tremendous. Eventually, it is likely that this bank will simply
stop paying out commodity money at all, declaring that the
circulating banknotes are the only real money. Money of that
kind, as we mentioned, is called fiat money—it is money
because the government has declared it so. Historically, the
U.S. moved to a fiat money system in two steps. The first took
place in 1933, when Franklin Roosevelt suspended domestic
redemption of gold and confiscated all privately held gold.
The U.S. completed the move away from gold as money in

1971 when Richard Nixon stopped exchanging U.S. dollars for gold with foreign countries as well.

INFLATION AND DEFLATION

*O*NE OF THE historical effects of the move from commodity money to fiat money has been greater volatility in prices. That has increased the importance of a proper understanding of *inflation* and *deflation*.

The standard definition of inflation is "too much money chasing too few goods," and the corresponding one for deflation runs something like "too little money chasing too many goods." These definitions are imprecise, because prices, given time, can adjust to any particular amount of money existing in the economy. There are practical limits on the amount of some good that must be available for it to be used as money. But goods not falling within those limits will not be chosen as money. Neither a metal so rare that it would need to be divided at the atomic level to make change, nor a commodity so plentiful that a shopping cart full of it is required to buy a pack of gum, will be suitable as money. For any good that might realistically be chosen as money, Murray Rothbard points out "there is no such thing as 'too little' or 'too much' money . . . *whatever the social money stock, the benefits of money are always utilized to the maximum extent*" (*Man, Economy, and State*).

Economist Paul Krugman frequently has cited what he believes is a simple, contrary example to that principle. He describes a baby-sitting co-op in the Washington, D.C., area. To ensure that each parent did his fair share of sitting, it used coupons as a "currency," each representing one hour of baby-sitting. It essentially created its own fiat baby-sitting money, which each participant could trade for baby-sitting from any of the other participants.

Krugman contends that the currency was too scarce. The residents hoarded it, even when they might have wanted to hire a sitter, because they couldn't get enough of it to guarantee they'd have some when they *really* needed a sitter. Because others were hoarding coupons, each person had difficulty acquiring more of them. So, Krugman concludes, all the residents had to do to get their baby-sitting economy going again was to circulate more coupons. The market had failed and the "government" (the sitters' association) had to step in and prime the pump.

His example actually illustrates the danger of price-fixing rather than the need for an active monetary policy. The problem the sitters' co-op had was that it had tried to arbitrarily set the price of baby-sitting in terms of coupons. If it had let people needing sitters bid whatever they wanted to for an hour of sitting, the price in coupons would have dropped until the amount of currency was completely adequate to meet their needs.[1]

The desire to hold cash alters prices. It is true that not everyone in the economy can put more dollars under their

---

[1] Krugman would answer by pointing to the "stickiness" of prices, especially wages, in the downward direction. We'll discuss *that* problem later. He might also contend that it was the *change* in people's desire for cash holdings that was the problem, although his article in *Slate* describing the co-op emphasizes the quantity of coupons.

mattress at the same time. As there are only so many dollars in existence, everyone's efforts to trade goods for a certain number of dollars cannot all succeed. They need someone on the other side of the exchange, trading dollars for goods. But even if all market participants are trying to trade goods for dollars, they *can* achieve their goal in the sense that the real value of each person's cash holdings can rise at the same time. Trying to gain cash by selling goods, people drive the price of money up and that of all other goods down. There won't be more dollars in the economy, but at the new, lower price level, each dollar can buy more.

The opposite effect occurs if people desire smaller cash balances. Everyone cannot achieve that in dollar terms. Unless they are burning their money in the yard, people will receive whatever money they trade for goods, making the recipients' cash balances larger. Economists say that the *nominal* value of the total cash holdings cannot be altered in such a fashion, where nominal means "measured in dollars." (If your country uses the pound, peso, mark, or lira, just substitute that for the dollar.) But in what economists call *real* (purchasing power, not dollar amount) terms, everyone *can* reduce his or her cash balance. Attempting to shed cash by buying goods, people drive the price level up. Although the dollar amount of the net cash balances will not have changed, each dollar is able to buy less.

The effects described in the previous two paragraphs do not make everyone, on the whole, wealthier or poorer. Although each person prefers his or her new level of cash holding to the previous one, it makes no sense to say "society" can increase or decrease its cash balance. If the net of everyone's decision to hold more cash has driven the price level down, that doesn't mean that "society" has a larger cash balance. For each individual, his cash balance is larger in that it can now buy more goods. But if everyone attempts, at the same time, to use his higher real balances to purchase more goods, it would be a reversal of the general desire to hold larger cash balances, and it simply would drive the price level back up.

Since, given time, prices can adjust to any particular amount of money in the economy, inflation and deflation are best viewed as rapid *changes* in the amount of money in the economy. Rapid increases in the money supply are called inflation, and rapid decreases are called deflation. It is the fact that it takes time for all prices to adjust to the new amount of money that makes inflation and deflation economically significant.

If the government is in charge of creating money, its interest generally will run toward inflating the money supply. It can use the new money for increased spending, without having to go through the unpopular measure of raising taxes. That helps explain why prices have been more volatile since governments have replaced the gold standard with fiat money. Gold must be dug up from the ground and processed, and that takes time and effort. It is much easier to set a printing press running. The adoption of fiat money has made inflation simpler to achieve than it had been under the gold standard.

Historically, deflation is less important than inflation, so we will concentrate our discussion on inflation. There have been few historical examples of governments deliberately deflating. (Britain's return of the pound to the prewar parity with gold after the Napoleonic Wars and World War I are notable exceptions.) That is because, as pointed out above, inflation is a source of revenue for the government that is doing the inflating. Since the government prints the money, it gets to spend it first. With more money in circulation, each dollar is worth less: Inflation acts as a stealth tax on the value of citizens' cash holdings.

Inflation also creates the illusion of prosperity, adding to its popularity. We will examine the relationship between inflation and the booms and busts of the modern economy further in Chapter 13. For now, I simply will point out that the relationship between economic growth and inflation frequently implied by the financial press is backward. Whenever aggregate measures of economic growth, such as gross domestic product (GDP), gross national product (GNP), and so on, rise at a relatively fast rate, we hear that the growing economy may "ignite inflation."

But prices rise in response to an increase in the value of money relative to other goods. Economic growth—in other words, more goods—cannot possibly cause inflation! The analysis of the process in the popular press reverses cause and effect. Inflation creates the illusion of rapid growth in the economy. Before it is realized that a general price rise is under way, some people feel richer, due to higher money profits and money wages, while other people really are richer, since they received the new money first, before a general rise in prices occurred. Those people will tend to spend more than they would have otherwise, making it seem that the economy is growing more rapidly.

Some people mistake this illusory prosperity for real growth and recommend constant inflation as a means to continuing prosperity. They call their policy "low interest rates." Since, when the Fed sets rates artificially low, it must increase the money supply to keep them low, it comes to the same thing. But inflation cannot really make society as a whole wealthier. Every transaction that is income for person A is an expense for person B. If we try to use a rise in prices to universally boost incomes, we must, simply by definition, also universally (and to the same extent) boost expenses. It is as though my wife and I tried to get rich by paying each other an increasing amount of money every week.

Similarly, deflation is not necessarily an evil. Even if nominal wages are dropping, standards of living can still rise, as long as prices for consumer goods are dropping even faster. The worker does not care about his nominal wage, but about what standard of living that wage will support.

Let's isolate the effect of inflation on the overall price level with the use of a thought experiment. We'll imagine an isolated village—we'll call it Walras. Walras has some important characteristics for our purposes—the stuff it uses as money has no other use, and it is, in every sense, perfect money: it is perfectly and effortlessly divisible, weightless, without volume, can't be lost or stolen, and so on. (Such money is, of course, impossible, but we want to abstract away all but one aspect of inflation in our tale.)

Walras is visited, late one night, by the legendary Ghost of Fisher. The phantom mysteriously doubles the amount of money held by every person in the village. What's more, the Ghost of Fisher is able to communicate, to everyone, an exact and complete understanding of what has happened to the money supply.

The result of the ghost's activities is that all prices in Walras will immediately double. We have postulated that every person has complete knowledge of the new state of the money supply. Therefore, everyone will understand that, with the new doubled quantity of money and nothing new to spend it on, buyers will bid up prices to twice what they were. But since our assumption also implies that everyone knows that everyone else knows that prices will double, there is no point in anyone bidding less than twice what he used to for something; the seller *knows* the price will double. As soon as the Ghost of Fisher transmits the knowledge of the inflation, the price of everything has, essentially, already doubled. There is more money in Walras, but the usefulness of each money unit has declined commensurately.

That is the world in which the quantity theory of money fully describes the effect of inflation. This theory, originated by Jean Bodin, John Locke, and David Hume, relates changes in the quantity of money to changes in the price level. Economist Irving Fisher formulated the algebraic expression of the theory in 1911: $MV = PT$, or the quantity of money M times the rate at which it circulates, V, equals the price level P times the volume of transactions T. If we regard the equation as a rough description of the equilibrium position toward which the market process will guide prices after a change in the quantity of money, it is a useful tool. Much like the evenly rotating economy, it can give us a picture of the general direction of a central tendency in the economy.

But it is highly misleading to regard the equation as a picture of the most significant effects of inflation in the real world. We have abstracted out the important elements of the picture, from the point of view of human action. Humans are uninterested in a phenomenon that will leave their state of satisfaction unchanged, such as the instantaneous doubling of cash holdings and all prices. Such a change could occur every night, and no one in Walras would give a hoot.

Human creativity in the face of the uncertain future means that the actors in our economy, who in reality do not all learn about all changes instantly, will strive to understand first the effects of economic changes. Those who comprehend early the nature of change will attempt to buy and sell before the new knowledge becomes widespread. Rather than complain that they are taking advantage of others, it seems more useful to note that it is only the entrepreneurial search for profit that drives prices toward equilibrium. There simply is no other way to discover equilibrium prices than by allowing people to employ their wits in trying to figure them out. Allowing them to profit from more accurate estimates and lose on less accurate ones is the only way to align their motivation with the need for price discovery.

The knowledge of the new state of monetary affairs will not be instantly in everyone's head. Nor will the new money be distributed proportionately into everyone's pocket. The new money cannot possibly hit all areas of the economy at the same time. Who it does go to first is determined, in a fiat money economy, by government policy. Curiously enough, quite often the answer seems to be large and politically well-connected banks.

The definitions of inflation and deflation we are using here are Austrian, not mainstream, definitions. When most economists talk about inflation, they are referring to an increase in the price level (the P of the Fisher equation), and by deflation, they mean a decrease in the *price level*. However, the Austrian definitions have two major advantages over those of the mainstream. First, the notion of measuring the price level is itself problematic, as we will see in the next section.

Even if we assume away that difficulty, a second problem exists: The mainstream definitions mask the most significant economic phenomena involved, pointing, instead, to a symptom of those phenomena. The Fischer equation shows *roughly* where the economy is headed, once all of the effects of the inflation or deflation have worked themselves out. It is the working out that is the more interesting topic. As we have seen above, the creation of new money in an economy inevitably alters economic relations among people, in addition to altering the relationship between goods and money. Those who get the new money first are aided; those who get it last, hurt. These are called *Cantillon effects*, named after the great Irish-French economist Richard Cantillon.

The first recipients of the newly created money are in a position to spend it before the inflation raises prices throughout the entire economy. They now have more cash, but, unlike the people in Walras, they have it before everyone else, and before the effect of the new money is fully felt throughout the economy. Unlike the people of our mythical village, the new amount of money they possess will buy them more goods than the previous amount they had.

The process by which new money flows into the economy is not like the neutral money image of a bathtub filling evenly from all sides. Rather, it is like the discharging of a liquid into a river. The chaotic flow of the turbulent market process carries the new liquid along paths that are inherently unpredictable, even by those creating the money. Human action is creative, and we cannot even say ourselves what course of action we might take if we awake tomorrow to a new world.

CAN WE MEASURE THE PRICE LEVEL?

*W*E MENTIONED THAT the concept of stable money has led to a desire for price indices that can measure the value of money. There are two common fallacies at the root of the desire for stable money. One is that money is a "measure of value," and the other is that it is a "store of value."

Value is subjective and cannot be measured. If two parties exchange $10 for a bag of onions, it does not mean that we have "measured" the value of onions to be $10. It means that the person who bought the onions valued them *more than* $10, while the person who sold the onions valued them *less than* the $10. No measurement is involved. It does not make sense to assign to the onions and dollars "equal" values. To whom are the values equal? Valuation means preferring one thing to another, never indifference between them. Prices are not measurements but historical facts, indicating that at such-and-such a place and time, two parties exchanged one bag of onions for $10.

Nor is money a "store of value." The phrase implies that money is some sort of container, into which value can be poured. When we have inflation, it seems that some of the value has "leaked out" of money, while in a deflation, value has somehow "seeped in" to money. What people who use that phrase are talking about can be indicated much more clearly: people value money, and they can store it. (The fact that it can be stored is one of the reasons a good emerges as money.) While they store it, its value may rise or fall. There is nothing special about money in that respect: you can store a painting or a book, and its value might also rise or fall while it is being stored.

Even if we ignore the fact that money is not a measure of value, the idea of a price index encounters a second difficulty. Economist Richard Timberlake, in defense of price indices in an article "Austrian 'Inflation,' Austrian Money," compares them to thermometers. True, his line of reasoning goes, they are not perfectly accurate—but neither are thermometers, yet we still use them.

But let us see whether the consumer price index (CPI) and other measures like it are really analogous to a thermometer. A thermometer is a measuring device that we can place in an environment where an independent phenomenon (in the case of a thermometer, molecular motion) is taking place. The measuring device responds to that phenomenon in a predictable manner, most often by some sort of visible display. The display is interpreted as having some correspondence with the quantity we want to measure. For example, the height of mercury in a thermometer corresponds to the temperature in the area where it is placed. The position of the needle on an ammeter corresponds to the current passing through the wires to which it is connected.

When it comes to price levels, what are we measuring? And what is the measuring device? Our readings are all in terms of prices, in other words, the exchange rate of various goods for money. For the thermometer analogy to hold we must take money itself as the measuring device.

But a price index is not measuring the monetary temperature of a good—or indeed, all goods—at a single point in time. It is an attempt to track the readings of our thermometer over time, to see if the readings are stable. A price index tries to track changes in the money price of the "same" basket of goods. Therefore, since money is our thermometer, a price index is *an attempt to gauge the stability of our measuring device.*

Now we can construct a more accurate thermometer analogy. We have a device, money, which we suppose is measuring the value of goods. That device gives us various readings—gold traded for $275 today, bread is $1.19 a loaf, and so on. What we are interested in is finding out whether, over time, that thermometer is drifting; is it giving us generally higher or lower readings for all goods on average, rather than just for some particular good?

If we had some "measure" of value besides money prices, our venture would be much easier. However, we don't. So those advocating price indices are recommending that we check for drift in our thermometer by wandering from place to place, checking the temperature from time to time—*with the very thermometer whose accuracy we are testing!*

We can see that we have arrived at a severe problem. There is no way to determine which changes in measured temperature are real, and which are caused by drift in our thermometer. Let's look at one example that illustrates the problem.

We'll say that we are trying to determine whether the cost of computer programming has risen in the last thirty years. The services of today's programmers, armed with significant advances in software engineering and capitalized with better tools, are just not the same good as those of the programmers of thirty years ago. (That is no comment on the people themselves—any particular person programming today should be vastly more productive than he was thirty years ago.) We can guess that an hour of programming today should be more valuable than an hour of programming was thirty years ago. In order to determine if the cost of programming has risen, we will have to establish some ratio between the goods—for example, one hour of 1972 programming is equivalent to fifteen minutes of 2002 programming—and compare the cost after applying this ratio.

However, there is no way to measure the change in valuation other than by comparing what employers are willing to pay for programmers now with what they paid in 1972. To try and gauge the value of programmers' labor by lines of code or something of the sort is to fall back into the fallacious labor theory of value. The only possible thermometer for measuring the change in valuation—money—is precisely the device whose accuracy we wish to check.

The attempt to measure the price level is not useless, as long as it is taken as a rough approximation of changes in the value of money. To return to the thermometer: If, in our peripatetic attempts to check its accuracy, we read 80 degrees, walk five feet, then read 40 degrees, we might suspect that something is up with the thermometer. Similarly, when the Consumer Price Index (CPI) shows 20-percent inflation, money is probably losing value. Such figures may be useful for economic history or for planning a year's business expenses. However, if CPI figures show that inflation has "ticked up" from 2.5 percent to 2.6 percent, we are justified in doubting that this .1-percent increase is really indicating anything about the value of money.

As Mises said in *Human Action*:

> The pretentious solemnity which statisticians and statistical bureaus display in computing indexes of purchasing power and cost of living is out of place. These index numbers are at best rather crude and inaccurate illustrations of changes which have occurred. In periods of slow alterations in the relation between the supply of and the demand for money they do not convey any information at all. In periods of inflation and consequently of sharp price changes they provide a rough image of events which every individual experiences in his daily life. A judicious housewife knows much more about price changes as far as they affect her own household than the statistical averages can tell. She has little use for computations disregarding changes both in quality and in the amount of goods which she is

able or permitted to buy at the prices entering into the computation. If she "measures" the changes for her personal appreciation by taking the prices of only two or three commodities as a yardstick, she is no less "scientific" and no more arbitrary than the sophisticated mathematicians in choosing their methods for the manipulation of the data of the market.

PART III

INTERFERENCE WITH THE MARKET

CHAPTER 10

A World Become One

ON THE DIFFICULTIES OF THE
SOCIALIST COMMONWEALTH

THE CALCULATION PROBLEM

*P*ICTURE YOURSELF AS the head planner of a worldwide socialist commonwealth. The Northern Hemisphere spring has been particularly hot and dry. Your subalterns come to you and ask you what to do about agricultural planning for the summer season. All of the farm managers are crying out for more water, but there is not enough to meet all of their requests, in addition to keeping the city folk supplied with drinking water and the factories running.

Your alternatives are legion. To better comprehend the choice you are faced with, it is useful to contemplate some of the numbers involved. In 1999, there were over two million farms in the U.S. If the growing season is dry across the Northern Hemisphere as a whole, we could certainly add millions more farms to the total affected. Since water is so divisible, you could allocate to each farm, let's say, millions of different amounts of water. But the water must arrive at the farm. And for each farm, there may be any number of ways to get water there. For any particular farm, you might decide to re-route city drinking water, build an aqueduct, establish a new salinization

plant, dispatch trucks, and so on. Each of these ways of real-
locating water will impact different nonagricultural users in
different ways. And a choice of how to acquire water to allocate on one farm will affect what is available for other farms,
as they may be on the same local water system, sharing an
aquifer, or near the same reservoir.

Each farm manager, given his allotment of water, can
choose to cope in a variety of ways. If the amount of water
allocated to a farm is less than the average year's supply, the
manager can choose any combination of installing water con-
servation devices, switching crops, producing less total weight
of crop, reducing the quality of the produce, and, I'm sure,
other things a farmer could tell you about but I can't. And you,
the central planner, might consider closing farms and sending
the workers off to other employment. What is the number of
possible solutions you face? Is it in the trillions? Quadrillions?

How can you decide what course of action you should
take? The answer is that you can't. That is to say that there is
no rational system by which you can allocate water. The best
you can do is to venture a guess and then order your minions
to implement it. The reason that you can't rationally arrive at
an answer to your dilemma is that you lack market prices for
the factors of production to which you must assign a use. It is
market prices that enable business accounting and rational
calculation of profits and losses. The key characteristic of
socialism is that the factors of production are not owned by
various individuals, but are monopolized by the state. The
market process—the ceaseless striving of entrepreneurs to
locate price discrepancies and profit from them, thus better
adjusting prices to the demands of the consumers—is absent
from the imaginary construction of the socialist economy.
Unfortunately for socialism, there is nothing that can substitute
for that process. The mathematical equations describing the

evenly rotating economy are of no use in determining how to move toward that state. Various attempts to set up "pseudo-markets" among socialist managers that arrive at "market-like" prices are akin to playing chess with oneself. It is competition among private property owners that generates real prices.

Now imagine a free market for water. (The U.S. water market is not a pure free market, as local, state, and federal agencies are very active in intervening in it.) In such a market, the drought is handled by the locally informed choices of myriad individuals. Farmer Joe has a bunch of black plastic in his barn. When water prices rise in response to the shortage, he finds it worth his while to unroll it and lay it around his crops, in order to conserve water. Farmer Mary has been thinking of installing a drip irrigation system anyway; in response to the price rise she calculates that it is now worthwhile. Other farms will dig deeper wells, or invest in a water cooperative in order to build an aqueduct, or plant a crop that needs less water. Entrepreneurs operating in the water market will be keenly sensitive to small local variations in price, reflective of differing demand for water from place to place, and will work to take advantage of any price discrepancies by routing water from areas where the price is lower to those where it is higher.

Some farmers may need extra cash to see them through the drought period. Which farmers are worth investing in because they can weather the crisis? The local water dealer can judge this to an extent by looking at how long a farmer has been his customer, how strong his ties to the community are, and how timely a fashion he has paid his bills. Anyone who has dealt with a local merchant long enough to become a "regular customer" knows that merchants try to gauge who is worth carrying through a temporary crunch to do business with again when the crunch is over.

Imagine that you are a central planner with a mountain of steel. You know how to make things with it, and you know that people want cars, tractors, microchips, strong buildings, and electrical wire, among a multitude of other uses. But because you don't have an infinite amount of steel (to say nothing of every other good and service that goes into making those items) you must make choices concerning economic priorities. You must allocate and produce at the least cost and in a manner consistent with the priorities of the consuming public, about which you know absolutely nothing.

It is a hopeless task! Lenin promised that under socialism "the population will gradually learn by themselves to understand and realize how much and what kind of work must be done, how much and what kind of recreation should be taken." But imagine doing this in a world without any pricing signals! And imagine doing it in a world that is constantly in flux. You end up with a situation like Mises described in 1920:

> There will be hundreds and thousands of factories in operation. Very few of these will be producing wares ready for use; in the majority of cases what will be manufactured will be unfinished goods and production goods. All these concerns will be interrelated. Every good will go through a whole series of stages before it is ready for use. In the ceaseless toil and moil of this process, however, the administration will be without any means of testing their bearings. It will never be able to determine whether a given good has not been kept for a superfluous length of time in the necessary processes of production, or whether work and material have not been wasted in its completion. How will it be able to decide whether this or that method of production is the more profitable? At best it will only be able to compare the quality and quantity of the consumable

end product produced, but will in the rarest cases be in a position to compare the expenses entailed in production. (Mises, *Economic Calculation in the Socialist Commonwealth*)

F.A. Hayek highlighted another aspect of the problem socialist planners face. In his famous essay, "The Use of Knowledge in Society," he pointed out the importance of "the particular circumstances of time and place" in making economic decisions. Hayek says:

Today it is almost heresy to suggest that scientific knowledge is not the sum of all knowledge. But a little reflection will show that there is beyond question a body of very important but unorganized knowledge which cannot possibly be called scientific in the sense of knowledge of general rules: the knowledge of the particular circumstances of time and place. It is with respect to this that practically every individual has some advantage over all others because he possesses unique information of which beneficial use might be made, but of which use can be made only if the decisions depending on it are left to him or are made with his active co-operation. We need to remember only how much we have to learn in any occupation after we have completed our theoretical training, how big a part of our working life we spend learning particular jobs, and how valuable an asset in all walks of life is knowledge of people, of local conditions, and of special circumstances. To know of and put to use a machine not fully employed, or somebody's skill which could be better utilized, or to be aware of a surplus stock which can be drawn upon during an interruption of supplies, is socially quite as useful as the knowledge of better alternative techniques. The shipper who

> earns his living from using otherwise empty or half-filled journeys of tramp-steamers, or the estate agent whose whole knowledge is almost exclusively one of temporary opportunities, or the arbitrageur who gains from local differences of commodity prices—are all performing eminently useful functions based on special knowledge of circumstances of the fleeting moment not known to others.

The contributions of Mises and Hayek to the theory of socialism are closely related. Mises showed the impossibility of all socialist schemes, because they leave the economic planners with no means by which to perform economic calculation. Hayek highlights the *reason* that market prices enable rational calculation: market prices for the factors of production reflect the best estimates of their role in filling consumers' needs, made by the previously most successful entrepreneurs. (It is the previously successful entrepreneurs who have the most influence on the price of the factors of production because they're the ones with the dough!) In bidding for the factors of production, each entrepreneur is able to use his own local knowledge of the circumstances in which he finds himself in estimating what to bid. Those estimates are not perfect. But the results of past estimates are the starting point from which the entrepreneur begins his calculations, and those calculations generate new estimates. (The evenly rotating economy is an image of a society in which all of the estimates *are* perfect, all of the time, for the rest of time. But, as we have seen, such an economy has no place left for human action—everything is already perfectly accounted for, and there is no room for further improvement.)

A central planning bureau has no mechanism that can fill the role that prices play in the market. As Mises puts it in *Human Action*:

Even if, for the sake of argument, we assume that a miraculous inspiration has enabled the director [of a socialist economy] without economic calculation to solve all problems concerning the most advantageous arrangement of all production activities and that the precise image of the final goal he must aim at is present to his mind, there remain essential problems which cannot be dealt with without economic calculation. For the director's task is not to begin from the very bottom of civilization and to start economic history from scratch. The elements with the aid of which he must operate are not only natural resources untouched by previous utilization. There are also the capital goods produced in the past and not convertible or not perfectly convertible for new projects. It is in precisely these artifacts, produced under a constellation in which valuations, technological knowledge and many other things were different from what they are today, that our wealth is embodied. Their structure, quality, quantity, and location is of primary importance in the choice of all further economic operations. Some of them may be absolutely useless for any further employment; they must remain "unused capacity." But the greater part of them must be utilized if we do not want to start anew from the extreme poverty and destitution of primitive man and want to survive the period which separates us from the day on which the reconstruction of the apparatus of production according to the new plans will be accomplished. The director cannot merely erect a new construction without bothering about his wards' fate in the waiting period. He must try to take advantage of every piece of the already available capital goods in the best possible way. (Mises, *Human Action*)

Lacking real prices, the director has no clue as to that "best possible way."

Of course, there are other telling arguments against the possibility of successfully organizing a society along socialist lines, such as the problem of motivation. In a market society, people are motivated to increase the satisfaction of their fellows because that is how they get paid. While Mother Teresa or Albert Schweitzer may have performed their work on purely humanitarian grounds, most people choose socially useful work because it pays. If a mason works hard at his trade and becomes eminent in his field, he can expect to directly reap much of the benefit of his hard work. But in the socialist commonwealth, the benefits of this hard work are diffused across the entire society. The mason can expect to receive a miniscule part of the extra value that his hard work generated.

Historically speaking, we can certainly see that this has been a problem in every society that has attempted to implement the socialist program. On a purely empirical basis, we might decide that it is highly unlikely that any socialist society could overcome this handicap. But, we must admit, there is no basic principle of human action that says that people couldn't all place the good of the society as a whole, *as seen by the central planners*, first on their list of values, however implausible we might think that this is in reality. Socialists could argue that in the yet unachieved glory of the socialist paradise, all men would act from a sense of altruism.

Mises's great accomplishment in analyzing socialism was to show that a rational allocation of the factors of production is impossible in socialism, even if all people were perfect socialist citizens. A race of saints would still be unable to perform economic calculation in the absence of market prices for the factors of production. Even though they all desired to fulfill the most urgent needs of society, without prices, they could not determine what means should be used to fulfill those needs. While the argument from motivation shows that it is highly unlikely that socialism could create a successful society, supporting the billions of humans who are alive in the world today, Mises's argument shows that it is impossible.

Some people have found it odd that Mises referred to socialism as "impossible." "Aren't there," they ask, "numerous examples of socialist societies? Perhaps we don't like the results, but surely we must admit that socialism is possible."

What Mises meant is that it is impossible that any large society could really implement socialism and achieve a rational system of production, not that some societies might not call themselves socialist. Attempts to implement the complete socialist program have quickly been abandoned. Sheldon Richman, in an essay entitled "To Create Order, Remove the Planner," notes:

> Immediately after the Russian revolution in 1917, the Bolsheviks under Lenin and Trotsky tried to carry out the Marxian program. They got planned chaos. Trotsky said they stared into the "abyss." Chastened by that experience, Lenin enacted the New Economic Policy, which was a reintroduction of money and markets. No Soviet leader ever tried to abolish the market again. That is not to say that the Soviet Union had a free market. It is to say that the Soviet Union's economy was a government-saturated market. There was no actual central plan. In truth, the plan was revised to reflect what was happening outside the planning bureau.

As George Mason University economist Peter Boettke points out in his book *Calculation and Coordination*:

> [T]he actual operation of the Soviet economy bore little resemblance to the predictions of these optimal planning models. Soviet "planning" seemed to mostly occur after-the-fact. With the break-down, and finally the collapse, of the Soviet state, it has become increasingly apparent that central planning authorities had little real power to manage the Soviet economy. . . .

> We argue that the mature Soviet system was not a hierarchical central planning system at all, but was really a market economy heavily encrusted with central government regulation and restrictions. The Soviet state employed these various interventions to extract revenue from the economy, as an alternative to collecting revenue via the use of taxation.

Furthermore, societies such as the Soviet Union and Communist China were embedded in a worldwide market order. They were able to rely on market prices from the countries with less-hampered markets in order to survive as long as they did.

The goal of most socialist movements has been to establish a worldwide socialist commonwealth. Many apologists for socialism have, in fact, blamed the continued existence of capitalist countries for many of the socialist countries' problems. Mises shows us that the reverse is true—if socialists had ever achieved their dream of global socialism, the result would have been a collapse into complete chaos. The communist countries copied the market countries' methods of production, their products, and their technologies. Soviet planners even copied commodity prices out of the *Wall Street Journal* so that they would be able to perform economic calculation. Lew Rockwell once told a wonderful story about

Mikhail Gorbachev's press secretary. Asked what his dream for mankind was, he replied that he wished to see all of the world embrace socialism, except for New Zealand. "Why not New Zealand?" he was asked. "Well," he responded, "we need someone to get the prices from."

THE CONCENTRATION OF POWER

*I*N MILAN KUNDERA'S novel *The Unbearable Lightness of Being*, the chief protagonist is a Czech surgeon named Tomas. Tomas writes a letter to the editor of a dissident publication, complaining about the Czech rulers. As a result of that letter, his boss at the hospital asks him to sign a retraction. When he fails to do so, he is "reassigned" from the hospital to a window washing crew.

Although Kundera's novel is not primarily an antisocialist tract, the above incident provides a moving portrait of life under a regime that pervades every aspect of one's life. An act of political protest puts one at odds with the current regime, true . . . but the current regime is also one's employer. Indeed, the regime is the *only* employer.

Many advocates of socialism overlook the pervasiveness of its control over the lives of its citizens. Ironically, today's socialists often have fringe interests in nonpolitical areas— health foods, new-age spiritualism, minority religions, avant-garde art, and so on. An advanced market society can accommodate a stunning variety of tastes and dispositions. Perhaps most people want white bread, but whole grain is still offered for sale. The masses may be more interested in a weekend in Las Vegas than one at a meditation retreat, but nevertheless, weekend meditation retreats are available. *Independence Day* may have been the bigger draw at the cinema, but *The Remains of the Day* still was made.

We must wonder if people with such fringe tastes have contemplated what would happen to their interests under socialism. As we saw above, a socialist state will have extreme difficulty supplying even the basics of life to the masses. Such a state will have few resources with which to indulge individuals' fancy for healing crystals or shiatsu-massage therapy. In a market society, no one will pay you to go on a month-long retreat dedicated to finding the warrior within you. Your current employer might even fire you if you take a month off. On the other hand, neither your employer nor anyone else can stop you from going, or stop you from trying to find other work once you return. But in a socialist society, the attempt to take a month off of work might well be considered treasonous. You can vacation where and when the state says you can.

THE RULE OF THE WORST

SOME OF THE advocates of socialism are surely very pleasant people, without a tyrannical bone in their bodies. They are motivated solely by a concern for the weak and powerless. They often discount the historical experience of utopian societies when proposing their own utopia. Yes, they admit, the Soviet Union, Communist China, Nazi Germany, and other utopian experiments have turned out to be tyrannical—but that was only due to the bad character of those who took over. They advocate a utopia ruled over by kindly, open-minded, tolerant people—like themselves. Despite the fact such socialist saints could still not solve the calculation problem outlined above, it is certain that their regime would be preferable to Pol Pot's. However, in what is probably the most famous book to emerge from the Austrian School, *The Road to Serfdom*, Hayek explained why such people are unlikely to rule under socialism.

Socialism requires that a single will direct the disposition of society's efforts. The will might be that of a dictator, of a ruling committee, or even of "society as a whole," as determined by polls or voting. In any case, all productive efforts must contribute to a single master plan.

However that determination is made, it is inevitable that there will be substantial portions of the population who disagree with various details of the master plan. The question arises as to what to do about such disagreement.

Let's say that the nation's coal miners feel the wage assigned to them in the plan is too low, and they refuse to work for such a "chintzy" amount. In a market society, workers are free to seek other employment that offers a better combination of pay and working conditions. The competition among employers for workers will tend to move wages toward the level of revenue provided by the marginal worker. (Remember that the marginal worker is the next one an employer is considering hiring, or, looked at from the other side, the last one chosen.) If a worker desires a certain wage but can't get it on the market, we cannot guarantee, in a market society, that his work isn't really worth that much—but we can say that entrepreneurs will have a tendency to discover any undervalued resource and bid up its price.

But the coal workers in a would-be socialist commonwealth are not free to go look for other work; the director has assigned them to the coal mines. If the plan calls for 10,000 coal miners, then 10,000 there must be—otherwise, the state's production plans become irrelevant. The director cannot simply raise the miners' wages until they agree to work—their wages are already in the plan, and raising them will require replanning the entire rest of the economy.

What can the directors of the socialist economy do? The inclination of the "nice" socialists will be "to enter into a dialogue" with the miners. The government should find out what their grievances are, determine what conditions will make them happy, try to sell them on their patriotic duty to produce coal, and attempt to adjust the plan based on the dialogue. Once a few of those "dialogues" get going, it's clear that production in the society will have come to a standstill.

The people of such an aspiring-to-be-socialist nation will be faced with a choice. They can either abandon the march toward socialism, or opt for a strongman who promises to get things done. If they do not turn toward a less-hampered market society, the strongmen will soon be in charge, as happened in Weimar Germany in the early 1930s. Then, when the coal miners refuse to dig coal at the wage allotted to them in the master plan, the solution is simple: "Shoot them!" As Hayek says, "the totalitarian dictator would soon have to choose between disregard of ordinary morals and failure." Under the strongmen, the people at least have a shot at being able to heat their homes, albeit at the cost of the liberty of the coal miners, and, ultimately, all other citizens.

A market-based society may seem harsh at times. If miners don't wish to accept the wage offered by a mine owner, the owner might simply fire all of them and find replacements. But at least the miners have a chance to go find work elsewhere, and to try for the highest wage they think they might get in those new opportunities. When the government is the one employer, there is nowhere else to go, and no one else with whom to negotiate.

The socially conscious hope "for the miracle of a majority's agreeing on a particular plan for the organization of the whole of society" (Hayek, *The Road to Serfdom*). Falling short of that miracle, Hayek says that it is "the lowest common denominator which unites the largest number of people." Whatever set of prejudices can most easily connect with the most ignorant members of society will tend to win the most allegiance. Society becomes a contest of who can mug whom most quickly.

Once society is operating on such a basis, it behooves minorities to carefully watch their backs. The temptation for the leaders to organize a pogrom against some minority group will be immense. Hayek points out that "it seems to be almost a law of human nature that it is easier for people to agree on a negative program—on the hatred of an enemy, on the envy of those better off—than on any positive task." Totalitarian regimes tend to promote the demonizing of some unpopular group: the Jews, the kulaks, the intellectuals, the East Asians, and so on.

THE CHIMERA OF EQUALITY

SIMPLE COMMON SENSE and everyday observation should convince us that every person is inherently, not just accidentally, different. The findings of genetic science and the teachings of most religions support that common-sense view. In *The Constitution of Liberty*, Hayek concluded that treating everyone equally, with the same laws applying to all, would inevitably result in people achieving very different outcomes in life. Therefore, "the only way to place them in equal position would be to treat them differently. Equality before the law and material equality are, therefore, not only different but in conflict with each other."

The idea that socialism can achieve material equality while suppressing only economic freedoms is untenable. The other freedoms we value—of speech, religion, assembly, and so on—all require the use of resources for their accomplishment. To be free to speak, we require at least a place to stand and talk. To really reach people, we will often have to publish our ideas in a book or newspaper. But when the state owns all publishing outlets, it must decide whose voice will be heard. The freedoms of religion and assembly require, among other things, places to worship and assemble—but in a totalitarian society, the state is the only construction company, and the only source of building materials.

In fact, it is only the differences among people's natural endowments, tastes, and learned skills that leads to exchange, the division of labor, and human society. As Murray Rothbard wrote in *Freedom, Inequality, Primitivism and the Division of Labor*:

> The glory of the human race is the uniqueness of each individual, the fact that every person, though similar in many ways to others, possesses a completely individuated personality of his own. It is the fact of each person's uniqueness—that fact that no two people can be wholly interchangeable—that makes each and every man irreplaceable and that makes us care whether he lives or dies, whether he is happy or oppressed. And, finally, it is the fact that these unique personalities need freedom for their full development that constitutes one of the major arguments for a free society.

Kurt Vonnegut's short story "Harrison Bergeron" satirizes the attempt to create a society where everyone is equal. In the world of the story, those who can jump higher than the average person must wear weights on their bodies. Those who are more attractive must make themselves uglier. And those who can think better than others can must wear a device that interrupts their thoughts with a loud noise every few seconds.

Short of measures like those in Vonnegut's story, the ideal of equality is a chimera. The Soviet Union was not a society in which all citizens were equal. The freedom of action and access to goods of a high-ranking Communist Party official was immensely greater than that of the average person. But attempts to create an egalitarian world have resulted in some of the worst tyrannies in history.

CHAPTER 11

The Third Way

ON GOVERNMENT IN THE MARKET PROCESS

THE DYNAMICS OF INTERVENTIONISM

*T*HERE HAVE BEEN many efforts over the years to develop a "third way" of managing social cooperation, a path that will take advantage of the efficiency of the market process while controlling its "excesses." The fascist movement in Italy, National Socialism in Germany, and the New Deal in America were all examples of the search for that path.

However, all attempts to improve market outcomes run into the same problem that cripples the attempt to create a socialist society, although to a lesser extent. Outside of market prices, based on private property, there is no way to rationally calculate how valuable an undertaking's contribution to society's well-being is. Arbitrary numbers can be assigned to gauge the costs and benefits of, for instance, a new environmental regulation, but they are just guesses. Only real market prices convey information on the freely chosen values of acting man.

Mises pointed out that all market interventions are likely to produce results that are undesirable even from the point of view of those forwarding the intervention. That is because the market participants are not supine in the face of interference with their wishes, and will act contrary to the intent of the interventionists.

SUNY Purchase economics professor Sanford Ikeda, in *Dynamics of the Mixed Economy*, extends Mises's analysis of interventionism. Ikeda explains the patterns that the interventionist process is likely to follow. His analysis begins with the Misesian insight mentioned above.

An unhampered market brings about its outcome through the voluntary choices of all people in that market. Any interference with the market process—such as rent control, farm subsidies, and so on—will, to some extent, thwart the realization of people's preferences. People, in the face of such interference, will act to reassert their desires. However, the process has been made less efficient. One reason is the overhead of the government program itself. Another is the fact that market forces will reassert themselves, though in unexpected ways. If apples would be priced at $1.00 a pound on the unhampered market, but government sets the price at 60¢ a pound, people will still tend to pay the market price. However, they will go to the market expecting to pay 60¢ for a pound, and be surprised by paying 60¢ plus 40¢ worth of time waiting in line.

Even the minimal state, which attempts to provide only protection from the violence of others, runs afoul of such difficulties. Since the minimal state must tax, it must set the level of taxes, or, looking at the other side of the coin, it must decide how much protection to provide. Whatever level of protection it chooses, some people will be unhappy with that decision. Since, in a constitutional republic, the level of protection will be set somewhere in the middle of the range of desired amounts, there will be a large group of people who feel they are getting, and paying for, too much of it.

It's not impossible that those people will choose to just grin and bear it, but it is very unlikely. Humans act in order to improve situations they find unsatisfactory, and the people paying too much in taxes, in their own eyes, have the motivation to act.

Not paying their taxes will subject them to violence from the state. But since those taxes were imposed on them by political means, it will occur to them that they can use the same means to try to gain some compensating benefit. Perhaps they will lobby to have extra protection for their neighborhood, to have a military base located nearby, thereby increasing local trade, or to get street lights on their road, in the name of increased security.

Whatever benefit they wrestle from the state will change the situation of those who were happy with the old amount of protection. They are paying the same amount in taxes as before, but some of their previous benefits have been shifted to others. Now *they* have a motivation to form an interest group and lobby the state to provide them with some new benefit as compensation for *their* loss. That creates a dynamic that tends to produce continual growth in state programs.

Furthermore, however wise and noble the founders of the state were, state service will act as a magnet for the person who wants to exercise power over others—as Hayek said, the worst rise to the top. In order to maneuver his way into a position of power, such a person will have every reason to rub salt in some interest group's wound. By goading "his" interest group on in its grievance, a politician can build a "constituency" that he can ride to power.

Such interventionism clouds the interpretation of prices, interest rates, profits, and losses. Jörg Guido Hülsmann points out that interventionism involves a falsifying of signs. The past price of a good is people's own best appraisal of the options available to them, and is a sign for people trying to estimate the future price. A legally fixed price is in some ways not a price at all, as it lacks that essential feature. It bears the same relation to a market price as a wax figure does to a living person.

With prices altered, entrepreneurs are discouraged from pursuing genuine opportunities in some areas. For example, farm subsidies will make the search for more efficient methods of farming less urgent. Meanwhile, entrepreneurs pursue other opportunities that, in the unhampered market, would have been considered superfluous—consider the proliferation of lobbyists and tax accountants.

Ikeda shows that the problems resulting from one intervention tend to lead to calls for other interventions to fix those problems. People sense that something is wrong, but unless they have a firm grounding in economics, it is difficult for them to trace the problem to the intervention. As each succeeding intervention moves the market further from its unhampered state, the process of tracing the problem back through the myriad distortions becomes ever more torturous.

Nothing could illustrate the situation better than the "health-care crisis" in the United States. Initial government interference, in the form of licensing requirements, restricted supply and drove costs up. A further government intervention, the wage controls imposed during World War II, led employers to offer "free" health insurance in order to attract employees. (Since employers could not raise wages, they competed for employees by offering more benefits.) The third-party provisioning of health insurance made health-care consumers less price conscious, driving up costs still further. The subsidy of demand through Medicare and Medicaid added yet another factor increasing costs. The market responded with strange entities such as health management organizations (HMOs). (Notice that we do not see AMOs in the automobile industry, or CMOs in the computer business.)

In answer to the problems that have developed, the major policy proposals involve, just as Ikeda predicts, further interventions to correct the unfortunate consequences of past interventions.

Even people who generally understand the benefits of the market cannot see, through the welter of distortions produced by interventions, any choice but more intervention as a cure for the worst problems of interventionism. Robert Goldberg of the National Center for Policy Analysis says:

> As most know by now, Medicare currently provides coverage for hospital therapy and doctor therapy, but not drug therapy. Failure to cover drugs in the current system creates perverse incentives that waste resources and endanger patient health. . . . Both the Gore and Bush plans [to cover drug therapy] would improve on the current situation. ("Continue the W. Revolution")

However, new interventions will add new distortions to those added by previous interventions. It is impossible to intervene the economy back onto the path that the unhampered market would have taken, as there is no way, in the absence of the market process, to discover what that path might have been.

Goldberg acknowledges that under either plan, certain drugs will be covered, and others that will not. He asks, "Under which plan will these lists of drugs be more likely to be used to limit access to new and better drugs at the price of increased risk to patients?" But he fails to note that either plan will certainly have the unwanted effect of focusing prescription and research on listed drugs, to the detriment of patients who might have benefited more from other, unlisted drugs. When that problem is noticed, there will surely be some politician recommending another intervention to correct it, perhaps asserting a patient's right to a greater variety of subsidized drugs.

Subsidizing drug purchases in any fashion only leads to further price distortions. While it is true that some of the new spending on drugs will be shifted from spending on hospitals and doctors, other shifts will occur from nonmedical goods into medical spending, where the marginal utility of an additional dollar spent will have been raised by the new subsidy.

Ikeda's subsequent work, following in the footsteps of Charles Murray and others, is exploring the ways in which the effects of interventionism on social attitudes are similar to its effects on the market process. In order to survive in a laissez-faire society, I must either exchange with others for what I need to survive or convince others to voluntarily support me. I may want to spend my whole day getting plastered, but I'm unlikely to survive too long if I do. That fact may motivate me to hold off on drinking until I've done at least a few hours of work.

But in a welfare state, that motivation is absent. With a minimum level of support guaranteed, I can drink the day away without worrying about starving to death. All of that drinking will further undermine my desire and ability to work, making it increasingly difficult for me to survive without state assistance.

The attitudes that are most successful in a market society—thrift, hard work, responsibility, trust—are gradually undermined by interventions that relieve people of facing the consequences of their own actions. They are replaced by increasing short-term thinking, laziness, dependence, and suspicion. These attitudes create social problems that lead to calls for further interventions to "fix" them, and those interventions further erode the values most important to a free society.

Our analysis of the intervention process might seem to counsel despair to those who favor a free economy. But Ikeda contends that the interventionist process inevitably leads to a crisis, where the effects of multiple interventions have become so pernicious that the possibility of a dramatic turn toward free markets becomes possible. The oil crisis of the late 1970s offers an example of such a turning point, when a deregulation of the oil industry that would have been unthinkable a few years before took place fairly rapidly.

When the crisis hits, a turn toward the free market is not inevitable. The other possibility is to turn toward socialism, in order to eliminate the remaining "market failures," and allow state regulation full sway. Which direction the system takes in a crisis will depend, to a great extent, on the ideological leanings of the public.

An important aspect of people's decisions is that they realize there is a choice. When the supposed defenders of the market order have been pushing a series of interventions as "free-market solutions," the public is likely to decide that laissez-faire has been tried, and has failed. That is exactly what occurred in the 1920s and early '30s, as documented by Murray Rothbard in *America's Great Depression*. Several Republican administrations, from the purportedly free-market party, engaged in an unprecedented amount of economic meddling. For instance, in his speech accepting the GOP nomination for president in 1932, Hoover noted:

> [W]e might have done nothing. That would have been utter ruin. Instead, we met the situation with

proposals to private business and to Congress of the
most gigantic program of economic defense and
counterattack ever evolved in the history of the
Republic. We put it into action. . . . No government
in Washington has hitherto considered that it held
so broad a responsibility for leadership in such
times. (Rothbard, *America's Great Depression*)

THE PROBLEMS WITH EFFICIENCY

*I*N THE NEXT several chapters we will look at some specific
government interventions into the market. Before we
leave this chapter, however, I'd like to examine a technique by which interventionism is often justified: the appeal
to efficiency. The basis of the technique is the employment of
equilibrium analysis to demonstrate that the free market has
produced an "inefficient" outcome, and to recommend some
government intervention that will rectify the situation, leading
to increased "social utility." A leading proponent of such
analysis, Judge Richard Posner, has "described the common
law as a tool to maximize aggregate social wealth." (I'm quot-
ing Steve Kurtz, interviewing Posner in the April 2001 issue of
Reason.)

Steven Landsburg, in *Price Theory*, gives an example of the
use of the *efficiency criterion* for resolving legal disputes
among individuals. A group of ten students would like to burn
down their professor's house, while the professor is not in
favor of the idea. Landsburg explains how to use the efficiency criterion to settle this dispute:

According to the efficiency criterion, everyone is
permitted to cast a number of votes proportional to

> his stake in the outcome, where your stake in the
> outcome is measured by how much you'd be will-
> ing to pay to get your way. So, for example, if ten
> students each think it would be worth $10 to watch
> the professor's house go up in flames, while the pro-
> fessor thinks it would be worth $1,000 to prevent that
> outcome, then each of the student's gets ten votes
> and the professor gets 1,000 votes. The house burn-
> ing is defeated by a vote of 1,000 to 100. (Landsburg,
> *Price Theory*)

Some of the problems with this approach should be obvious. First of all, what if it is just the professor's tool shed the
students want to burn? Perhaps they really love to watch fires,
and would be willing to pay $100 each to watch the shed
burn. Meanwhile, the shed is only worth $500 to the good
professor. It's "efficient" for the students to go ahead and burn
down the shed, even if they never have to pay the professor.
One thousand dollars of utility has been gained at the expense
of a loss of only $500 of utility. Let's momentarily set aside any
moral compunctions we might have about allowing people to
destroy or abscond with others' property because they enjoy
that more than the owner suffers from the loss. Even on its
own terms, such efficiency analysis is a failure, because it
doesn't take into account the loss of "efficiency" in society
when people don't feel that their property is secure. Of
course, the magnitude of such a loss is incalculable, because
different social arrangements do not appear as goods for sale
on the market.

Just because we can't calculate such a figure doesn't mean
that secure property rights have no value—we might suspect,
in fact, that their value is enormous. Several authors have
recently written books stressing the importance of property
rights for prosperity, including Tom Bethell (*The Noblest*

Triumph: Property and Prosperity Through the Ages) and Hernando de Soto (*The Mystery of Capital: Why Capitalism Triumphs in the West and Fails Everywhere Else*). De Soto, for instance, says that the ordinary people of Third World countries have a great deal of property, but that they are hindered in exploiting it because they do not have a clear, recognized title to the land. He estimates that 81 percent of the rural land in Peru is owned without legal title, and in Egypt, over 80 percent of all land is owned in such a fashion. The lack of secure property rights is a major cause of the poverty in those places. A calculation of efficiency that leaves out the negative effects of nebulous ownership is like an estimation of the effect of a nuclear bomb that includes the weight of the bomb but leaves out the nuclear reaction.

The second problem with such analysis is that the "prices" used are not prices at all. The parties involved are only asked to say how much something is worth to them. Why not just pick a really big number? If you're not going to have to pay the price, just name it, then what the heck—say that it's worth a billion dollars to you to see the prof's house burn.

Various tricks, involving possible consequences for lying, can be used to try to get around this problem, but none of them solves a more serious problem: We don't know how much we value something until we *really* have to pay for it. Imagine, if you will, that we visit a children's swim club and ask the kids if they're willing to make the sacrifices necessary to become Olympic champion swimmers. We'd probably get many positive responses, despite the fact that perhaps only one in ten thousand young swimmers really is willing to pay the costs of becoming an Olympian. Efficiency analysis implies that we'd be better off if we just asked the swimmers what they *would* sacrifice to make the Olympics, and then appointed those who bid the highest to the Olympic team. Think of all the training time that would be saved!

It is only in the process of moving toward a goal and experiencing the costs ourselves that we discover what those costs really are. A smoker suffering from a bad cold may swear he'll never smoke again, but it is not until he feels better and is offered a cigarette that even he discovers whether that oath is real. Without actually undertaking the discovery process, "costs" are only guesses as to what the costs *might* turn out to be.

Efficiency analysis also assumes that the prices we arrive at by such quizzes are equilibrium values or final prices. For that to be true, everyone would have to agree on the future usefulness of all of the factors of production. But Austrian economist Peter Lewin points out:

> The whole [market] process is driven by *differences* in opinion and perception between rival producers and entrepreneurs. . . . The values they place on the resources at their disposal or which they trade, are not, in any meaningful sense, equilibrium values. They reflect only a "balance" of expectations about the possible uses of the resources. One cannot use such values meaningfully in any assessment of efficiency. (Introduction to *The Economics of QWERTY*)

The use of *Pareto improvement* as a criterion for justifying intervention is plagued by similar problems. Per the Pareto criterion, a policy is considered good if at least one person affected by the policy is better off because of it, while absolutely no one is worse off. In simple cases where we can clearly see a Pareto improvement, we can just voluntarily implement it. If I'm sitting around with three of my friends, and we all feel we'd be better off if we were playing bridge, then we can just play bridge. We don't need a "policy" implemented to get the game going. In real-world policy situations, it's almost impossible to conceive of finding Pareto improvements. Even a policy that would unambiguously result in everyone in the country having more goods would not meet with the approval of many environmentalists and ascetics.

As market prices are the sole means by which we can calculate economic efficiency, it is ironic that efficiency considerations are often used to justify government intervention in the economy. It is only when people must actually pay the cost of their choices that we can be sure that, at least in their eyes, the choice was worth the cost. The only way we can know how much it is worth to the students to burn the professor's house is if the students *really* have to pay the professor enough that he agrees to let them go ahead. State intervention destroys the very mechanism by which the market achieves efficient outcomes.

The Pareto criterion and other measures like it are attempts to formulate a "scientific" gauge of better economic outcomes, standing apart from the value judgment of the person who is classifying the outcome. But human judgment creates the categories of "better" and "worse," and all judgment is individual judgment.

CHAPTER 12

Fiddling With Prices While the Market Burns

ON PRICE FLOORS, PRICE CEILINGS, AND OTHER INTERFERENCES WITH MARKET PRICES

*G*OVERNMENTS HAVE FREQUENTLY felt the need to interfere with market prices. Such interference can take a number of forms. *Price floors* set a legal minimum on the price of some good or service. *Price ceilings* set a legal maximum on the price. *Price targets* try to keep a price with a narrow range: examples include foreign currency exchange rates "pegged" within a band, and the Federal Reserve targets for interest rates. And *fixed prices*, such as the price of taxi service in many cities, allow no price flexibility at all.

We'll examine a few, particularly popular cases of interference with market prices.

A PRICE FLOOR

A COUPLE OF years ago, I went to my friend Dick to show him a proposal I was working on. Dick happens to be a die-hard interventionist. Since it forwarded a new plan for the government to help the underprivileged, I was sure he would approve. My proposal ran as follows:

Today, many corporations in our strong economy have been left behind by the general prosperity. They may be old-industry stalwarts who have not been able to gain the skills necessary for a smooth transition to the electronic economy. Or, perhaps, they are new companies, just getting going in industry, whose penny stocks are undervalued by investors. Perhaps, through no fault of their own, those companies have had a run of hard luck: the CEO died, a major customer went belly-up, or a new product from a competitor rendered what they produce obsolete.

Many employees, suppliers, investors, and customers are relying on those very companies. Meanwhile, those businesses are suffering from a simple lack of capital. If they had sufficient funding, they could invest in new plants or modern technology and could then aid other players in the economy by buying more of their goods, supplying them with better products, or employing them at higher wages. Not only is it compassionate to help out those companies, but it will help the economy as a whole by boosting purchasing power.

Therefore, I forward a proposal. I recommend that the government set a national floor for stock prices. A reasonable first estimate of where it should be set might be $10 per share. Once my law is passed, it would be illegal to buy or sell the stock of any company for less than the chosen amount. (Naturally, it would be $10 per share for the full number of currently outstanding shares—we can't have ruthless exploiters trying to skirt the law by forcing a company to do a reverse stock split or buy back its own shares.)

The effects of the law would be entirely beneficial. No capitalization would be taken from any other company to boost the capital of the most-needy corporations. Those corporations, now able to float shares at least at the minimum price, would quickly become more prosperous. The flow of funds to those enterprises would ripple throughout the economy, spreading wealth all around.

"But wait a second, Gene," Dick said. "You're not serious about this, are you?"

"Yes, quite serious," I reply. "Why wouldn't it be a good idea?"

"Well, first of all, your point about 'boosting purchasing power' is ridiculous. If anyone is buying those stocks at the new price floor, they now have less money than they would have had at the old, lower price. In fact, they'll have as much less as the company in question now has more. So there is no increased purchasing power at all."

"Hmm, you may have a point there. I'll have to try and work around that. But do you see any other problems with my plan?"

"Of course! You heard me say, 'If anyone is buying the stocks at the new mandated price'. . . . But why would they? If yesterday, I was only willing to pay $5 for a share of Dotty Dotcom, why in the world would I suddenly be willing to pay $10, just because some new law is passed? I'll still only pay what I think an item is worth! Aren't you the one always going on about that theory of subjective value?"

"Well, I guess I am. But what do you think would happen to the shares of Dotty?"

"Well, they would simply stop trading. Dotty, far from being able to raise more capital, would no longer be able to raise any money at all."

"You have some good points there, Dick. But the funny thing is, I showed my plan to a few CEOs, and they all loved it."

"Were these the CEOs of companies whose stocks were trading below $10 per share?"

"Well, no, in fact, everyone of them has a stock trading above $10 per share."

"Then of course they'd love it! They're trying to eliminate competition. Since their shares are currently above $10, *their* stock will continue to trade. In fact, without the competition of the lower-priced stocks, demand for their stock will go up. They're simply trying to enrich themselves at the expense of the less fortunate. They're a bunch of scoundrels."

"You know, Dick, you've convinced me. My plan is kind of dopey. Thanks! But you've left me with one question."

"Sure, anything I can do to help." Dick was feeling quite confident, having thoroughly debunked my proposal.

"Since you can see how bad my plan is, why do you support raising the minimum wage? In fact, why do you support having a minimum wage at all?

"Aren't low-wage workers analogous to the low-priced stocks I was describing? Aren't employers equivalent to the investors in my scenario, in that they will only pay wages that seem worth parting with? And aren't the labor unions, the main supporters of minimum wage legislation, the same as the CEOs of the higher-priced companies that I described to you, enriching themselves at the expense of the less fortunate?"

It took me a while to revive Dick, but when he finally came to, he claimed that he couldn't remember a word of our conversation.

Minimum wage laws, at least temporarily, will help those who already make *more* than the level at which the wage is set. But those who would only be hired at a wage below the minimum wage will simply be shut out of the employment market. (Recall that employers will hire workers only up to the point where they expect the revenue from the marginal [last] worker hired will just exceed his wage.) "Well," some will say, "no one could support themselves on such a wage anyway. Rather than allow businesses to exploit them by paying below-subsistence wages, it's better they're on relief so they can go to school or care for their kids."

No doubt some people have been able to make themselves productive while they were on relief. (J.K. Rowling, who started the *Harry Potter* series while on relief, is a prominent example.) But for most people, it is a trap. For those at the bottom of the economic ladder, generally the best thing to do is to start working, at whatever wage they can.

I spent eight years playing in reggae bands. Over time, we were able to find steady work in local clubs. But that was only because, when we started out, we were willing to work for whatever a club would pay—sometimes for nothing! By gradually demonstrating that we could attract and satisfy a crowd, our wage steadily rose. If the minimum wage law had been strictly enforced at all of those clubs, we never would have gotten going at all.

That is the situation of the least-experienced workers. The most important thing to their economic future is that they learn that a job is not a right, but an exchange of valued goods—their labor for the employer's money. Signs of having gotten the notion include showing up on time, being polite to customers, completing assigned tasks, and so on. Once they have demonstrated that they understand that central idea then their wages will rise. I don't know of any employers who consider receiving government assistance, no matter for how many years, as a plus on a resume.

A PRICE CEILING

*T*HE WINTER OF 2000–2001 was much snowier than the previous four that we had spent in our current house. Given the mildness of those previous winters and the lack of snowfall, we hadn't bothered to look for a plowing service.

But in the winter of 2000–2001, four different storms each dumped over a foot of snow in our yard. Now, I sure as heck wasn't going to go out there and shovel away that mess—hey, I've been busy writing this book! (I'd send my wife out to do it, but our driveway is visible from the neighbors' houses, so that's out of the question as well.) So clearly, we needed someone to plow.

After the first storm, I spotted two men plowing my neighbor's driveway, and asked them if they would do ours after they had finished hers. They named a price—one that seemed fairly high for a small driveway like mine. It was clear to me that, since these fellows were already going to be across the street from my house every time it snowed, and it would take them less than five minutes to clear out my driveway, that they were each making well over $100 an hour for their work.

I readily agreed. Why? First of all, their price was still lower than what it would have cost me to clear the driveway myself,

given the value of my time to me—my opportunity cost. That
condition is, of course, the basis for any exchange—a person
considers what they are giving up less valuable than what
they receive. Further, I understood that all of the plow-truck
operators would be quite busy, and that I would spend time
searching for another operator who might be cheaper. In fact,
I might not find anyone else who would want to take on such
a small driveway at all. I could take their price or leave it.

A common reaction to such situations, in both the popular
press and among politicians with an election coming up, is to
charge that the consumer is being "gouged" by a businessman
making "windfall profits," taking unfair advantage of the consumer's predicament. The businessman didn't do anything to
earn the high profits—instead, he is taking advantage of an
accident of nature that is entirely beyond his or the consumer's control in order to line his own pocket.

But we should apply Bastiat's dictum, and contemplate
what is not seen as well as what is seen. In the midst of a
snowy winter, it was true that the plow operators are making
a very high wage *right then*. But what about the previous four
winters, when they had gotten very little business? During
those winters, the potential supply of plowing had exceeded
the demand for it. Many plow trucks sat idle. Why didn't the
majority of those truck owners abandon plowing? It is precisely the possibility of "cleaning up" in a bad winter that persuades people to maintain their plows and trucks during mild
winters.

In fact, the plow operators might just as well complain that
I had taken advantage of them during the previous four winters! After all, the lack of snow was neither their fault nor the
result of any efforts of mine. Wasn't it "unfair" that their business should suffer while I was able to save the money that, in

a normal winter, I would have spent on plowing? From the point of view of the plowing services, it might be quite acceptable for the state to legally limit the price they could charge in bad winters, if it would also mandate that everyone with a driveway have it plowed several times every winter, even if it hadn't snowed. This would even out the income flow of the plowing services and make their business more predictable. (Of course, their support for such a law would depend crucially on how high the legal price was set.)

Whether we like it or not, the vagaries of the natural world often have a high impact on our lives. No form of social organization can dodge that fact. The market does have a means of dealing with it, however: the activities of speculators in stockpiling reserves, from which they hope to profit should an emergency occur. In a market system, stockpiles of food, oil, clothing, snow shovels, rock salt, plywood, and many other items needed during severe conditions exist because of the possibility of large profits should they be needed. Politicians often complain that oil companies are making "excess" profits during a shortage, from oil that they held off the market in good times. But ask yourself, where we would be if they hadn't been holding a reserve? Clearly, the shortage would only be worse! Measures to restrict prices to some "normal" amount during a crisis only serve to discourage stockpiling—producers are also subject to time preference—and make it likely that we will lack a reserve during future shortages.

Not only are alternate forms of social organization unable to remove the influence of the natural world on our lives, they cannot eliminate the speculative nature of stockpiling goods for unusual circumstances. We do not know what nature has in store for us next month or next year. Speculation is action in the face of the uncertain future: entrepreneurship. The question is who should be doing the speculating: business-men who specialize in the relevant market, and who have their own money riding on getting supplies correct, or government bureaucrats, whose skills are mostly political and who are betting the taxpayers' money that they are right?

SPILLED MILK[1]

*L*ET'S CONSIDER AN economy in which the price of farm products is declining. Farmers may begin pleading for the government to stop the price drop. "Wealth is being wiped out of the economy," they will complain, "the value of our farms has fallen 50 percent in the last year. That will make everyone poorer, since we can't spend as much on goods produced by others." Their reasoning makes their pleas seem to be for the good of the whole nation, instead of just a matter of self-interest.

Surely, most economists would debunk such wrong-headed thinking. The conclusion that wealth has disappeared from the economy is unjustified. The same farms, the same fields, the same tractors are here today as were here last year. If some farms have shut down, it is only because consumers valued some alternative uses of the resources necessary to run the farm more than their use in farming. They chose the products requiring that alternative use over the products of the

---

[1]The section "Spilled Milk" was co-authored with Robert P. Murphy.

farm. Therefore, they will be less wealthy, in their own eyes, should the government intervene to keep the farm running.

We can sympathize with those farmers who have had a hard time. But propping up their business is wasting scarce resources. The law of comparative advantage tells us that there is some other role for them in the economy, to which they are better suited in the eyes of the consumers.

All that we definitively can say has occurred is that there has been a change in relative prices. A bushel of wheat buys fewer dollars, but the flip side of the coin is that a dollar buys more wheat. Those holding wheat are hurt, but those holding dollars (or any other good that did not decline along with wheat) are helped. This constant adjustment of prices by market participants, so as to bring supply and demand into balance, is the essence of the market process. There is little further we can say about whether "everyone" is better off with the new price configuration than they were with the old one. Certainly, though, we can point out that it will not help most people to try to maintain the old prices by government manipulation in the face of the new data of supply and demand.

Or consider the continuous, twenty-year decline in the price of personal computers. Economists have (quite correctly!) heralded it as a sign of the wondrous powers of the market. Certainly, computer manufacturers would like to have seen a thirty-year rise in the price of PCs. I haven't heard any economists worrying about the wealth that was disappearing as the value of my old NeXT Workstation headed to zero. That price decline occurred because better opportunities appeared on the market. In other words, we were becoming wealthier during the price decline, not poorer.

So why do so many economists have such difficulties when the fall in prices occurs in the stock market, instead of in the market for agricultural commodities or personal computers? When stock indices fall, we hear repeated worries that "wealth is being wiped out." On the surface, that seems too obvious to argue. When, during the year 2000, the NASDAQ plunged from 5,100 to 2,400, the total capitalization of the index shrank by over $3 trillion. It looked as though that wealth had simply vanished into thin air.

However, as we have seen above, that view is the result of confusion between the money prices of goods and the amount of wealth in the economy. The NASDAQ decline did not level any buildings or render any machines inoperable. America was just as full of farms, warehouses, railroads, and oil wells as it had been when the NASDAQ was at its peak. The dot-com wipeout did not suck the knowledge of Java programming out of anyone's head. Certainly, some companies shut down. But those were the companies that it no longer seemed worthwhile to operate, in light of new market data.

A stock market decline represents a shifting of wealth. Those who were holding cash, bonds, or gold are now wealthier, as their assets can buy a greater share of various corporations. Those who were short shares of companies they judged to be overpriced are wealthier. The largest group made better off by the decline is the non-asset-holding consumer. Before the stock market decline, the stock-rich had been bidding up the price of various goods—homes, carpenters, plumbers, massage therapists, domestic help, private schools, and so on. After the decline, they are no longer able to bid as much, making such items more affordable for others.

Cries for the government to stop a stock market decline are no less special-interest-group pleading than are attempts by farmers to boost wheat prices. Those holding stocks have come to expect that they have the right to see the prices of their assets continually rising, and call for the government to intervene when that expectation is disappointed.

Usually, the request for intervention takes the form of the cry, "Lower interest rates!" But such a change in a key market price does not add a single new good to the economy. It simply shifts wealth from those who are intending to lend money to those who are intending to borrow money.

The price of securities must ultimately rest on their prospective future yield. While American productivity has been increasing, and we would therefore expect higher future yields on stocks, this explains only a small portion of the 85-percent rise in the NASDAQ in 1999 and the further 20-percent increase at the beginning of 2000.

A good deal of the NASDAQ run-up was due to the Fed flooding the market with liquidity in preparation for Y2K. That liquidity entered the capital market first, creating a classic *market bubble.* The bubble was concentrated, as bubbles tend to be, in the fad of the era: hi-tech stocks, in the '90s.

In addition, as Professor Roger Garrison has pointed out, the Fed has attempted to create a "firewall" to protect the "real" economy from the securities markets. But firewalls work both ways. We might reasonably suspect that holders of securities have begun to feel that they would be protected from changes in the rest of the economy. The government would step in to bail them out, as during the Mexican and Long-Term Capital Management crises.

Freely established market prices are not arbitrary: they serve an important social function. At any particular time, the market price of a share of stock reflects the best estimates of experts—where "experts" are those who have demonstrated the greatest foresight in the past—of the *future* price of the share (adjusted for interest). The critic of a price movement is implicitly asserting that *he knows better* than those actually risking their own money in the market.

In any discussion of share prices, we must also keep in mind the social function of the stock market itself. The price of a stock is closely connected with the present value of the expected future revenues of the company. Thus, unlike stamp collectors, those buying stocks are not *merely* guessing what everyone else thinks the future price of the good purchased will be. (In this respect, Keynes's analogy of a beauty contest in which each judge tries to guess which contestant the *other* judges will rate highly—rather than which contestant is actually most beautiful—is dangerously misleading.) A surprisingly poor performance will invariably reduce a company's share price. That is vitally necessary, in order for the market to accurately price *the company itself.*

If a company's market price is less than the sum of its assets, to some market actor, the company becomes vulnerable to the much-maligned "corporate raider." The corporate raider—epitomized by Danny DeVito's character in the movie *Other People's Money*—may then execute a leveraged buyout, liberating the underutilized assets (including labor) and transferring them to the highest bidders (i.e., those expecting to use the assets in a manner that better fits consumer preferences). While small alterations in the structure of capital can often be made within a firm, large alterations usually take place by capital moving *between* firms. It is the stock market that enables those adjustments to occur.

Before condemning a fall in a stock index, we must first ask, "*Why* has the stock market plummeted?" The answer to that question demonstrates why any interference with the process is harmful. Many people seem to think the market drop in 2000 and 2001 was simply a case of an "irrational," self-fulfilling prophecy. But to the extent that was true, the real wealth of the economy (as argued above) had not changed.

But what if the stock market plunge was due to something more fundamental than prophecies? In that case, the euphemism "correction" would be accurate. If people realized with dismay that they had been overly optimistic about future corporate earnings, that must necessarily reduce share prices. However, the decline in prices is merely a symptom of the previous errors, not their cause. If Americans change their minds about the justice of the Union cause in the Civil War, the value placed on the Lincoln Monument will fall considerably. That loss of a patriotic symbol would not be offset by anyone's gain, but it certainly would not justify any attempts to interfere with the adjustment. We need prices to reflect what we value today, not to be an image of what we valued yesterday. People might regret their previous value judgments, but there is no use crying over spilled milk.

Of course, none of the above should be taken to mean that the government should deliberately try to lower security prices, either! Rather, the market should be allowed to price securities in accordance with supply and demand. As Mises said in *Human Action*:

> It is easy to understand why those whose short-run interests are hurt by a change in prices resent such changes, emphasize that the previous prices were not only fairer but also more normal, and maintain that price stability is in conformity with the laws of nature and of morality. But every change in prices furthers the short-run interests of other people. Those favored will certainly not be prompted by the urge to stress the fairness and normalcy of price rigidity.

CHAPTER 13

Times Are Hard

ON THE CAUSES OF THE BUSINESS
CYCLE

*I*N THE ECONOMIES of most modern industrial nations, a central bank manages the nation's money supply and attempts to control the level of interest rates, at least to some extent. (In America, that central bank is called the Federal Reserve. Since it is the most powerful and famous central bank in the world, we will focus our discussion on "the Fed.") Various rationales have been put forward for central bank interference in the market: to supply sufficient currency and credit to "meet the needs of commerce," to ensure a "stable value" for the currency, to "fight inflation," to smooth out fluctuations in the economy, and so on.

In light of our discussion of money and credit so far, those reasons are suspicious. We have seen that prices can adjust to whatever amount of currency is in the economy. Certainly, the adjustment process takes time and has associated costs. Therefore, we'd prefer gradual to rapid change, giving us more time to adjust. The need to dig up gold from the ground in order to create money acted as a regulator on the growth of the money supply during the period of the gold standard. That regulator led to a century-long period of remarkably low volatility in prices. Being able to create new money almost at will, as central banks can, obviously makes it easier to create rapid changes in the money supply. The various hyperinfla-tions that have occurred in the last century, under fiat money regimes, attest to that fact.

Similarly, we have every reason to believe that the best mechanism for matching the businesses' perceived credit needs with the available savings is the interest rate market. What really matters to a business is that it can acquire the goods, the knowledge, and the services it needs to complete its plans during their progress toward producing consumer goods. The cash a business borrows is important only as a means to help acquire those factors of production. If the real factors are not available, because people have not saved a suf-ficient amount out of current and past production to bring them into existence, then neither increasing the amount of dollars in circulation nor artificially lowering the interest rate will magically bring them forth from the void.

And we have already covered the reason that the search for a stable currency is hopeless: valuation is an aspect of human action, and there are no constant numerical values in human action. Every freely chosen value implies the possibility of a change in valuation. And, far from fighting inflation, the Fed is the main cause of it.

In this chapter, we will examine the final reason listed above, "smoothing out fluctuations in the economy," in some depth. Over the course of the chapter we will see that the cen-tral bank tends to be the *creator*, and not the *dissipater*, of economic fluctuations. When it is putting on the brakes and deflating a bubble, it was usually the one that inflated the bubble in the first place.

OUT OF GAS

*I*MAGINE THAT YOU are a bus driver, at the edge of a desert, about to take a busload of passengers across it. You have left all gas stations behind. Your destination is a town on the other side of the wasteland before you. You are faced with a trade-off: the faster you try to reach the town, the less the passengers can use the air-conditioning to alleviate the desert heat. Both higher speeds and higher air-conditioning settings will use up the gas more quickly. And since, in our luxurious bus, each passenger has his own temperature control for his seat, you, the driver, cannot control the total amount of air conditioning used on the trip.

In order to make your decision, you look at your fuel gauge and determine how much gas you have. You tell the passengers that they must now make a trade-off between comfort on the way and speed traveled, as the more air-conditioning they choose to use, the faster the bus will consume fuel. Then you collect statements from the passengers on what temperature they will keep their seat. You perform some calculations on mileage, speed, and fuel consumption, and pick the fastest speed at which you can travel, given the amount of gas you have and the passengers' statements about their use of the air-conditioning.

The passengers had to decide whether to cross the desert in greater comfort but arrive later at their final destination, or in less comfort but with an earlier arrival. The science of economics has little to say about the combination that they picked, other than that it seemed preferable to them at that moment of choice.

However, also imagine that, before you began your calculations, someone had sneaked up to the bus and replaced the passengers' real choices with a fake set that chose a higher temperature, in other words, one that makes it seem they will use *less* fuel than they really will. You will make your choice on travel speed as if the passengers will tolerate an average temperature of, say, 80 degrees, whereas in reality they will demand to have the bus cooled to an average of 70 degrees. Obviously, your calculations will prove to be incorrect, and the trip will not come out as you had planned. The trip will begin with you driving as if you have more resources available than you really do. It will end with you phoning for help, when the sputtering of your engine reveals the deception.

I offer the above as a metaphor for the Austrian business cycle theory (ABCT), which explains why most modern economies tend to swing through boom times and recessions. You, the driver, represent the entrepreneurs. The gas is the sum of the resources available in the economy. The trip across the desert is some period of production. The passengers represent the consumers. Their choice on how much to use the air conditioning is analogous to how much consumers want to consume now at the expense of saving for the future (i.e., their time preference). The speed of the bus is the amount of investment spending the entrepreneurs will undertake. The ultimate destination is the satisfaction of as many of the consumers' wishes as possible. And it is the central bank—for instance, the Federal Reserve—that has sneaked up and tampered with the consumers' choices.

What the central bank tampers with is the market's reading of the consumers' average time preference, which is the rate of *originary interest*. Consumers' time preferences tell us how much capital will become available through consumer saving, or, in our metaphor, through cutting back on the air-conditioning. When the central bank artificially lowers the rate of interest—we hear on the news that the Fed has cut rates to "stimulate the economy"—entrepreneurs make their plans as if consumers were willing to delay consumption and save more than they really are. As the bus driver, you act as if the passengers are willing to endure the heat enough for you to drive 70 miles per hour. In reality, they will force the bus to consume gas so rapidly that you should have planned to drive only 55. Your attempt to cross the desert will fail, leaving you out of gas.

Of course, the real economy does not simply come to a halt. At some point in the trip, it becomes apparent that the bus is using fuel too rapidly. The Fed, expressing a concern about "overheating," will raise rates. The entrepreneurs will slow way down so that the bus does not simply die—they lay off employees, cancel investment projects, and reduce spending in other ways. The economy, after the boom at the start of the trip, has fallen into a recession.[1]

Our metaphor also allows us to differentiate between a "soft landing," a "hard landing," and a full crash. The further the bus has gone before the discrepancy between the market interest rate and consumers' real time preference is accounted for, the "harder" a landing the economy will undergo. If the entrepreneurs discover the error early (or the central bank cuts short the expansion quickly), the bus may only have to slow to 50 miles per hour to complete the trip. If the credit expansion is continued for a long time the bus may wind up having

---

[1]For those familiar with mainstream macroeconomics, Roger Garrison's way of putting this may be helpful. In his book on Austrian macroeconomics, *Time and Money*, he says that the economy had been pushed beyond its *production possibilities frontier*, or PPF, during the boom, and falls back inside the PPF during the bust.

to coast down hills with the engine off—and we have a full-scale depression, or crash.

As we saw in earlier chapters, the rate of originary interest reflects consumers' time preference because it is what borrowers must pay lenders, in order to persuade the lenders to delay their own consumption. If I have $100, I could spend it today on a nice dinner with my wife. Or, I could lend it out for a year, at the end of which I could spend it on a somewhat nicer dinner. Exactly how much nicer a dinner I must expect to receive before I will lend the money is an expression of my preference for current consumption over future consumption. If I demand a rate of interest of at least 5 percent, that means that a $105 dinner next year is marginally more valuable to me than a $100 dinner this year. On the other hand, if my friend Rob demands 10-percent interest, he is demanding a $110 dinner. He values current consumption compared to future consumption more highly than I do.

The net result of all lenders and borrowers expressing their time preference by offering and bidding on loans is the market rate of interest. In any real interest-rate market, that rate will include, besides originary interest, added interest to account for inflation (or subtracted interest to account for deflation), as well as a risk premium to account for the chance that the venture or person that the money has been lent to will go belly-up.

The rate of interest tells entrepreneurs whether a particular investment is worth making or not. In an unhampered market, without inflation or deflation, that rate would be approximately equivalent to what is termed, in finance, the risk-free rate of interest. Since entrepreneurs can earn that return on their money simply by buying high-grade bonds, they will not undertake capital projects if they estimate that their return will be lower than the risk-free rate of interest. In terms of our analogy, it makes no sense to plan to travel 70 miles per hour on our trip if the consumers are only willing to turn off the AC (put off current consumption) enough for us to travel 55 miles per hour. For any project that returns less than the risk-free rate of interest, the consumers are indicating that they would, in fact, prefer that the resources necessary be used for current consumption rather than being invested in that project.

THE FED STARTS A PARTY[2]

*L*ET'S LOOK BRIEFLY at the recent Internet boom-and-bust as an example of using the Austrian theory to explain an episode in economic history.

It's been said that the Fed's job is to take away the punch bowl once the party gets going. The aphorism doesn't mention that it was usually the Fed that had filled it in the first place. ABCT has sometimes derisively been referred to as a "hangover theory." In fact, the metaphor is fairly apt. The Fed gets the party ginned up on cheap credit, then has to cut everyone off before disaster strikes.

MZM (money of zero maturity, one of a number of money supply measures) increased at a rate of less than 2.5 percent between 1993 and 1995. But over the next three years it shot

---

[2]Parts of the "The Fed Starts a Party" were co-written with Roger Garrison, and first appeared in our article, "A Classic Hayekian Hangover," in the January 2002 edition of *Ideas on Liberty.*

up at an annualized rate of over 10 percent, rising during the last half of 1998 at a binge rate of almost 15 percent.

Sean Corrigan, a principal in Capital Insight, a UK-based financial consultancy, details in "Norman, Strong, and Greenspan," the consequences of the expansion that came in

> autumn 1998, when the world economy, still racked by the problems of the Asian credit bust over the preceding year, then had to cope with the Russian default and the implosion of the mighty Long-Term Capital Management.

Corrigan continues:

> Over the next eighteen months, the Fed added $55 billion to its portfolio of Treasuries and swelled repos held from $6.5 billion to $22 billion. . . . [T]his translated into a combined money market mutual fund and commercial bank asset increase of $870 billion to the market peak, of $1.2 trillion to the industrial production peak, and of $1.8 trillion to date [August 2001]—twice the level of real GDP added in the same interval.

The party was in full swing. The Fed had kept the good times rolling by cutting the federal funds rate a whole percentage point between June 1998 and January 1999. The rate on 30-year Treasuries dropped from a high of over 7 percent to a low of 5 percent.

Stock markets soared. The NASDAQ composite went from just over 1000 to over 5000 between 1996 and 2000, rising over 80 percent in 1999 alone. With abundant credit being freely served to Internet start-ups, hordes of corporate managers, who had seemed married to their stodgy blue-chip companies, suddenly were romancing some sexy dot-coms that had just joined the party.

Meanwhile consumer spending stayed strong—with very low (sometimes negative) savings rates. Growth was not being fueled by real investment, which would require the putting aside of current consumption to save for the future, but by the monetary printing press.

Buoyed by the stellar stock market returns, consumers built massive additions to their houses and took trips they otherwise would not have taken. Real estate, especially in the "dot-com areas" such as Silicon Valley, soared in price.

As so often happens at bacchanalia, when the party entered the wee hours, it became apparent that too many guys had planned on taking the same girl home. There were too few resources available for all of their plans to succeed. The most crucial—and most general—unavailable factor was a continuing flow of investment funds. (Of course, a continual supply of such funds by the Fed would only extend the boom and worsen the ensuing crash.) There also turned out to be shortages of programmers, network engineers, technical managers, and other factors of production. Internet startups, which had planned to operate at a loss for years by raising capital, found that not only was there less investment money available than they had hoped, but the cost of staying in business had gone up as well!

The business plans for many of the start-ups involved negative cash flows for the first ten or fifteen years, while they "built market share." To keep the atmosphere festive, they needed the host to keep filling the punch bowl.

However, the Fed knows that such a boom cannot be sustained indefinitely without eventual price inflation. Ultimately, if credit expansion continues, it will lead to the *crack-up boom*, where the economy enters into a period of runaway inflation. Fears of inflation led to Federal Reserve tightening in

late 1999, which helped bring MZM growth back into the single digits (8.5 percent for the 1999–2000 period). As the punch
bowl emptied, the hangover—and the dot-com bloodbath—
began. According to research from Webmergers.com, at least
582 Internet companies closed their doors between May 2000
and July of 2001. The plunge in share price of many of those
that remained alive was gut wrenching. For example, shares
of Beyond.com, split adjusted, went from $619 to $0.79. The
NASDAQ retraced two years of gains in a little over a year.
Unemployment shot upward, and the economy slipped into a
recession.

In the fall of 2001, Enron exploded in the largest corporate
bankruptcy in U.S. history. It appears, at the time of writing,
that some at Enron were at least morally and perhaps crimi-
nally culpable in the meltdown. But Enron's rise took place
during a period of free-flowing credit, and it crashed once the
last call was made. Ponzi schemes, too, thrive when credit is
easy.

Another prominent explanation for booms and busts, one
that has been applied to the Internet craze, might be called
"mania theory." Investors become entranced by some particular investment—tulip bulbs, French colonial trading ventures,
Florida real estate, the "nifty fifty" stocks, or Internet companies—and begin a self-perpetuating process of bidding more
for the asset, seeing its price rise, bidding even more, and so
on. Like a manic-depressive who can only maintain his manic
phase so long before crashing, eventually people begin to
have doubts about the mania, and it all blows up.

Commenting on the psychology of the theory is beyond the
scope of this book. Nevertheless, we can say that there is
nothing in the mania theory that contradicts the Austrian
account. They look at the same phenomenon from the vantage

point of two different sciences: social psychology and economics. They may, in fact, prove to be complementary. The
Austrian theory offers a coherent explanation of the onset of
the mania—a credit expansion—and the onset of the depression—the cessation of the expansion. After all, the mere fact
that people are excited about the Internet cannot create a
speculative bubble by itself. The funds to speculate with must
come from somewhere, and the Austrian theory identifies just
where. On the other hand, the mania theory might help
explain the reason that booms often do seem to be channeled
into certain faddish investments.

BOOM, BUST, AND THE STRUCTURE OF CAPITAL

*T*HE AUSTRIAN THEORY is concerned primarily with *malinvestment*, not with *overinvestment*. Entrepreneurs have
spent time and resources on projects that they cannot
actually complete and that they would not have undertaken if
there had been an accurate reading available of consumers'
time preference. As Mises put it in *Human Action*,

> A further expansion of production is possible only
> if the amount of capital goods is increased by addi-
> tional saving, i.e., by surpluses produced and not
> consumed. The characteristic mark of the credit-
> expansion boom is that such additional capital
> goods have not been made available.

Differentiating overinvestment from malinvestment is only
possible because of the key Austrian insight that capital has
structure, which we examined in Chapter 8. Many entrepreneurial plans count on complementary capital goods being

available sometime in the future. For example, as I launch my e-commerce business, my plan may have a step such as: "Six months after start-up: hire 100 web programmers at $100,000 each annually." But in the intervening months the boom is proceeding. Other companies are flush with cash from the credit expansion as well. As we all begin to hire our programming staffs, it turns out that web programmers are not available in the quantity and at the price we thought they would be. Any company that can't afford to put its plan on hold must bid more for those services.

The new credit tends to flow first into the higher-order capital goods—things like business plans, new buildings, new plants, and so on. It is later, when those goods require complementary goods to continue production on their road toward consumer goods, that the transitory nature of the boom becomes apparent. If real saving had occurred, there would have been a much better chance of the complementary goods being available. Take our example of my e-commerce business: If enough people had been setting aside enough time to learn web programming (a form of saving), then perhaps there would have been enough web programmers available for both my plans and those of my competitors to succeed.

Yet another metaphor for the process by which the Fed "manages" the economy would be that of a hyperactive pediatrician, who never feels that the children under his care are growing at the "right" rate.

The body grows by a process we do not consciously control, based, in ways we only partly comprehend, on genetic makeup, nutrition, rest, exercise, and so on. Each cell responds to its own local conditions, and the net result of all of these responses is the body's overall rate of growth. Similarly, each individual in the economy makes local decisions based on his unique circumstances, the net of which is the overall state of the economy. By using this analogy I do not mean to contend that the economy is "really" some sort of organism, only that the process of economic growth is in some ways similar to that of organic growth.

The Fed, the pediatrician of our analogy, feels it can improve on its patient's natural state. It doesn't alter any of the real inputs to the process, such as the number or nature of capital goods available, or the willingness to save. Instead, it fidgets with the economy's "hormonal levels" by adjusting the interest rate. When it makes credit easy, the economy's apparent growth speeds up. In fact, what has occurred is that certain visible manifestations of growth have accelerated, while other, equally necessary but less visible growth processes have suffered as a result. Without the necessary "nutrients" being present, the "growth" is not built on a solid foundation. The "bones" weaken and cannot support the body. The central bank, fearing a collapse, then tries to reduce the rate of growth through tightening credit. That in no way undoes the damage done during the period of credit expansion, but, rather, adds a new set of distortions to those already present. Of course, once the central bank has engaged in credit expansion, it is foolish to blame it for reining in the boom. The only alternative is eventual economic collapse in the crack-up boom: hyperinflation and the breakdown of the indirect exchange economy.

The proponents of Austrian business cycle theory do not hold that credit expansion unsupported by savings is the only way an economy can come upon hard times, or that, even when ABCT does apply, that it accounts for all of the hardships experienced in a downturn. For instance, although many Austrian theorists contend that the path to the Great Depression was paved by expansionist central bank policy in the 1920s, they generally acknowledge that ABCT does not fully account for the depths of the crash.

For instance, in the U.S., both the Hoover and Roosevelt administrations disastrously attempted to hold post-crash prices, especially wages, at pre-crash levels. That halted the adjustment process of the bust in its tracks and created the mass unemployment that made the Great Depression so notorious. (W.H. Hutt did extensive work on this aspect of busts.) Milton Friedman feels that Fed blunders led to a collapse of the money supply. Austrians acknowledge that further Fed errors would exacerbate the downturn. And at the same time the stock market crashed, the system of international division of labor, made possible by the free trade policies of the late nineteenth century, was collapsing in an international trade war among the increasingly interventionist states of the 1930s. (The infamous Smoot-Hawley tariff was the main American salvo in that war.)

Nor is the Austrian business cycle theory a deterministic one, in that we can exactly determine where the distortions from fixing the interest rate will appear. The story we have given here is a typical one, but not the only one possible. When the government sets the price of eggs too low, we cannot say exactly where distortions will appear, but we can say it is likely they will. Piero Sraffa objected to ABCT as stated by Hayek: Why, he asked, couldn't relative wealth changes from the rate cut drive marginal time preferences down to exactly where the central bank had set the rate? Well, we suppose, they could. So could the wealth changes from price-fixing in the egg market just happen to set supply and demand equal. But it would be pure chance and would happen very rarely.

BUT WHAT ABOUT EXPECTATIONS?

As ECONOMIST RICHARD E. Wagner of George Mason University says, in a paper published in the *Review of Austrian Economics*, "Austrian Cycle Theory: Saving the Wheat while Discarding the Chaff,": "the primary criticism that has been advanced against Austrian cycle theory . . . is that the Austrian theory assumes that entrepreneurs are foolish in that they do not act rationally in forming expectations."

Wagner goes on to point out that "a variety of occupations and businesses have arisen that specialize in forecasting the timing and extent of all kinds of governmental actions, including those of the central bank." Presumably, entrepreneurs now have better information with which to form their expectations.

The idea of rational expectations entered into economic theory chiefly through the work of Robert Lucas. Justin Fox, in a *Fortune* magazine article entitled "What in the World Happened to Economics?" explains Lucas's theory as follows:

> He argued that if people are rational . . . they can form rational expectations of predictable future events. So if the government gets in the habit of boosting spending or increasing the money supply every time the economy appears headed for a downturn, everybody will eventually learn that and adjust their behavior accordingly. . . . But the deductive logic of Lucas and other "new classical" economists led them to the stark conclusion that government monetary and fiscal policy should have no effect on the real economy.

As Austrian theory posits central banking as the primary cause of the cycle of booms and busts that have characterized modern market economies, it is easy to see why a wholesale acceptance of rational expectations theory entails a rejection of Austrian business cycle theory. For instance, Gordon Tullock, in his article "Why the Austrians Are Wrong about Depressions," says:

> The second nit has to do with [Austrian's] apparent belief that business people never learn. One would think that business people might be misled in the first couple of runs of the [Austrian] cycle and not anticipate that the low interest rate will later be raised. That they would continue unable to figure this out, however, seems unlikely.

What can Austrian theory say to this objection? If business people, aided by legions of "Fed watchers" and econometricians, could tell just what the Fed (or any other central bank) is up to, would we see a disappearance of the cycle?

To begin an examination of that question, I would like to recall the metaphor of the hyperactive pediatrician. Unsatisfied with how his patients were growing, the doctor kept administering doses of hormones that alternately sped up and slowed down that process. Let us imagine that we visit one of these patients after ten years of "treatment."

What do we know about this child's height compared to what it would have been without the treatment? Very little, I contend. The child might be taller than he would have been at his natural rate of growth, shorter, or even, by chance, exactly the same height. We might know that, at present, the doctor is applying growth-promoting hormones. But are they merely boosting growth up to where it would have been without the previous round of growth-retarding hormones, or are they boosting it above that?

Entrepreneurs are in a similar situation vis-à-vis the central bank and the rate of interest as it might have been on an unhampered market. When, exactly, could we point to a time when we saw that rate on the market? The Fed is always intervening, attempting to establish *some* rate. We might assume that, at least some of the time, the Fed-influenced rate has been close to the market rate, but how do we know at *which* times? Even if we somehow did know that on, for instance, July 12, 1995, the interest rate was at its natural level, how could we relate that fact to what the rate should be *now*? Fed watchers might be able to tell entrepreneurs that the Fed is easing. But is it easing toward the market rate of interest from some level above it, or further past the market rate from some level already below it? The idea that entrepreneurs are committing significant errors by not somehow divining where the rate ought to be is to criticize them for lacking superhuman capacities.

Entrepreneurs do know, however, whether the Fed is currently easing or tightening. But here the knowledge that is most important to them is how long that policy will be pursued. The Fed has a motivation to act contrary to whatever expectations the business community forms. If businessmen feel the Fed will raise rates, and therefore they refrain from hiring, undertaking new projects, making new capital good orders, and so on, then the Fed, watching the statistics collected on new hires, capital good spending, etc., will be *less* likely to raise rates. The Fed will explain that the economic growth seems "under control." Of course, the reverse is true as well: If the Fed thinks businesses, busily hiring, undertaking new projects, and so on, are not anticipating a rate increase, it will be *more* likely to raise rates—the economy is "overheating."

Wagner's point, mentioned above, that businesses have become better at watching the Fed must be complemented by the observation that the Fed has become better at watching businesses. Entrepreneurs and the Fed have entered into a sort of poker game, and it is hard to see how entrepreneurs can be faulted for not always guessing correctly which card the Fed is about to play.

We must also look at the issue of which entrepreneurs will have the strongest motive to first take advantage of easier credit, and in what position that will place the remaining entrepreneurs.

Let us, for simplicity, divide entrepreneurs into classes A and B. (Such a sharp division is not crucial to our analysis, as you'll see; it is merely a device to simplify our picture.) Class A entrepreneurs are those who are currently profitable, i.e., those most able to interpret the current market conditions and predict their future. Class Bs are struggling, money-losing, or, indeed, unfunded "want-to-be" entrepreneurs, less capable at anticipating the future conditions of the market.

Now, let us go to the start of the boom. It is 1996, and the Fed begins to expand credit. To where does this new supply flow? The As are not necessarily in need of much credit. If they wish to expand, they have available their cash flow. In the state of the market prior to the expansion, they were the ones most able to secure loans. They quite possibly have been through several booms, and, adept at interpreting the state of the market, suspect that they are witnessing the start of another one. They are cautious about expansion under such conditions.

The situation for the Bs is quite different, however. Their businesses are marginal, or perhaps nonexistent. They have previously been turned down for funding. Even if they *could* tell that they are witnessing an artificial boom, it might make sense for them to "take a flier" anyway. As it is, they are either not capitalized, or on the verge of failing. If they ride the boom, they will have a couple of years of the high life. And who knows, their business just might make it through! Or, perhaps, they will build a sufficient customer base to be purchased, maybe even enough to retire on. In that case, it might not matter to them if their company ultimately fails.

They use the easy credit to expand or start their business. We should notice that the *A*s are much less susceptible to such a motivation—they expect to be "living the high life" anyway, since their businesses are already doing well.

As the *B*s create and expand businesses, the boom begins to take shape. However, we can see that the actual situation of the *A*s has changed:

> Of course, in order to continue production on the enlarged scale brought about by the expansion of credit, all entrepreneurs, those who did expand their activities no less than those who produce only within the limits in which they produced previously, need additional funds as the costs of production are now higher. (Mises, *Human Action*)

Although the most skilled entrepreneurs suspect that the expansion is artificial, most can't afford to shut down their business for the duration of the boom. But if they can't, they must increasingly compete with *B*s for access to the factors of production. Take, for instance, the *A* company Sensible Software, Inc., and the *B* company, Dotty Dotcom.

Dotty Dotcom, flush with venture capital and an "insanely great business plan," is luring top Java engineers with salaries matching Sensible's while throwing in stock options that could be worth millions after the IPO. (That is an investment in higher-order capital goods, as top engineers are needed chiefly for more complex projects, which typically can take several years to complete.) Sensible simply cannot afford to lose all of its best programmers to Dotty. It must bid competitively for them.

However, in order to do so, Sensible must take advantage of the same easy credit that Dotty is using to back its bids. At the market rate of interest existing at the start of the boom, Sensible was already bidding as much as it deemed marginally profitable for producer goods. So the *A* entrepreneurs, willy-nilly, are forced to participate in the boom as well. Their hope is that, in the downturn, the basic soundness of their business and the fact that they have expanded less enthusiastically than the *B*s will see them through, perhaps with only a few layoffs.

Or, take the case of a class A mutual fund manager who suspects that stock prices are artificially high. If he simply puts his funds in cash and attempts to sit on the sidelines, he's sunk. All of his customers will leave, and he'll never survive to see the bust that proves he was right. In order to stay in business, he will continue to invest in stocks, perhaps keep a bit more money in cash than usual, and watch carefully for signs of the turn.

Our analysis of the banks proceeds in the same fashion. It is precisely the marginal lenders, those with the least ability to evaluate credit risks, that have the least to lose and the most to gain from an enthusiastic participation in the boom. They will tend to have the strongest motivation to expand credit. The more prudent lenders are eventually sucked in, in order to compete. The problem is compounded by the tendency of the International Monetary Fund, central banks, and other government bodies to jump in and bail out large investors when they get in trouble. We've already mentioned the Mexican loan bailout and the bailout put together after the collapse of Long-Term Capital Management as two prominent examples of the problem of moral hazard. If you are promised all of the upside of making a risky loan, should the borrower being funded succeed, but are protected on the downside by the likelihood of a bailout, you are much more likely to make the loan!

Our *A/B* division of entrepreneurs adds to the explanation of the radical difference between an artificial boom and a savings-led expansion. In the latter, the *A* entrepreneurs are able to sense that the consumers really do desire a lengthening of the production process and an increased investment in capital goods, as demonstrated by increased saving. Therefore, they are eager to take advantage of new credit. There is no reason to turn to the *B* entrepreneurs to find takers for the new funds.

Of course, there is no sharp *A/B* division in entrepreneurial ability. That was introduced only to simplify the discussion above, but the fundamentals remain unchanged under a more realistic assumption.

Another source of investment maladjustment from the boom, in addition to the intertemporal one, is the interpersonal one—the *B*s are those entrepreneurs that the consumers least want to have capitalized! One of the corrective forces operating to bring on the downturn is the fact that capital must be wrested back from the *B*s and into the hands of the *A*s, who can better satisfy the desires of the consumers.

The Austrian explanation fits well with the experience of real booms and busts. For example, an architect I worked with several years ago was quite aware that we were in a boom phase. He told me stories of witnessing a previous wipeout in

Connecticut real estate in the late eighties. He expected another downturn, yet he had expanded his business anyway. There were simply jobs that he couldn't afford to turn down coming his way.

Meanwhile, with the established builders so busy, new builders popped up everywhere. When the downturn came in 2001, one local contractor told me, "Some guys are going broke—but they're the ones who should not have been in the business in the first place." As Auburn University economist Roger Garrison said, in commenting on this chapter:

> In lectures more so than in print, I have often referred to the "marginal loan applicant" in explaining it all (your Class *B* entrepreneur). At the operational level, the relevant margin is the creditworthiness of the borrower and not an eighth of a percent difference one way or another in the rate of interest.

THE RATE GAME

A s WAGNER POINTS out, the idea that the Austrian cycle depends on systematic, foreseeable errors on the part of entrepreneurs arises from confusion between individual outcomes and aggregate outcomes. Certainly, an omniscient socialist planner in perfect control of the economy, who had by some miracle solved the problem of economic calculation in the absence of a market for capital, would not choose to misalign the time structure of production. But in a market economy, as Wagner says, the "standard variables of macroeconomics, rates of growth, levels of employment, and rates of inflation, are not objects of choice for anyone, but rather are emergent outcomes of complex economic processes."

I'd like to introduce one last metaphor to clarify Wagner's point. Picture a small town centered on a village green. It is an ordinary town, except that the town council has acquired an odd ability and has chosen to use it in a most curious way. Somehow, the council has devised a way to abscond with 50 percent of each resident's store of goods, including money, every evening at midnight. No effort to hide wealth from the council is of any avail. In a redistributionist fantasy, the council has decided that it will deposit this pile of stuff in the middle of the green every morning at six o'clock, available to anyone who wants to grab some.

It is obvious that this activity cannot make the town as a whole better off. In fact, as everyone will now be spending time trying to grab back as much wealth as they can, the town will be worse off. (They obviously had better things to do before this program started, as they weren't all hanging out on the green at six.) Some less-well-off residents may occasionally do OK, but as time goes on, the net effect of the lost productivity will tend to punish them as well. Our process also will alter the distribution of wealth, with wealth moving from those who are best at meeting the needs of the consumers to those who are best at grabbing things from the green.

Still, it is not an economic error on the part of residents to plop down on the green at 5:55 every morning. They are subject to a phenomenon that they cannot control. Each of their micro-level decisions leads them to participate despite the fact that, at the macro-level, the activity is wasteful. There is only one error necessary to generate this wasteful activity, and that is the error of the town council's foolish policy.

During a credit expansion, the entrepreneurs are in a similar position. On the one hand, they may suspect the frantic activity around the green is in the long run unproductive. On the other hand, they cannot produce without resources, without being able to secure access to the factors of production. To the extent that those factors are being placed out on the green every day, the entrepreneurs must go and participate in the competition to employ them. There are many long-term plans already under way that count on access to those factors. In many cases it is not financially feasible to halt those plans until the central bank's expansion has ended.

Anthony M. Carilli and Gregory M. Dempster, in a paper in the *Review of Austrian Economics,* look at ABCT from a game theory perspective. As I mentioned earlier, Austrians tend to view game theory as having limited applicability to market exchange. But the relationship between investors and the Fed is like a game in many ways.

Carilli and Dempster employ a simple game theory model to help explain expectations and ABCT. The Fed acts as "the house." The players are the investors. The best net result for all of them is when no one takes advantage of artificially low rates. But for any individual player, the worst result is when he fails to take advantage of the low rate while all of his competitors *do* take advantage of it. And the best result for each individual player is when he does take advantage of the credit expansion while his competitors don't. Since no entrepreneur can count on all of his competitors to abstain from the easy credit, his best move is to get "his bus" heading across the desert first.

Earlier, we had a single bus driver, representing the entrepreneurs, driving a single bus, representing the economy. The passengers (the consumers) had voted on a level of air-conditioning for the trip, but the Fed had replaced their vote with its own.

To incorporate the game theory perspective, we need to have many buses crossing the desert, each with its own driver. Meanwhile, scattered across the desert are several gas stations, with limited supplies of gas, where the drivers can refuel. The drivers are competing for passengers, who will, to a great extent, board a particular bus based on the combination of comfort and speed that the driver offers them. The drivers, while knowing that they do not have the passengers' real preferences on air-conditioning, do not know what those preferences are, or how the temperature they have been handed actually relates to those preferences.

In particular, the drivers (entrepreneurs) who first take advantage of a low apparent time preference from the passengers have the best shot at making the crossing. They will arrive at the intermediate gas stations first, and have the first shot at the scarce gas available to complete the crossing. Meanwhile, the drivers who hesitate to use the low apparent time preference may not attract any passengers.

In addition, as the supposed air-conditioning preference (the interest rate) is lowered, it lures more drivers into the business, many of whom are not really qualified, but may have no better shot at "making it" than to attempt the desert crossing. Perhaps, after all, they will get across!

It is clear that the situation is far from optimal. Whenever the Fed sets a supposed demand for air-conditioning (current consumption) that is too far below the real one, many buses will fail to make the crossing. Recovering from the problem (liquidating the failed investments, or, we might say, sending out the tow trucks) adds unnecessary costs to production, creating the losses of the downturn. But it is hard to see why the bus drivers are to blame.

One of the most famous theories in economics is *Say's Law*, first formulated by Jean-Baptiste Say: the supply of a good on the market always represents the demand for other goods. If I am selling apples, this is because I intend to use the proceeds to purchase bananas. Of course, there may be too much or too little of some particular good on the market at a particular time, *given its current price.* But we have seen that on the unhampered market such situations soon correct themselves: If the price for some good is too high, some sellers will be disappointed in their attempt to sell their goods, and will be motivated to lower their prices. If the price is too low, some buyers will be disappointed in their attempt to acquire goods, and will be motivated to bid more.

In the absence of interference with the market, such as a legal floor or ceiling for a price, sustained gluts and shortages will not occur. But, as we saw in the previous chapter, price-fixing can change that. The setting of a minimum wage, and the fact that governments allow unions to employ coercion to achieve nonmarket wages for their members, result in an ongoing glut of labor on the market, or, as we usually refer to that glut, unemployment.

While it is true that all goods supplied represent a demand for other goods, not all of the goods are demanded immediately. Some supply is a demand for present goods, and some a demand for goods that the supplier hopes will be available at various times in the future. The supplier (i.e., the worker, capitalist, or entrepreneur), having successfully exchanged his product for money, expresses a future demand by saving part of the proceeds. It is precisely the setting aside of immediate demand that makes available resources that can be used to create capital goods, that will be employed making consumer goods, that will satisfy future demand.

Capital has a structure because our plans have structures. All plans are executed over time. A particular capital good will enter a plan at some specific stage on the way toward a consumer good. We can call this the time structure of supply. Demand will have a similar structure: some goods will be consumed over long periods of time, some goods are set aside for later use, and money is set aside by people planning to use it to purchase consumer goods at a later time. The better aligned are the time structure of supply and the time structure of demand, the more smoothly the economy will function.

The market price that generates that alignment is the interest rate: the price for time. When the central bank sets an interest rate, it is engaged in price-fixing in the market for time. The essence of the situation is not particularly different than any other sort of price-fixing. But because the market is for time, the negative effects of the artificial price take time to appear. (The state would not be likely to undertake, deliberately, interventions in the time market for which the negative effects appeared immediately but the positive ones only much later!) And because of that time lag, it is harder to trace the later problems to the earlier intervention—after all, the initial results of an artificially lowered interest rate appear to be entirely salubrious.

The Austrian theory of the business cycle does not rely on entrepreneurs being slow or unable to learn. Of course, error is a key part of the theory—the error being the conceit on the part of the central bank that it can guess the "correct" interest rate better than the free choices of those lending and borrowing.

CHAPTER 14

Unsafe at Any Speed

ON IMPROVING THE MARKET
THROUGH REGULATION

PRODUCT SAFETY

*W*HEN CONSIDERING THE possibility of an unregulated market, one question that arises frequently is how consumers can be protected against unsafe products without government intervention.

Safety is not an absolute value that automatically trumps all others. Highway safety would go up if everyone drove a multi-million-dollar armored-personnel carrier or if everyone was forced to drive at two miles an hour. The mere fact that no one is suggesting those ideas illustrates that even the most die-hard of consumer protectionists realize that safety must be traded against other factors. Products need not be "absolutely safe," whatever that would mean, but merely "safe enough." However, government efforts to ensure that products are safe enough run into an insurmountable barrier. Having crippled the price mechanism via its intervention, the government has no means by which to gauge what trade-off consumers desire between safety, cost, convenience, and other product features.

In an unhampered market, it is the effort on the part of entrepreneurs to make profits by satisfying consumer demand that guides that trade-off. Let us imagine the market for chain saws to be in a plain state of rest, where it also happens to be the case that all producers are manufacturing saws that are equally safe. Now the producers, in their efforts to make profits, have reduced the costs to produce such saws to the minimum level that they could, given the means available to them. Competition will also drive those entrepreneurs to make the best saws that they can at any given cost. Thus any safety improvements can come about only with an increase in costs.

Let us further imagine that there are safety improvements that at least some consumers value more than the cost of adding them. This will mean that there are factors of production, be they safety engineers, quality inspectors, automatic shut-off devices, or so on, that are underutilized in meeting consumer demand, and therefore are priced below the level that would fully account for their value in yielding consumer satisfaction. The discrepancy between the prices of the factors of production and the prices of the final consumer products they might yield creates an opportunity for entrepreneurial profit. An entrepreneur can purchase those undervalued resources and use them to create a product that will sell for more than his costs. We have good reason to suspect that some entrepreneur, in the endless quest to find further sources of profit, will realize that the discrepancy exists and act to eliminate it.

True, the market process does not guarantee that every such opportunity will be found. However, aside from the search for profits, there is no possible procedure, other than guessing, to discover those opportunities. Furthermore, guessing without prices, while it might occasionally get the right result, does not even provide a way to detect success after the fact! Entrepreneurs have feedback as to whether they did a good job of estimating consumer demand; was the venture profitable? On the other hand, if the government steps into the chain saw market and mandates a certain feature, it destroys the very mechanism by which we might discover whether consumers valued such a feature more than its cost. Since *all* chain saws will now have the feature, consumers must pay for it whether they want it or not. No one can say whether consumers find this to be a reasonable trade-off, since they no longer are able to express their preferences by choosing between saws with and without the feature.

There is not even any guarantee that in requiring some safety feature the government will not make us less safe, as it might have overlooked another, more important element of safety. Michael Levin, in his *Free Market* article "Labeling and Consumer Choice," talks about his surprise at finding his son's new jacket had no drawstring. The reason the manufacturer had removed this feature was pressure from the Consumer Product Safety Commission. Apparently, some children had gotten their drawstrings caught in something and been injured. But perhaps the risk of pneumonia in cold climates is greater than the (minimal) risk of getting the string caught. Who knows? The government found a couple of cases of harm and saw the opportunity to "act decisively." But, as Levin points out: "Meanwhile, in the chilly New York wind, my son can't figure out how to tighten his hood."

When presented with these arguments, a friend of mine commented: "OK, but I don't have the time to research the safety of every product I buy, while the government can employ people to do so full time."

That is certainly true. If every consumer were left entirely to his own devices in determining product safety, the world would be a riskier place. But implicit in this concern is the idea that if the government does not fulfill such a role, then no one can. It overlooks other important sources of safety information, which would function even more effectively in an unhampered market than they do at present. Not only do such sources exist, but they have the distinct advantage that the decision whether to use them or not is voluntary. Perhaps I don't care how safe my chain saw is, as long as it chops up trees "real fast." In that case, why should I be forced to pay for safety evaluations that don't interest me?

One source of privately supplied safety information is independent consumer publications, such as *Consumer Reports*. While they provide consumers with good information today, the demand for safety information, and hence the supply of it, is dampened by the fact that these groups are competing with the "free" consumer information and protection from the government. (It's not free to us as taxpayers, of course, but since we pay for it whether or not we use it, there is no additional cost in making use of it in our role as consumers.) Some religious or ethnic groups have a tradition of private safety standards as well, such as the "kosher" designation on foods.

Or have a look at nearly any electric item you own and you will see a "UL Mark." It stands for "Underwriters Laboratories." The UL Mark is applied to as many as 17 billion products every year, to show that the product meets some standard of safety. UL has been providing the service for more than 100 years, long before the regulators got into the business. It's also completely private, a company with 6,000 employees that examines 20,000 different types of products. Its marks are forced on no one. The existence of organizations like Underwriters Laboratories depends on the fact that most businesses consider it disadvantageous to kill their own customers, both because it *will* tend to give one a bad name, and because marketing studies have consistently shown the dead to be far less avid consumers than the living.

There is always the risk that a testing organization might become beholden to some big client, and grow less than rigorous in testing that client's products. However, using that fear as a justification for government safety standards is flawed in two respects. First of all, it simply assumes that government agencies are free from such difficulties. The Public Choice School has long since debunked that idea.

The second problem is that it ignores the fact that competition is the consumer's best friend, here as elsewhere. In an unhampered market, if a testing organization is not performing up to snuff, there is an opportunity for competitors to draw away customers and make a profit by pointing that out. That is, in my estimation, the most significant source of safety information on any company's products: *its competitors*. No one else in the economy has as much motivation to study Company *A*'s widgets as competing widget-maker Company *B*. The means by which such knowledge can be propagated to the consumer is advertising. Examples of companies that have relied heavily on advertising the high safety standards of their products include Volvo and Michelin.

Empirical work on product safety bears out our theoretical considerations. Economist Ronald Coase describes the results of an extensive study of U.S. drug regulation by Sam Peltzman as follows: "The gains (if any) which accrued from the exclusion of ineffective or harmful drugs were far outweighed by the benefits foregone because effective drugs were not marketed" (*Essays on Economics and Economists*). *Reason* magazine contributor Jacob Sullum, in his article "Safety That Kills," contends that federal airline safety regulations most likely cost lives. Sullum also points out, in "Alcohol Blindness," that because of federal regulations, there are strong restrictions on mentioning the health benefits of moderate alcohol consumption. Dickinson College economist Nicola Tynan has done extensive research indicating that the socialization of the water supply in nineteenth-century London, done in the name of public safety, often created the large epidemics it was supposed to alleviate. In addition, private water suppliers were increasing water safety well before the government acted.

People have different tolerances for risk, and different views of the benefits of risky activities. Government regulations, with their one-size-fits-all view of this trade-off, are simply an attempt by some people to make that choice for everyone else. They are unsafe at any speed.

IN PRAISE OF BUGS

*P*RODUCT QUALITY IS closely akin to safety—in some cases, such as bungee cords, "quality" might even be a synonym for "safety." It is also another area where some people have claimed that there is market failure, and a need for the government to "step in and correct" the outcome of the market process.

One particular product that has often been accused of unconscionably poor reliability is computer software. *Wall Street Journal* tech columnist Walter Mossberg wrote a column a couple of years ago entitled "I'm Tired of the Way Windows Freezes!" in which he indicts the reliability of his PC software. As Mossberg puts it, "[Computers] should just work, all the time." In a similar vein, *San Jose Mercury News* tech columnist Dan Gillmor complains, "the attitude [of the technical industry] toward reliability and customer service has been scandalous."

Over the years, any number of other writers have sounded similar themes: computer systems are too buggy, there's no excuse for a single defect in software, if programmers built bridges we'd be afraid to drive on them, and so on. In their view, software defects are a moral issue, instead of simply a result of the well-known trade-off between schedule, cost, and quality. For them, there is no trade-off possible—defects are a moral failing, and a complete absence of defects must be assured, whatever achieving that goal does to the cost and the schedule.

What all of these writers allege, knowingly or not, is that, in the market for software, consumer sovereignty has been violated. The consumers would prefer bug-free software, *whatever the cost*, but greedy companies, thinking only of their profits, somehow force the current, inferior breed of software on them.

But is achieving bug-free software always in the consumer's best interest? Let's contemplate an example. I once went to work for a partnership that trades stocks with the partners' capital. There, the people who specified the software, the people who managed its development, the people who paid for that development, and the end users were all the same people. There was little risk that those people, in their role of managing development, were misrepresenting their own interests as users of the end product. Nevertheless, I was shocked at the haste with which the traders put my first, practically untested, development effort into use. One of the partners explained to me that this was not recklessness or ignorance, but simple accounting sense. For a company creating an automated trading system, one measure of its quality would be the ratio of good trades (i.e., trades the designers intended the system to make) to bad trades. If the average cost for a bad trade is $6,000, and the average benefit of a good one $4,000, then once the system generates 61 percent good trades, it is profitable. Any pre-release testing beyond that point is costing the firm money. Further testing may make the system more profitable, but once it achieves 61 percent reliability it is worth releasing.

After the publication of Mossberg's column, one woman wrote in, saying, "I never have to reboot my refrigerator, no matter what I put in it." But a refrigerator does the same thing with all input—keeps it cold. It doesn't have to connect to your head of cabbage, format your waffles, recalculate the spiciness of your horseradish, or spell-check the labels on your pickles. In fact, it keeps cooling even if you have nothing in it—something that we would consider a bug in a piece of software. A refrigerator is a fairly simple device, and a refrigeration engineer could explain the inner workings of one to us in about half an hour. On the other hand, modern computer systems are among the most complex devices humans have ever constructed. To achieve a moderate understanding of the inner workings of Windows NT or Linux, starting from scratch, would take years.

Complaining along the same lines, Gillmor writes, "The appliances we use at home do not crash." He seems blissfully unaware of the existence of washing machine repairmen, plumbers, electricians, telephone repairmen, and the dozens of other trades that help maintain our homes.

Fantasies about life in an ideal world where there is a surplus of everything are irrelevant to economics. In such a world there would no longer be economic goods, and the science of economics would cease to be of importance. Consumers would no doubt love to have software that contained every feature they might ever want to use, was completely without defects, and merely appeared on their hard drive at no cost. But here in the real world, where resources are scarce, we must choose *A* while foregoing *B*. Software can be made more reliable only by leaving out features, or increasing the cost of developing it, or both. Consumers' preferences in regard to this trade-off are embodied in their actual purchases.

Gillmor says: "[Consumers] just don't want to consider the possibility that low prices can mean not-so-great service. . . . People have to patronize the companies that provide quality, and have to be willing to pay more." He doesn't contemplate that consumers might be well aware that there is a trade-off between price and service, and could rationally choose a lower price at the expense of service. Someone using an on-line brokerage might decide that saving $15 a trade is worth suffering the service being down for one hour a month. Why shouldn't a consumer make that trade-off if he feels it is in his interest?

Even in the market most thoroughly dominated by Microsoft—desktop operating systems—consumers are able to make their own choices on quality in software every day. There were, at the time Gillmor was writing, two major varieties of Windows on the market. Windows 98, the cheaper of the two, was much more prone to crashing than Windows NT, the more expensive (in terms of learning time and administration costs, as well as initial price). This fact was publicized in reviews and advice columns. Yet consumers overwhelmingly opt for Windows 98. Shouldn't they have that option?

Whatever one thinks of the degree of "market power" that Microsoft wields, it certainly spends a great deal of time and effort putting out new releases of its products. As is often lamented, the releases tend to focus on new features, and generally contain about the same number of bugs as previous ones did. But if customers truly cared more about the bugs than the new features, then even from a monopoly position, wouldn't Microsoft want to focus on that area, so as to sell more upgrades?

There is no reason to conclude that consumers are not getting roughly the level of software reliability they prefer, given the scarcity of resources available to produce software. (I say roughly because Austrians do not believe that we can possibly arrive at the "equilibrium always" state of the evenly rotating economy.) But let us imagine that entrepreneurs have made a general mistake, and badly misestimated the desire for quality software. Either explicitly or implicitly, views like those described above contain calls for the government to do something about the problem. Many interventionists believe that once they have found an area in which the market's behavior is, in some sense, less than optimal, they have fully justified the case for government intervention. But as Ronald Coase points out, they have barely begun: Even if most software is, in some sense, "too buggy," what evidence exists that some government intervention could improve the situation? A common suggestion is to enforce a licensing system for software engineers. However, such schemes, by driving up the cost of entry, serve to protect the salary of those who can acquire the licenses, and to raise the cost of software. There is no evidence that practitioners who have, for instance, a bachelor's degree in computer science produce software that is more reliable than those who have entered the field with no formal training. Who can better judge the competence of software engineers for the task at hand than the entrepreneurs who hire them? Who better knows "the particular circumstances of time and place"?

The attempt to replace the actual preferences of consumers, as expressed in their willingness to pay real prices for real products, with fanciful musings about an ideal world in which ends are achieved without expending any means (except jawboning!) is doomed to disappoint. Such frivolity is not an attempt to strive toward an unrealizable standard, as there is no striving involved on the part of the daydreamer. Instead, these ideas, when acted upon by the state, only serve to cripple our ability to create the most desired of the less-than-perfect goods that we less-than-perfect beings actually can create.

CHAPTER 15

One Man Gathers What Another Man Spills

ON EXTERNALITIES, POSITIVE AND NEGATIVE

THE THEORY OF EXTERNALITIES

B RITISH ECONOMIST A.C. Pigou was instrumental in developing the theory of *externalities*. The theory examines cases where some of the costs or benefits of activities "spill over" onto third parties. When it is a cost that is imposed on third parties, it is called a *negative externality*. When third parties benefit from an activity in which they are not directly involved, the benefit is called a *positive externality*. The study of externalities, a part of *welfare economics*, has been an active area of research since Pigou's efforts early in the twentieth century.

There are standard examples that illustrate each type of externality. Pollution is a typical case of negative externality. Let's say I operate a factory along a river, making foozle dolls. As a by-product of my manufacturing, I dump lots of foozle waste into the river. That imposes a terrible cost on the people downriver, because, as everyone knows, foozle waste stinks to high heaven. If neither my customers nor I have to pay that cost, our choice as to how many foozle dolls should be made will be, in a sense, incorrect. If I had to pay those costs, I would have chosen a smaller number of dolls. Instead,

I chose to produce "too many" dolls while the people down-river are forced to foot the bill for part of my activity.

Pigou recommended taxing activities that produce negative externalities. Emission taxes on factories are an example of his approach. Another common policy adopted has been to regulate the amount of the activity legally permitted, for example, laws that forbid loud parties after a particular time of night.

A positive externality will arise when some of the benefits of an activity are reaped by those not directly involved. A typical example would be improving the appearance of one's property. If I paint my house, not only do I benefit, but so as well do all of my neighbors, who now have a nicer view. When such a positive externality exists, it can be contended that I will produce "too little" of the activity in question, since I don't take into account the benefits to my neighbors.

The traditional policy responses to positive externalities have been for the state to subsidize or require the activities in question. For example, the U.S. government subsidizes research into alternate energy sources. Primary education, often said to have positive externalities such as producing informed citizens, is mandatory (as well as subsidized) in most countries.

Lionel Robbins challenged Pigou's analysis in the 1930s. Robbins pointed out that, since utility is not measurable, it is invalid to compare levels of utility between different people, as Pigou's theory required. Robbins recommended using the criterion of Pareto improvement, which we met in Chapter 11, as the basis of welfare economics. A policy had to make at least one person better off (in that person's own estimation) and none worse off before economists could say it was unambiguously better. But Robbins held that if we just assume people have an equal capacity for satisfaction, economists still can recommend certain state interventions.

The notion of justifying economic intervention on the basis of welfare analysis was dealt a severe blow in 1956, with the publication of Murray Rothbard's paper, "Toward a Reconstruction of Utility and Welfare Economics." Rothbard showed that it is only through preference demonstrated in action that we can gauge what actors really value, and that to try to deduce values from mathematical formulas, without the evidence of action, is a hopeless cause. Only when people demonstrate their preferences by exchanging can we say with any certainty that both parties felt that they would be better off in the subsequent state than in the prior one. Since Pigou's solution involves imposing taxes and subsidies by fiat, without voluntary exchange, the numbers arrived at are mere guesswork.

Nobel Prize-winner Ronald Coase further undermined interventionist welfare analysis with the publication of his paper, "The Problem of Social Cost," in 1960. Coase demonstrated that as long as property rights are clearly defined and transaction costs are low, the individuals involved in a situation can always negotiate a solution that internalizes any externality. Consider the case of river pollution from the foozle factory, which we noted above. If the people downriver from the factory have a property right in the river, the factory will have to negotiate with them in order to legally discharge waste through their property. We can't say what solution the participants might arrive at—the factory might shut down, the people downriver might be paid to move, the factory might install pollution control devices, or it might simply compensate those affected for suffering the pollution. What we can say is that, within a system of voluntary exchange, each party has demonstrated that it prefers the solution arrived at to the situation that existed before their negotiations. (After all, either party can maintain the status quo by refusing to negotiate.)

Furthermore, we should note that negotiating between the parties affected allows them to use the "particular circumstances of time and place," with which they alone are familiar, to arrive at a solution. The factory owner may be aware of an alternative foozle input that does not pollute the river. The people downriver might know that the river is stinky anyway, and it's best to move. Regulators generally cannot take such specific knowledge into account in their drafting of edicts.

If transactions costs are high, it may be difficult to negotiate a solution. In those cases, the best solution again is to have clear property rights. For instance, it is hard for a factory creating air pollution that spreads over a wide area to negotiate with each person affected. In such a case, we might want to define property rights so that each person has a right to be free of airborne pollutants that exceed a certain level on his property.

Case studies have illustrated the resourcefulness of voluntary exchange in accounting for potential externalities. A common example of a positive externality in economics was the production of fruit trees and beekeeping. The growers of fruit trees provide a benefit to beekeepers: flowers. And beekeepers provide a benefit to the growers: pollination. However, the standard analysis contended that neither party had an incentive to take account of the benefit to the other. Thus, there would be "too few" orchards and beekeepers. However, economist Steven Cheung studied those markets and found that the parties involved had accounted for the externalities quite well, through contracting with each other to raise production to preferable levels. As Cheung pointed out, previous economists had only to look in the Yellow Pages to find "pollination services."

Social pressure also plays a role in handling potential externalities. If I don't paint my house, my neighbors will start to grouse. I may not get invited to the next block party. Hayek contends that those who value liberty should prefer social pressure directed against "deviant" behavior to outright bans. ("Deviant," in our case, meaning simply behavior of which many people disapprove, but which does not violate anyone else's right to life or property.) If I highly value having a house painted mauve, I can ignore my neighbors' mocking glances and jeers. But if the government regulates house colors, I'm stuck.

Loyola University economist Walter Block has continued work on externalities in the tradition of Rothbard. Block has challenged the traditional distinction between public goods, which must be produced collectively because of the positive externalities they create, and private goods, the production of which may be left to the market. The proposed list of public goods has included such items as postal delivery, roads, schools, garbage pickup, parks, airports, libraries, museums, and so on—just think of the activities your city government undertakes. The consensus has run that unless such goods are provided through government action, people will attempt to become *free riders*, enjoying some of the benefits of such goods while letting other people pay for them.

Block points out that the flaw in such analysis is that almost any good might be viewed as providing some benefit to third parties. What about socks? Doesn't the fact that other people wear socks, and I don't have to smell sweaty feet all day, provide me with a benefit for which I'm not paying? Must socks, therefore, be considered a public good, that only the government can supply in adequate quantities? Such logic, followed to its conclusion, would lead to a centrally planned economy, as the price and quantity supplied of all goods would be set based on the state's cost-benefit analysis, not on consumer evaluation.

WHO COOKED THE JAM?

*P*AUL KRUGMAN ADDRESSED energy policy and traffic problems in his 2001 *New York Times* article, "Nation in a Jam," saying:

> But you don't have to be an elitist to think that the nation has been making some bad choices about energy use, and about lifestyles more generally. Why? Because the choices we make don't reflect the true costs of our actions.

We'll let his contention that "the nation" makes choices slide. Krugman contends that "the nation" does too much driving, since each additional driver produces negative externalities for other drivers. Let's set aside the question of how Krugman can tell what the cost of those externalities is, apart from market prices. We'll grant him his estimate that the cost of traffic congestion in Atlanta was $2.6 billion in 1999. Each additional person's decision to drive cost other people $14 in lost time.

Krugman fails to ask *why* those costs are not borne by the drivers in question. We don't go to the opera expecting to find several other people vying for our seat. We never encounter two-hour delays in the checkout line at the supermarket. Those resources are privately owned, and, in the interest of making a profit, the owners have a strong incentive to ensure that their customers have a pleasant experience. While it is true that private businesses usually desire more customers and sometimes fail to plan adequate capacity for those who show up, such situations are most often corrected quickly. No one wants to own the business that's "so crowded that no one goes there anymore." If a private road owner found that his road was overcrowded, he would simply raise the price of using the road.

Recall the last time you met unexpected highway construction on the way to work. In my area, encountering such a project can easily add an hour to one's commute. Multiply that hour by the number of people stuck in the jam, and you can see that a whole heap of costs have been imposed on drivers by the road operator: the government.

Why is the government free to impose those costs? Both because we pay for government roads whether or not we use them and because the government has made it very difficult for private companies to build roads, the government has a near monopoly on routes for car travel. With the market process for evaluating the relative importance of roads, travel speeds, established property uses, pollution, and so on severely crippled, the government cannot rationally allocate scarce means among desired ends. Political pressure comes to dominate the allocation of resources.

For example, John Rowland, the governor of my state as I write this, commented on the Connecticut's branch rail lines in 1997: "Given the ridership on these lines, it is by no means outrageous to say it would be cheaper for the state to purchase cars each year for most of the riders." On some lines each passenger was being subsidized more than $18 per trip. But when his plan to eliminate those lines was faced with strong opposition, mostly from wealthy individuals who relied on the lines for access to New York City, the plan was dropped. We are entitled to wonder if the campaign contributions of the individuals in question didn't play a role in calculating the "cost" of closing those lines.

As Sanford Ikeda points out, such interventions also have the effect of making political action increasingly attractive, when compared to voluntary exchange. The more my economic well-being is determined by the political process, the more likely it is that I'll increase profits by lobbying than that I'll increase profits by producing. Further, the more my neighbors are using political pressure, the less resistant I will be to the idea of doing so. If no one else is using politics to achieve his personal ends, then I may be very reluctant to become the first to do so. But if many other people are pursuing that avenue, my resistance to joining them is likely to decline dramatically—after all, I can tell myself, I'm only trying to "even the score."

The state has repeatedly intervened in the transportation market. Roads are often provided at no extra cost to the users. The property on which the roads were built was often seized by eminent domain, so that the supposed construction cost did not reflect the true cost of acquiring the needed land. The supply of taxis and jitneys, which can to some extent substitute for having one's own car, has been artificially limited. Of course, other modes of transportation have had their own history of interventions. We have no idea of what a transportation market that had developed unhampered for the last several centuries would look like.

But it might strike us as odd that the very process that created the externalities in the first place—interventionism—is usually what is offered as the solution to them. Instead of seeking ways to allow the market in transportation to do its job, most recommendations call for further interventions intended to clean up the unwanted effects of past interventions.

For instance, Thomas Sowell, in his book *Basic Economics*, suggests that a law requiring mud flaps on cars is justified, because:

> Even if everyone agrees that the benefits of mud flaps greatly exceed their costs, there is no feasible way of buying those benefits in a free market, since you receive no benefits from the mud flaps you buy . . . but only from mud flaps that other people buy.

But Sowell's problem arises only because roads are publicly owned. The owner of a private road could internalize the benefit by requiring mud flaps and advertising the fact. Those who preferred that they pay for mud flaps as long as everyone else does, as well, can make use of roads requiring them.

Krugman does not explicitly call for a particular policy in his column. But when he says that the government should place a high priority on "getting those incentives right," we are to understand that he means imposing new taxes on fossil fuels, on car ownership, and other interventions into the transportation market.

But there is no way for the government to "get incentives right" without market prices, the very thing eliminated by intervention. It is simply not possible for the government to guess the prices that might have arisen on an unhampered market. Each subsequent intervention intended to fix an earlier one will add new distortions and generate new unintended consequences.

Regulations that require a certain average miles-per-gallon figure for a manufacturer's sold cars led directly to the explosion of sport utility vehicle (SUV) sales. Since SUVs are considered to be trucks, not cars, they are held to less stringent fuel-efficiency standards. Government efforts to increase overall gas mileage steered consumers into buying less efficient trucks, instead of station wagons, which were subject to the regulations. The general response has been, predictably, a call for new regulations on SUVs. Ford, for one, has tried to head off new legislation by increasing the fuel efficiency of its SUV fleet.

Often, some proponent of new regulation will contend that following the regulation will actually increase profits, and is the right thing to do for purely business reasons. For example, Steve Gregerson of the Automotive Consulting Group said of Ford's decision in the *Houston Chronicle*: "It's a smart business decision. They're creating a vehicle that is going to be accepted in the marketplace and has better fuel economy but offers some of the utilitarian functions of the SUVs."

But if it really is a smart business decision—and perhaps it is!—then surely some entrepreneur will do it without legislative pressure. Only if one believes that our best entrepreneurs just happen to be legislators does the argument make sense.

The free market is not a panacea. It does not eliminate old age, and it won't guarantee you a date for Saturday night. Private enterprise is fully capable of awful screwups. But both theory and practice indicate that its screwups are less pervasive and more easily corrected than those of government enterprises, including regulatory ones.

CHAPTER 16

Stuck on You

ON THE THEORY OF PATH DEPENDENCE

MARKET FAILURE AGAIN?

*P*ATH DEPENDENCE HAS recently and prominently been forwarded as an example of market failure. The idea is that markets can get "stuck" on a path that is clearly inferior to another option. However, no individual market participant is in a position to change things—that is the sense in which the market is stuck. For each individual, the cost of switching to the better path is too great. But if a person knew that everyone else would switch, he would prefer to do so.

A simple example would be the choice of which side of the road to drive on. Let's say it's discovered that driving on the left, as in the U.K., is significantly less stressful than driving on the right, such as in the U.S. Knowing that, I might prefer to drive on the left. But I surely don't want to be the *first* person to start driving on the left! Since everyone else is in the same boat, we keep driving on the right.

Therefore, conclude those alleging market failure, only the government is powerful enough to move the market off of the inefficient path. Popular literature parades out a trio of cases to illustrate path dependence.

The three stars of this show are:

- The Dvorak keyboard, a "superior" alternative to our current QWERTY standard.
- The Betamax video cassette format, which lost out to VHS in the consumer market.
- The Macintosh operating system, supposedly preferable to the dominant Windows/Intel (Wintel) platform.

The term "superior," economically speaking, means superior in satisfying the consumers' needs, given the current configuration of the factors of production. An engineer may view a Mercedes as superior to a Honda, but the fact that Mercedes does not outsell Honda is not a failure on the part of the market. It is a reflection of the market's ability to meet the needs of the mass of consumers. From an economic perspective, the claim that the "unlucky loser" technologies listed above are superior turns out to be false. There is no evidence that the triumph of alternate standards was a violation of consumer sovereignty. What's more, we have no reason to suspect that government supervision of the development of those technologies could have resulted in a better outcome.

A few examples illustrate how commonplace the idea is that Dvorak, Betamax, and Macintosh were superior products, that the market capriciously rejected:

Jared Diamond, writing in the April 1997 issue of *Discover Magazine*, tells us:

> The infinitely superior Dvorak keyboard is named for August Dvorak. . . . QWERTY's saga illustrates a much broader phenomenon: how commitment shapes the history of technology and culture, often selecting which innovations become entrenched and which are rejected.

The August 1998 issue of *Wired Magazine* contains the claim: "But of course, 'fittest' in technology does not always mean 'best'—hello, Macintosh and Betamax."

Paul Kedrosky introduces us to a leading proponent of such arguments, again in *Wired Magazine*, as follows:

> Brian Arthur . . . is the founding father of "increasing-returns economics," a new branch that is examining how dominant players in emerging markets can stifle innovation by locking people into inferior technical standards. Think of the old battle between VHS and Beta, and you begin to understand why superior technologies don't always win the tug of war for market share.

Our triumvirate is the major evidence put forward by the proponents, such as Arthur, of "strong path dependence," the keystone of "increasing return economics." The theory is that in the high technology world, as opposed to older manufacturing industries, a company's profit margin often increases with each additional customer. A typical example used is that of Microsoft, where it is contended that, while each additional sale of Windows adds a diminishing amount to Microsoft's costs, each sale adds an increasing amount to the value of Windows. (The claim itself is questionable. It only takes into account the physical cost of the product, ignoring the fact that each additional customer will be a harder sell than the previous one.) Increasing-return economics claims that because of the putative size advantage, the early market leader will be able to crush late arrivals. That leads to strong path dependence, because although the late arrivals may have better products, they won't stand a chance in the market.

It is useful to differentiate between claims of weak path dependence and strong path dependence. The weak case says

little more than that the future is, to some extent, dependent
on the past. For instance, the presence of nonconvertible capital goods in an economy will lead to more conservative
choices of methods of production than if they were absent.
But that is for the best, because it is only in the case where
investments in new technology more than repay the cost of
abandoning existing capital goods that they make efficient use
of society's scarce resources. Mises points out that from our
present vantage point, we might wish that past entrepreneurs
had made different choices about production. But that is
merely an inevitable consequence of the fact that the future is
uncertain, and that humans can make mistakes. What we are
now faced with are decisions about the best way forward,
given that the past was what it was, and that it created the
present situation, which we must take as a given. It is only the
future that holds open the opportunity to replace what is with
what ought to be.

However, the strong case goes much further than the weak
one, and contends that we often get stuck using inferior products, even when "society" could benefit from switching to better ones. The first product to market can win out against significantly superior competitive products. Those forwarding the
theory contend that path dependence can lead to a situation
where the government could usefully intervene to steer the
market toward better standards.

The first flaw in this argument based on strong path
dependence is that there is no objective yardstick by which to
gauge whether some technology is "better for society," other
than the profits and losses of the entrepreneurs who chose it.
As we saw in examining the calculation problem faced by
socialism, we cannot measure whether consumers have
received a net benefit from some macro-level change to the
technological landscape. Some consumers will gain, some will

lose, but we cannot "sum up" these changes to yield a total for "society's profit."

Just because we cannot calculate or measure that society is better off with one standard than another does not mean that it is impossible to employ human understanding for that purpose. We might, for instance, judge that society is better off having made knives the standard cutting implement in restaurants, rather than axes. But even under that looser standard, there is little evidence that the supposedly superior standards mentioned above actually were better. Let's examine the three popular cases put forward by the proponents of strong path dependence, and see how their evidence stands up under closer scrutiny.

BETAMAX VS. VHS

SONY (THE DEVELOPER of the Betamax format) and Matsushita (one of the VHS developers) chose to give different weight to the importance of ease of transportability (which meant small tape size) and recording time (which increases with tape size). Sony thought that consumers would want a paperback-sized cassette, even though it would limit recording time to one hour, while Matsushita opted for a larger tape and a two-hour recording time. Otherwise, the two technologies were nearly identical. In essence, each side had made a bet as to what would be more important to consumers, with Sony betting on small tape size, and the VHS folks betting on recording time.

Sony had a monopoly in the market for two years before VHS arrived on the scene. But with the VHS format allowing the taping of full-length movies, it quickly began to gain market share. The two formats started a price war. Sony also countered the VHS onslaught by increasing the recording time of Betamax to two hours. In response, VHS upped its recording time to four hours. Betamax went to five hours, and VHS to eight. (With the larger tape size on their side, the VHS contingent could always achieve a better trade-off between recording time and quality than could Sony.)

As we all know, the ultimate outcome was that VHS came to dominate the market for home video equipment. Betamax hung on as a niche format in broadcasting, where its advantages in editing and special effects were more important than in the consumer market. Stan Liebowitz and Stephen Margolis, the authors of *Winners, Losers & Microsoft*, point out that:

> [T]he market [did] not get stuck on the Beta path. . . .
> Notice that this is anything but [strong] path dependence. Even though Beta got there first, VHS was able to overtake Beta very quickly. This, of course, is the exact opposite of the predictions of path dependence. . . . For most consumers, VHS offered a better set of performance features. The market outcome . . . is exactly what they wanted.

QWERTY VS. DVORAK

THE SUPERIORITY OF the Dvorak keyboard to the standard QWERTY model has been taken for granted by many writers. Yet the myth largely has been constructed around a single study, performed by the U.S. Navy during World War II. The study, it turns out, was conducted by none other than the Dvorak keyboard inventor himself, August

Dvorak. He was the Navy's top expert in the analysis of time and motion studies during that war. The study he conducted used inadequate controls, and allowed no real comparison between the two training groups. The Navy study ignored the fact that additional training on QWERTY will also increase typing speeds.

The QWERTY keyboard, far from being deliberately designed to slow down typists, as the apocryphal story goes, actually had to win many typing-speed contests to eventually triumph in the market. Liebowitz and Margolis say:

> The QWERTY keyboard, it turns out, is about as good a design as the Dvorak keyboard, and was better than most competing designs that existed in the late 1800s when there were many keyboard designs maneuvering for a place in the market. (*Winners, Losers, & Microsoft*)

In asking whether our QWERTY-dominated world is an inefficient outcome compared to one in which Dvorak had won, we must keep in mind that the past cannot be undone: bygones are bygones. We are not faced with the task of reconstructing human society from scratch. "Society," meaning either the entrepreneurs of a market order or the central planners of a socialist order, must decide how best to use the current array of resources in going forward. If we were to start society over again, with the benefit of our current knowledge, we would make different choices. Factories would be located in different places, different transportation facilities would be available, different materials chosen for construction projects, and so on. Unless we wish to plunge mankind back to the subsistence economy that supported only a few million humans on the entire globe, we must make effective use of our current resources. That means that we can only afford to abandon older tools and techniques when the benefits gained by the switch outweigh the cost of switching.

The proponents of strong path dependence theory contend that in the cases we are discussing, the switch would more than pay for itself, but we have become "locked in" to inferior standards. If Dvorak is "infinitely superior," as Jared Diamond contends, switching to it as a standard would certainly be beneficial. But if that were really true, why hasn't it happened? It doesn't take long to recoup an investment offering infinite returns!

The supposed superiority of the Dvorak keyboard has been touted as so great that the extra productivity in *ten days of work* would repay the cost of training typists on Dvorak. But if that were true, it would hardly be necessary to get the rest of the world to go along on the switch. A single entrepreneur who employed a large pool of typists could lead the way out of the "efficiency trap" by himself.

In fact, more recent studies show that switching to Dvorak does *not* repay the cost of retraining. If a company needs to increase typing speeds, it is better off adding training on QWERTY keyboards.

In a world of rivalrous competition, where entrepreneurs seek out every opportunity for profit, we have good reason to suspect that they would not overlook an investment that they could amortize in ten days, but which offered years of returns. Liebowitz and Margolis, while not self-professed Austrian economists, forward an Austrian-like critique of the static models employed by the path-dependence theorists:

> In [Paul David's] model [of markets] an exogenous set of goods is offered for sale at a price, take it or leave it. There is little or no role for entrepreneurs. . . . In the world created by such a sterile model of

> competition, it is not surprising that accidents have
> considerable permanence. (*Winners, Losers, &*
> *Microsoft*)

Notice that the new "ergonomic" keyboards, from Microsoft and others, belie the notion that we are locked in to a particular keyboard choice. Although they use the same key order as the traditional QWERTY keyboard, the ergonomic models use a very different layout for the keyboard as a whole. Yet, despite the retraining necessary to use them, they are apparently quite viable in the marketplace.

MACINTOSH VS. WINTEL

As VIRGINIA POSTREL pointed out in *Reason*, calling the Macintosh superior to "Wintel" computers ignores many dimensions of what users want from their machines: expandability, a good price/performance ratio, a wide choice of peripherals, a wealth of software, and so on.

The first Macintosh was a 128K machine with no option for RAM expansion, no parallel port, a single floppy drive, no hard-drive option, little available software, and a limited choice of printers. It was simply not an acceptable business machine. Although Apple improved on the original Macintosh in many respects, it also continued to charge high prices.

Apple also erred in failing to realize that a large portion of the early PC adopters were tinkerers who wanted to be able to get inside their machine, trying to hook a piece of lab equipment to the computer's internal bus, for example. The early Mac was simply not to be tinkered with. The case was designed so that the consumer could not even open it.

That was a crucial mistake, for it is the tinkerers who develop the peripherals and applications that a platform needs to succeed. Tom Steinert-Threlkeld, writing in *Inter@ctive Week Online*, summed up Apple's failure: "Open up your architecture to all comers and win—or keep it closed, like the Macintosh, and lose."

A common charge leveled against Microsoft is that they used their monopoly over the operating system to attain dominance in application software. It is belied by the fact that Microsoft dominated the spreadsheet and word processing markets for Macintosh computers, where it did not control the operating system, several years before it achieved such dominance on MS-DOS machines.

Far from stifling innovation, as the proponents of path dependence contend will happen, Microsoft has had to innovate constantly to maintain its position. Consider that just a few years ago, "Microsoft Bob" was, according to Redmond, the "easy-going software that everyone will use." But it turned out that it was actually a Web browser that everyone would use, and Microsoft quickly switched strategies. The market process does not rely on altruistic motives on the part of entrepreneurs—Microsoft may have wanted to stifle innovation in that case, but they were simply unable to do so.

In the beginning of the personal computer revolution, consumers frequently complained about the bewildering variety of incompatible software and hardware on the market. I worked in technical support for a software product in 1985. We had to keep extensive lists of different hardware and software combinations available to us, as we found printing didn't work on manufacturers X's PC, graphics wouldn't function with graphic card Y, and so on. Bill Gates had the vision necessary to see that consumers would be much happier with standardized products they could mix-and-match without worry. By creating the Windows standard, Microsoft was able to internalize many of the network externalities in the personal computer market, earning it years of high profits.

CALCULATION AGAIN

*E*VEN IF WE *really don't like* some market outcome, which is what the majority of charges of market failure come down to, we must realize that in any effort to rearrange this outcome we must rely on opinion and guesswork, and cannot make use of economic calculation.

Imagine again that you are the economic dictator for your country. Usually, you let the market run its course. But once in a while, some market outcome really ticks you off, and you decide to act. Let's say that you feel there are too few operating systems available for personal computers, and you're going to change things.

How do you proceed? Perhaps you'll fund new operating system development. But how much funding should you provide? Over how many different companies should you spread the funding? If the development effort were profitable, we might expect that someone would be funding it already. Therefore, you will probably lose money in the venture.

But how much is it reasonable to lose? What is the right price to set for how much the public is "suffering" from having "too few" operating systems? And whom do you fund? The findings of the Public Choice School tell us that policymakers will almost inevitably be influenced by factors other than economic efficiency in making such decisions.

Perhaps the dominant operating system manufacturer should be penalized until it reduces its market share. What is the right amount of penalty to compensate for what you see as the cost of its dominance? What is the maximum market share that should be allowed?

The plain answer is that, other than pure guesswork, it is not possible to answer such questions other than by exchange based on private property. It is only when confronted with really paying the cost of something that we make choices that reflect our true values. Furthermore, if truly inefficient standards have been adopted, then the market presents entrepreneurs with the opportunity to profit by moving consumers to superior standards.

CHAPTER 17

See the Pyramids Along the Nile

ON GOVERNMENT EFFORTS TO
PROMOTE INDUSTRY

DOMED MONUMENTS

A COUPLE OF YEARS ago, in my home state of Connecticut, Governor John Rowland agreed on a deal to bring the New England Patriots to Hartford. To quote Diane Scarponi of the Associated Press, "At $374 million for a Hartford waterfront stadium and amenities, it was considered to be the richest stadium deal in National Football League history." Carole Bass of the *New Haven Advocate* noted: "[U]nder the deal struck by Rowland and Patriots owner Robert Kraft, the team will pay no rent, property tax or insurance on the stadium for 30 years." (The deal later fell through when Massachusetts made Kraft an offer that was, in his estimation, even better.)

While Connecticut's deal with the Patriots would have been expensive, the proposal just barely exceeded the $360 million Denver agreed to spend on a new stadium for the Broncos. Similar projects are common across the country. Writing in *The Brookings Review* in 1997, economists Roger G. Noll and Andrew Zimbalist described the then-current situation:

New facilities costing at least $200 million have been completed or are under way in Baltimore, Charlotte, Chicago, Cincinnati, Cleveland, Milwaukee, Nashville, San Francisco, St. Louis, Seattle, Tampa, and Washington, D.C. and are in the planning stages in Boston, Dallas, Minneapolis, New York, and Pittsburgh. Major stadium renovations have been undertaken in Jacksonville and Oakland. Industry experts estimate that more than $7 billion will be spent on new facilities for professional sports teams before 2006. Most of this $7 billion will come from public sources.

By subsidizing sports facilities governments are taxing the "average Joe" and increasing the earnings of some very wealthy individuals: pro athletes and sports team owners. What justification exists for such a practice? The usual explanation is that such largesse will, in the long run, provide a boost to the local economy, more than paying for itself. This explanation fails to heed Bastiat's warning to consider what is not seen, as well as what is seen, when contemplating an economic policy.

What is seen is the activity around the stadium on game day. People buy tickets to the game, producing revenue for the team. The tickets are taxed, producing revenue for the state. Inside, they buy hot dogs and beer, with money going to both the vendors and the state. They may go out for a meal before or after the game, enriching area restaurants. Perhaps they will also stop at a local museum, or see a show afterward. Both while the stadium is being built and after it is in use, local construction companies will have more work, first constructing and later maintaining the stadium, access roads, parking lots, and so on.

When we look at what is seen, it appears obvious that the stadium has been a boost to the local economy. It is only when we focus on what is not seen that the picture looks less rosy. The resources being expended around the stadium had to come *from* somewhere.

"Ah," the supporter of the stadium deal may reply, "but the state is going to borrow most of the money—so it's really creating the resources necessary for the project simply by being creditworthy."

However, Bastiat pointed out that in any loan, money is only the intermediary. What is being borrowed is ultimately always a currently existing good. When the government lends money to a farmer, he spends it on a tractor. (Bastiat used a plow in his example, but we might as well be more up-to-date.) What the farmer has really borrowed is the tractor. And since there are only so many tractors in existence at one time, someone else does not have that tractor as a result.

And so it is with these stadium deals, and all similar government efforts to "boost industry." If construction companies are building the stadium, there is something else they are *not* building. If steel is being used to support the structure, that steel is unavailable for other projects. If people are spending their money at restaurants around the stadium, there are other places—perhaps restaurants in their own neighborhood—where they are *not* spending that money. And the money spent by the state, whether raised through taxes or borrowing, to be repaid by later taxes, would have been spent by someone on something else.

Of course, all of that is true of any private investment as well: to commit resources to project *X* is always to withhold them from some other project *Y*. So the question becomes:

Who is likely to be better at picking projects in which it is worth investing, the government or private investors?[1]

Once we examine the incentives presented to those involved, the answer should be clear. Private investors will personally suffer a loss if their project fails and personally profit if it succeeds. Recall that a profit is a sign that the entrepreneur has better assessed the desires of the consumers as they relate to the resources expended for the project than others bidding for those resources did. A loss is a sign that the entrepreneur was mistaken—the resources were more in demand for some other use than the one to which he put them.

Given his intense personal interest in the project, the entrepreneur has strong motivation to ensure that resources are used in a manner conforming to the wishes of the consumers. And he has knowledge of the "particular circumstances of time and place" that he faces. Furthermore, those entrepreneurs who are best at assessing the future state of the market are the ones who will increase the resources at their disposal. Those who frequently misestimate will soon cease to have resources to invest. Entrepreneurs will make mistakes, but there is a weeding-out process in the market that rewards the entrepreneurs who are most often correct.

---

[1]There is an important issue relating to the morality of the government forcibly extracting money from Bill to invest in Joe's project. Ludwig von Mises, Henry Hazlitt, F.A. Hayek, Murray N. Rothbard, Hans-Hermann Hoppe, Walter Block, Stephan Kinsella, and other Austrians have dealt with this issue at great length. Without meaning to downplay the importance of this aspect of the problem, I will simply say that a discussion of it is beyond the scope of this book.

The incentives for government "investors" are quite different. Governor Rowland of Connecticut would neither garner the profits nor suffer the losses from any stadium project. Of course, the voters could have indirectly made him suffer a tiny fraction of the potential loss by voting him out of office. That is a very weak incentive. For one thing, he might have already left office long before the ultimate outcome of the project became clear. At that point, the voters would have no recourse whatsoever.

The Public Choice School has pointed out another force weakening that incentive, indeed, in most cases, completely negating it. Strong incentives exist for politicians to favor special-interest groups at the expense of the general public. Those upon whom benefits are concentrated are motivated to campaign hard for those benefits. As the costs of most political actions are spread across the public as a whole, the average person has little motivation to become involved.

In the context of the stadium project, we can see that, even at a total cost of $374 million, the cost to each Connecticut resident is only about $100. It is simply not worth much of any individual citizen's time to become devoted to the cause of stopping the stadium. However, for the construction companies who hope to get work on the stadium and the owners of businesses and land nearby, the potential benefits are enormous. They have a strong incentive to lobby hard for the project, to donate to the campaigns of politicians who support it, and to sponsor studies that will make the project look good.

In fact, if there were a profit to be made in some particular investment, private investors would be likely to act quickly to take advantage of the opportunity with their own funds. For instance, Chicago Bulls owner Jerry Reinsdorf and Chicago Blackhawks owner Bill Wirtz privately financed the

United Center in Chicago. Between hockey games, basketball games, conventions, ice shows, and other events, the arena is kept busy many nights out of the year.

Private investors will turn to the risky business of lobbying the government to support a project only when it is not clear to them that it is profitable without taxpayer subsidies. Thus, the government is likely to specialize in money-losing projects.

Empirical work backs up these theoretical considerations. In their Executive Summary, the Heartland Institute of Chicago, which has studied the sports stadium issue in depth, found:

> Between 1954 and 1986, the 14 stadiums for which sufficient data were available had an aggregate net accumulated value of *negative* $139.3 million. This loss of wealth to the host city's taxpayers ranged from $836,021 for Buffalo's War Memorial Stadium to $70,356,950 for the New Orleans Superdome. The only facility to have a positive net accumulated value was privately built, owned, and operated Dodger Stadium.

Larry Margasak of the Associated Press, in a June 1, 2001 article entitled "Producing a Farm-Fresh Flop," describes a U.S. Agriculture Department program:

> The idea was to invest government money in agricultural start-ups to turn sugar cane into furniture, sunflower seeds into motor oil and milkweed into comforters—with taxpayers reaping the returns.
>
> But some $40 million later, the Agriculture Department's much ballyhooed experiment to create the government equivalent of a venture capital firm has delivered hardly any return, according to documents

obtained by the Associated Press. Congress has given up and shut the doors to new spending.

Investment money to 16 companies has been written off as a total loss, and an additional 28 companies have failed to produce any significant returns—although there's still hope for some of them. All told, investments totaling $40.3 million have brought just $1.2 million in returns since 1993, the documents show.

AND OTHER CAUCUS RACES

*T*HE DIFFICULTIES FACED in justifying the use of public funds for stadium construction apply to all such public investment. In a recent review of, *Nothing Like It in the World: The Men Who Built the Transcontinental Railroad, 1863–1869*, Newt Gingrich wrote:

> This book is also a useful reminder to its modern audience that much of American success has been a public-private partnership. . . . The government played the most critical role by providing finances and incentives. Without those public contributions the [transcontinental] railroad could not have been built for at least another generation.

Using similar reasoning, we could say that without slave labor, the pyramids in Egypt might not be built even yet.[2] But

---

[2]Some scholars have recently questioned whether the construction of the pyramids relied on slave labor. If it turns out that it didn't, simply substitute some other project that *did* rely on slave labor for the pyramids.

no critic of such "public-private partnerships" ever doubted that at some time some particular project would be completed sooner with government intervention than without it. Gingrich is paying attention to what is seen, and ignoring what is not seen.

The resources necessary to build the railroads had to be diverted from other uses. Were those uses more or less valuable than the railroad? If what Gingrich says is true, and the intercontinental railroad would not have been built privately for a generation, we must conclude that entrepreneurs thought there were many, many projects that the consumers demanded far more urgently than the rails. No doubt, a transcontinental railroad is a handy thing to have around, but so are many other items. In a world of scarce resources, we must choose among a multitude of desirable items. Some we can have soon, but, in order to have them, other satisfactions will have to be delayed. Gingrich simply assumes that a transcontinental railroad ought to have come before the alternatives that entrepreneurs might have created with those same resources.

Gingrich places special emphasis on the role of the Army in "protecting" the rail line. That seems to be a polite way of saying, "Killing lots of Indians who were in the way." We might be excused for having serious doubts as to whether those Indians thought the railroad was the best use of resources at that time.

Contemplate a situation in which Newt Gingrich comes to American citizens and proposes that the government sponsor a regular shuttle to the planet Pluto. When we object, he asserts that his project would not be realized for another few millennia if not for government intervention. He is probably correct. But how is that a justification for undertaking this project? Isn't it, instead, a reason for rejecting the project from the start?

Another way in which government "promotes industry," in the United States and many other countries, is to aid exporters. (If you, dear reader, are not American, simply substitute your own country's name for "America" in what follows. The odds are high that your government is also engaged in similar shenanigans.) The think tank Foreign Policy in Focus reports:

> Examples of grants and subsidies for exporters include the Market Access Program (MAP) and the Export Enhancement Program (EEP) of the U.S. Department of Agriculture. The MAP, established in 1990, has an annual budget of $100 million and provides partial defrayment of the costs of market building and product promotion overseas. Some recipients, including Sunkist Growers, Sunsweet, Dole Foods, and Gallo Wines, have collected more than $1 million in a single year.

Certainly Dole Foods, a multi-billion-dollar corporation, appreciates the dough. But why should the rest of us pay for its marketing? One reason given is that the subsidies will create American jobs. Now, it is no doubt true that Dole can employ some greater number of workers than it could have without the subsidy. That is what is seen. On the other hand, the funds for the program came from other people, who presumably would not have been burning their cash in the backyard. (And if they did, it would lower the price level. While the economy would need time to adjust, as long as the adjustment is allowed to proceed there is no reason to believe that we would find ourselves in a "liquidity trap.") We can assume that some portion of their spending would have gone to pay someone's wages. We can also venture a guess that in most cases, the jobs lost to taxes were more valuable than those gained through the subsidies. After all, if Dole thought that this marketing was profitable, it would have undertaken it without the subsidy. If it didn't think so, that is because it estimated that consumers valued the resources necessary for the marketing campaign more highly in other uses.

Another, related, justification is that America needs to "level the playing field" its own exporters face, because many other countries subsidize their exporters. But no country can subsidize all domestic producers! The benefit to subsidized industries comes at the expense of higher taxes on those not subsidized. The closing of one door to American manufactures opens another door even wider. It is true that particular domestic industries may suffer as a result of another country's trade policies. But to attempt to compensate for that by introducing further distortions in the structure of production initiates a downward spiral in the satisfaction of all consumers. It is as though, because you have cut yourself and are now bleeding on my shoes, I will also cut myself, in order to bleed on yours.

Who is likely to benefit from such protectionist programs? It is not the family farmer or small business owner, who lack the resources to lobby Congress and to conduct foreign marketing efforts. Public Choice theory, common sense, and history all tell us that powerful, wealthy interests will come to control such programs. True, a populist revolt might succeed in limiting some programs to small concerns. However, there is no reason to suspect that the result would be better than the current crop of programs. In many cases, it might really be the largest corporations that should be devoting resources to export marketing. Again, the issue is who can best decide how much to spend on such marketing: The owners of the exporting companies, who have their own money on the line, or government bureaucrats, betting other people's money on the outcome?

MY TRACTOR AND BASTIAT'S PLOW

*W*HEN I PUBLISHED the above section in excerpt form, prior to publication of this book, I received a good deal of mail about it. A few correspondents were puzzled (or even distraught) over my use of the farm-equipment example from Bastiat's "What Is Seen and What Is Not Seen."

The complaints about that example were interesting and worth addressing. They illustrate the difficulty in perceiving the real economy through the "fluttering veil" of money, and the difficulty in clearly seeing the difference between the economy at a point in time and the progress of the economy over time. Furthermore, they point to an important distinction between the Austrian and neoclassical approaches to economic analysis.

We'll take up that difference between Austrian and neoclassical analysis first. One correspondent wrote to ask whether it wasn't "simplistic" to use a model with no inventory to describe this phenomenon?

There is a basic misunderstanding of the Austrian approach at work in that remark. Many neoclassical economists try to produce models of the economy that will "behave" as much like the real economy as possible, in the sense that they will produce numerical predictions that are close to the prices and quantities that really emerge. In the attempt to create such a model, more of the complicating factors of the real world that can be brought into play, the more realistic the approach is thought to be.

Austrian analysis is quite different. We employ imaginary constructions that (hopefully) allow us to see the essence of economic phenomena operating beneath the bewildering complexities of the real economy, not models that attempt to mirror that complexity. Having grasped those essences, we use them to navigate our way back to an analysis of more complex situations. Carl Menger set out this method in his *Principles of Economics*, as noted in Chapter 2.

Bastiat, usually considered an Austrian precursor, anticipated Menger's method. Commenting on his example of the plow, Bastiat wrote:

> True, I have reduced the operation to its simplest terms, but test by the same touchstone the most complicated governmental credit institutions, and you will be convinced that they can have but one result: to reallocate credit, not to *increase* it. In one country, and in a given time, there is only a certain sum of available capital, and it is all placed somewhere.

Bastiat's construction is not *simplistic*, but *simple*, just as it should be. Yes, he could have included unsold inventories of plows in his story, just as he could have included the price of the plow, what color it was, where the farmer lived, and how many pigs he had. But none of these things, including inventories, are relevant to understanding the essence of the phenomenon in question. (I'll address inventories more below.)

What about the example itself? Does it really capture that essence? I'll take up the various questions I received about that aspect of the example one at a time:

In what sense could Bastiat contend that the essence of the loan was the borrowing of a plow, and not the borrowing of money?

Bastiat was able to peer through the fluttering veil of money to see that people borrow it for the goods they can acquire with it. (The desire to hold cash balances is a complicating factor, but it does not change the essential analysis.) He wrote:

> In this question it is absolutely necessary to forget money, coin, bank notes, and the other media by which productions pass from hand to hand; in order to see only the products themselves, which are the real substance of a loan.

> For when a farmer borrows fifty francs to buy a plow, it is not actually the fifty francs that is lent to him; it is the plow.

> And when a merchant borrows twenty thousand francs to buy a house, it is not the twenty thousand francs he owes; it is the house.

> Money makes its appearance only to facilitate the arrangement among several parties.

> Peter may not be disposed to lend his plow, but James may be willing to lend his money. What does William do in this case? He borrows money of James, and with this money he buys the plow of Peter.

> But actually no one borrows money for the sake of the money itself. We borrow money to get products.

> Whatever the sum of hard money [gold] and bills that circulates, the borrowers taken together cannot

get more plows, houses, tools, provisions, or raw
materials than the total number of lenders can fur-
nish.

**But can't manufacturers just produce more plows (or
tractors) in response to increased demand, rendering
Bastiat's analysis a moot point?**

Well, certainly, over time, they can. But where did the
resources to produce more tractors come from? If the government has been specializing in tractor loans, then all it has
done is to shift resources, against the wishes of the consumers, from the manufacture of other goods to the manufacture of tractors. If the government is lending money to all lines
of manufacturing, it should be clear that this does not magically call more factors of production into existence. Only real
savings from real production can create new capital goods.

The money the government is lending ultimately comes
from one of two sources: taxes or the printing press. If the
government is using tax revenues to make such loans, then all
it has done is shift resources from those taxed to those who
are receiving the loans.

But it seems as though there may be a way out of this bind.
If the government prints up the money and lends it out, it
doesn't appear to have taken the resources from anywhere—
they just appear! That is the "magic" of Keynesian economics.

In reality, the government has taken the resources from
everyone in the economy who is holding cash. Real demand
in the economy is precisely the supply of real goods and services viewed from the other side of every exchange. If I produce corn, that corn *is* my demand for tractors, seed, TV sets,
cars, and so on. What someone hopes to receive in exchange
for their production is a certain amount of *real* goods and

services, not a certain number of pieces of paper with presidents' faces on them. A swift, unexpected increase in the amount of such paper in circulation may briefly fool people into believing they will receive the real goods they are demanding, creating a temporary boom, but the subsequent disappointment creates the bust afterward.

Well, just why *aren't* inventories relevant?

Here is the trump card in the Keynesian deck. "Ah," the Keynesians will claim, "the above analysis is fine when the economy is at full employment and comprises no unused capacity. But if the economy is in a slump, the increase in paper money will prime the pump, prodding those idle resources (i.e., inventories, idle factories, and unemployed workers) back into the cycle of production."

But *why* are certain resources idle? The owners of those idle resources expect to receive more for them than they currently are being offered. They are holding out waiting for a better price. (Or, in the case of workers, they may be legally prevented from even offering a lower price.) When such a situation is prevalent in the economy, Austrians would contend that it is the result of the false expectations created by the previous boom. In any case, as W.H. Hutt pointed out, what is needed to restore full productivity is for individuals in the economy to adjust their expectations to better align with the real demands for their products and services. The Keynesian solution is to try to fool producers (including workers) into thinking that their unrealistic demands *are* being met.

Keynesians contend that without government stimulus the adjustment process will be stalled—indeed, things will get worse—due to a spiral of economic despair. Laid-off workers will lower their demand for consumer goods. That will cause employers to lower their expectations and lay off more work-ers. The newly laid-off workers will now lower *their* demand for consumer goods. And so on.

It is true that a general malaise may settle on people dur-ing a downturn. But successful entrepreneurs are precisely those people who are able to see that the general opinion of the current situation is, in some sense, wrong. As Mises says:

> [T]he entrepreneur is always a speculator. He deals with the uncertain conditions of the future. His suc-cess or failure depends on the correctness of his anticipation of uncertain events. If he fails in his understanding of things to come, he is doomed. The only source from which an entrepreneur's profits stem is his ability to anticipate better than other people the future demand of the consumers. If everybody is correct in anticipating the future state of the market of a certain commodity, its price and the prices of the complementary factors of produc-tion concerned would already today be adjusted to this future state. Neither profit nor loss can emerge for those embarking upon this line of business. (*Human Action*)

In the downturn, certain factors of production are under-priced and may be idled. The deeper a downturn goes, the more underpriced they become. Those who can peer forward past the storm, through the dark forces of time and ignorance, and see the sun returning stand to profit from their foresight. They are the ones who buy when there is panicked selling and sell when there is manic buying.

To whatever extent that the Keynesian solution of stimulat-ing demand "works," it prevents the needed adjustments in expectations from taking place. Certain lines of manufacture *should* be shut down, since they are using resources that consumers demand more urgently in other places. Some workers *should* lower their wage demands, since they are unemployable at the wage they currently expect. Instead of an overall movement of the price level, what is really needed is for certain prices to be adjusted relative to others.

The Keynesian solution to a slump attempts to prop up prices (including wages) that are too high. When the economy has been on a bender and wakes up with a crashing headache, the Keynesians recommend having a few drinks, when what is needed is for the poison to be purged from the system. Real demand will only be restored when the structure of prices moves back toward a configuration more closely reflecting consumer's wishes. Printing, then lending, money only delays that adjustment.

PART IV

SOCIAL JUSTICE, RIGHTLY UNDERSTOOD

CHAPTER 18

Where Do We Go From Here?

ON THE POLITICAL ECONOMY OF
THE AUSTRIAN SCHOOL

WHERE WE ARE

*W*E HAVE OUTLINED an economics for real people, studying real choices as they are made by you and me.
Economics does not need to regard us as automatons, to assume we are only interested in monetary matters, or
to treat us as atomistic, pleasure-seeking narcissists. It can
acknowledge that we are embedded in a social context and
that we are influenced by faith, despair, hope, fear, love, hate,
superstition, and all of the other "irrational" aspects of human
nature. Economics proceeds based on the solid foundation of
the logic of choice. Many factors enter into human choice.
Psychology, genetics, history, ethics, and religion may all have
something to say about the origin and degree of influence of
those factors. But economics can accept those factors as given
and study the implications of the fact that we *do* choose.
Those implications are significant.

The fundamental problems that human actors solve in the
moment of choice are not of the sort that a computer can
solve. That is because, unlike in the models of mathematical
economics, the ends are not given to acting man: It is ultimately the ends themselves that we are creating with our

actions. We must imagine the world as it ought to be, then act to make that imagined scenario real.

That is captured in a variety of commonsense nostrums—"Watch what you wish for," "Once you start down that road, there's no turning back," "Choose your friends carefully," etc. If you are choosing between killing your neighbor and praying for his forgiveness, you are not choosing different means toward a given end: you are choosing among ends. It is true, as the logic of choice points out, that we can always affirm that what you choose is regarded by you as better than what you do not choose. But in the act of choice you are, in fact, deciding what you will regard as better: Is it revenge or peace that you are after?

THE AUSTRIAN APPROACHES TO POLITICAL ECONOMY

*T*HE INTERRELATIONSHIP OF politics and economics has existed since the first hints of economic thinking arose in human history. Policies have propelled the research of economists just as that research has propelled the development of policy. For many years the very name of economic science was "political economy."

Are there particular approaches to politics implied by the Austrian conception of the market? To help answer that question, I will take four great Austrian economists as representative of different political positions adopted within the Austrian School: Ludwig Lachmann, F.A. Hayek, Ludwig von Mises, and Murray Rothbard. These positions form a spectrum, and it will be useful to contrast them while taking note of the reasoning that led them to their positions.

LUDWIG LACHMANN

A S LUDWIG LACHMANN'S career progressed he focused increasingly on the uncertainty of the future. The fact that we can't say today what we might learn or create tomorrow means that uncertainty is a fundamental aspect of human action. It is the very quest for knowledge, with the surprising results it brings, that is the prime source of economic uncertainty. Because of his focus on uncertainty, Lachmann came to doubt that, in a laissez-faire society, entrepreneurs would be able to achieve any consistent meshing of their plans. The economy, instead of possessing a tendency toward equilibrium, was instead likely to careen out of control at any time. Lachmann thought that the government had a role to play in stabilizing the economic system and increasing the coordination of entrepreneurial plans. We can call his position "intervention for stability."

F.A. HAYEK

H AYEK REJECTED THE radical uncertainty of Lachmann, based on his perception that the market *does* exhibit regularities. As Bastiat would say, Paris *does* get fed. We might account for those regularities by the actions of entrepreneurs. Hayek found no reason to suspect that governments could outperform profit-seeking entrepreneurs at achieving plan coordination.

The evolution of F.A. Hayek's thought toward a system distinct from that of his mentor, Ludwig von Mises, involved a focus on evolutionary perspectives and the limits of reason.

Mises centered his system on the idea that every choice is rational insofar as choice itself means conscious, purposive behavior. Hayek turned his attention to the customs, habits, institutions, morals, prejudices, and so on, which make up the substratum of choice. Hayek saw them as evolving below the radar of abstract reason, as a result of the evolutionary selection of group traits, operating on many societies across many generations. While Hayek did not regard those traditions as being off-limits to intellectual exploration, he felt we should be cautious about concluding that we fully understand them. As a corollary, we should also be cautious about tossing them out just because we so far don't see a good reason for their existence. His exploration of the evolutionary aspect of society lent his generally libertarian thought a significant strain of conservatism. Where government interventions had existed in society for some time—poor relief, support for education, road building—Hayek was likely to be cautious or even negative about abandoning them. On the other hand, he was even more skeptical about proposals for new interventions. We could call Hayek's position "traditionalist interventionism."

LUDWIG VON MISES

*L*UDWIG VON MISES focused on the nature of human action itself. He took a more rationalist approach to human institutions than did Hayek. He acknowledged that they often arose as the unintended outcome of action directed toward other ends. But he held that reason should be used to examine such institutions and evaluate their efficacy. (As we've mentioned, Hayek did not argue against employing reason for social analysis. He was simply more cautious than

Mises was about the results it would achieve.) Stressing that human action always involved the employment of means toward some end, he asked whether particular interventions were the suitable means to attain the end sought. He held that, by destroying the price mechanism and interfering with peaceful cooperation, all economic interventions eventually would have repercussions that were undesirable, even to those initially favored by the intervention. Mises concluded, however, that the state was necessary to establish the rule of law and the property rights that the market needed as its foundation. Mises's ideal state is *minarchist*: it is the "night-watchman" state that acts only to prevent violence and theft. Mises's position might be characterized as "intervention to create the necessary condition—the rule of law—for a market society."

MURRAY ROTHBARD

*M*URRAY ROTHBARD PUSHED Mises's rationalism a step further. He contended that reason should be used to evaluate not just the means of social policy, but the ends as well. His politics arose from his marriage of Austrian economics and a rationalist, libertarian system of ethics. Starting from the basic idea of ownership and the premise that everyone owns himself, Rothbard developed a system in which the state was seen to have no legitimate role at all. All necessary social institutions, Rothbard contended, including police, courts, and military, could be established, without coercion, through peaceful cooperation. Rothbard's intellectual heirs, including Hans-Hermann Hoppe, David Gordon, Jörg Guido Hülsmann, Walter Block, and others, have sought to develop the rational base of his edifice and have begun to describe what a world without the state might look like. The Rothbardian view is *market anarchist*, or, as Rothbard called it, *anarcho-capitalist*: "no intervention, and no state that could consider intervening."

Lachmann, Hayek, Mises, and Rothbard all recognized that the main problem facing economics is not to describe what the market would be like in equilibrium—an impossible state of affairs, anyway!—but to examine the interplay of forces that generate the market process. To a great extent, their political economy reflects their opinion about the robustness of that process. Lachmann, the most interventionist of the four, also was the most doubtful that the market was self-stabilizing. Rothbard, the least interventionist, felt that the market could provide even law and defense better than the state.

The common idea in Austrian political economy is to use the minimum of coercion necessary to create a functioning society. The above Austrians' opinions on what that minimum might be range from "not too much" through "very little" to "none at all." But all of them saw the value of freeing the individual human mind to set its own course, and preferred that freedom as far as their theoretical musings led them to believe it was feasible. Even Lachmann, the most interventionist of the four, recognized the tremendous power of voluntary cooperation and the profound limitations of central planning.

ECONOMICS AS THE SCIENCE OF WEALTH

AN ALTERNATE VIEW of economics, dating back to the mercantilists and promoted by Adam Smith, is that it is the study of how to make a society wealthier. Many economists who are thought of as "right wing" hold to such a view, at least implicitly. While economists from the left generally recommend state interventions to alleviate inequality, the interventions most frequently recommended from the right are those that "promote growth" (see Chapters 12, 13, and 17). From the Austrian perspective such views are problematic, given the subjective nature of "wealth," "growth," and so on. Who is to say if a town is wealthier located next to a prosperous factory or next to a beautiful forest? Am I wealthier if I have more cash in the bank, or more time to spend with my children? The insights of the Austrian School demonstrate that economics can't answer those questions for us.

Schemes where property rights are violated in the interest of "promoting growth" are distinctly non-Austrian. Let's imagine that economists conclude that the uncertainty and loss of savings generated by a mild inflation has historically spurred people to work harder, resulting in higher growth. For an economist of the "science of wealth" school, it would be clear that we should pursue that policy. We can hear similar opinions voiced by some *supply-side economists*, who seem to feel that the Fed cannot set interest rates too low, nor can economic expansion possibly be too rapid.

That view is foreign to Austrian economics. Instead of realizing that wealth is a subjective concept—you're as wealthy as you think you are—economists favoring intervention to promote growth believe wealth can be measured by the dollar value of goods exchanged or some physical quantity of output. Instead of acknowledging that the market is the emergent outcome of the interaction of all participants' values, the growth economists feel they know better than others how much we should sacrifice now to provide for the future. They would override individuals' decisions as to how leisure, time with the kids, spiritual pursuits, and so on, are valued relative to having more "stuff." Instead of seeing each person as an individual who is in the best position to plan for his own happiness, people are seen as subprocesses in a production function, to be tuned so as to maximize the output of the function.

Here, we must acknowledge a valid criticism from the left of many "free-market" economists. "The supporters of free markets," their critique runs, "fail to admit how much their philosophy is a justification for the strong exploiting the weak." Professor Hans-Hermann Hoppe of the University of Nevada, Las Vegas contends that Marxist historical literature on exploitation is highlighting a genuine historical phenomenon, but has misidentified its source. The term "exploitation," when applied to a voluntary market exchange, simply means that the person using the term disapproved of that exchange. But when the government uses its monopoly on legitimatized coercion to force exchanges on people, the term takes on a more objective meaning. Again and again, expansive governments, generated around the rallying cry of protecting the weak, have been captured by the strong and used by them to fortify their own positions. (Their ability to exert their power is, after all, why we refer to them as "the strong"!)

An all-too-typical example recently occurred thirty miles from where I live, in New Rochelle, New York. Ikea wanted to put up a superstore. Town officials, excited by the "growth" this would promote (and the kudos and campaign contributions they might be able to garner?), enthusiastically backed the idea. (They eventually were forced to abandon it.) As reported by Jacob Sullum of *Reason* in his article, "Parcel Delivery":

> The site that Ikea had in mind for its new store happened to be occupied by 34 homes, 28 businesses, and two churches. Instead of trying to buy the land

> fair and square, Ikea asked the city to force the
> owners to sell, at whatever price the city considered
> reasonable.
>
> If Ikea did that sort of thing on its own, it would be
> called extortion. But when the government does it, it's
> called exercising the power of eminent domain. . . .
>
> "Is it right to tear people from their homes?" one res-
> ident, Dominick Gataletto, asked ABC's John Stossel
> in an interview that aired on January 27. "All the
> memories I've had all these years. . . . I've been here
> 67 years, and you just don't wipe that away simply
> because a furniture store wants to come in. This is
> America."

If the neighborhood in question was more valuable to Ikea
than to the residents, Ikea could have paid them all enough
to move out. The market allows individuals to carefully (or
carelessly!) weigh their alternatives and to find their own balance between material prosperity and other values. If you feel
the average person values his community too little, a free society allows you to engage in an unlimited amount of persua-
sion in order to convince him to value it more highly. Political solutions to questions of value force one set of values, typically those of some interest group, on everyone else.

A system where "government-business partnerships" run
roughshod over property rights is not the free market as
meant by Austrians. In our view, private property is essential
in rationally estimating value. Using the best system we have
of gauging such matters—market prices—we can conclude
that the "growth" such measures promote is, in fact, a reduction in the wealth of many of those affected, in their own
value judgments.

THE MARKET SOCIETY AND ITS DISCONTENTS

*T*IMUR KURAN, IN his book, *Private Truths, Public Lies: The Social Consequences of Preference Falsification*, suggests that supposedly voluntary choices are overly influenced by the fear of disapproval and the desire for approval. Kuran's book is, in fact, an excellent study of the interaction between tradition and individual autonomy. But he has chosen his primary term badly.

If I do not go to work dressed in only ostrich feathers, despite the fact that I love wearing them, it is misleading to call that "preference falsification." Rather, it shows that my preferences are influenced by my social milieu. I prefer not looking ridiculous even more than I prefer wearing ostrich feathers.

Imagine a Moslem woman living in a society that legally permits her to appear in public without a veil. If she chooses to wear one anyway, due to social pressure, she has not "falsified" her preferences. She has, in fact, expressed her preference for complying with social norms instead of "letting it all hang out."

Of course people are influenced by their social circumstances. Of course they adopt fads, take on "nutty" ideas from their environment, and are creatures of their time in history, their social class, and so on. But a man who would replace other individuals' choices with his own must answer the question of whether *he* isn't also a creature of *his* circumstances.

Those who criticize the choices of others based on the fact that those choices are overly influenced by social pressure imagine themselves to be standing outside of society passing judgment on those "trapped" inside. But man as we know him is inherently a social creature, a fact that all of the great Austrian economists have recognized. The intellectual critic of society is no exception—he is himself embedded in his society.

Looking at the other side of the coin, communitarians such as John Gray contend that market behavior is *inadequately* influenced by customs, manners, traditional morals, habits, and so on. Many of those at the recent "globalization" protests in Seattle, Washington, and Quebec City subscribe to somewhat similar views. Gray complains about the market society as follows:

> The celebration of consumer choice, as the only undisputed value in market societies, devalues commitment and stability in personal relationships and encourages the view of marriage and the family as vehicles of self-realization. The dynamism of market processes dissolves social hierarchies and overturns established expectations. Status is ephemeral, trust frail, and contract sovereign. This dissolution of communities promoted by market-driven labour mobility weakens, where it does not entirely destroy, the informal social monitoring of behaviour which is the most effective preventive measure against crime. (*Enlightenment's Wake: Politics and Culture at the Close of the Modern Age*)

But "consumer choice" (or freedom, as we might put it) allows one to make one's own decisions between "commitment and stability in personal relationships" and a new microwave. As Mises says, consumers in the market society are not choosing only among material objects or things for sale. The nature of free choice is that the chooser is deciding what to value. Commitment, stability, love, status, and all other "human values are offered for option."

Where has Gray been as governments have forced reset-
tlements of vast numbers of people, leveled neighborhoods in
the name of renewal, and seized property, forcing people to
move, through eminent domain?

And just what will Gray do about all of the people who
might move around willy-nilly if left to their own devices?
Why, he must stop them, of course! Intellectuals like John
Gray will flit around the world to various think tanks and con-
ferences, while a blue-collar worker is expected to stay put, in
the place he was born. Gray cannot eliminate the fact that life
involves trade-offs and that better opportunities might only be
available far from home. He cannot eliminate tough decisions,
but he would be happy to make them for you.

Who should decide how much importance someone should
place on such traditional values, "the authorities" or the individuals whose lives are in question? Although the communitarians have a point in faulting many current government-business
partnerships as disrupting prevailing ways of life, their distress
ought to lead them to reject interventionism, instead of hoping
that future interventions will be more hospitable to communi-
ties. "We" cannot decide how much to innovate and how much
to respect tradition—each of us individually decides this. As
political philosopher Paul Gottfried says in "The Communitarians":

> Even if the state were to carry out policies that
> seemed pro-community, such as changing the
> income tax so as to favor large working families, this
> would not serve the long-term interest of communi-
> ties. It merely provides another cover for political
> management, albeit one marketable to the middle
> class. But for those serious about communities, the
> goal of protecting their institutional integrity is
> inseparable from guarding their independence and
> their property from political invasion.

Another common complaint against the market society is that "we" have lost control of social life to "the market," which is now making our decisions for us. For instance, in his book, *The Illusion of Choice: How the Market Economy Shapes Our Destiny*, Andrew Bard Schmookler calls the market

> a monster run amok . . . [that], because of its biases and distortions, *carries us to a destination chosen by that system and not by us.* . . . [T]o conclude . . . that the market allows people to choose their destiny is a widespread and enormously influential fallacy.

If Schmookler desires a system where everyone can wish for any destiny that we desire and it will come to us, then he is wishing for the impossible. Means are scarce, ends are not, and acting man must somehow cope with the disparity. Those scarce means must be allocated among competing ends. The market society allows us to do so based on the prices that consumers are willing to pay for various consumption goods. On what basis would Schmookler allocate these resources?

When he says that "we" should choose our destination, instead of "the market," by "we" he means the political process. But we have seen that politics is inherently controlled by special interest groups. So, what Schmookler's request amounts to is that, rather than each of us making our own choices, various lobbies and power blocs should make our choices for us.

A market society does not prevent its members from forming a commune, going on meditation retreats, buying land and turning it into nature preserves, or any other "nonmaterialist" pursuit. If we do not do so, but wish we had, it is merely an attempt to escape responsibility to blame "the market" for our choices.

If it turns out that consumers prefer "trashy" and "vulgar" goods, it is not the fault of "the market." As Mises says in *Human Action*:

The moralists' and sermonizers' critique of profits misses the point. It is not the fault of the entrepreneurs that the consumers—the people, the common man—prefer liquor to Bibles and detective stories to serious books, and that governments prefer guns to butter. The entrepreneur does not make greater profits in selling "bad" things than in selling "good" things. His profits are the greater the better he succeeds in providing the consumers with those things they ask for most intensely. People do not drink intoxicating beverages in order to make the "alcohol capital" happy.

It is true that we are often at the mercy of the decisions of others. If I wish to buy an ounce of gold for two dollars, the fact that others are willing to pay more than two hundred dollars for that same ounce will doubtlessly prevent me from carrying out my plan. But it is not some gigantic being called "the market" that presents me with this difficulty—it is the fundamental fact that human desires are unlimited, but the means to fulfill them are scarce. "The market" is merely a name for the emergent outcome of myriad individual choices. Other social systems cannot get around the fact that everyone cannot have as much gold as they'd like to have. Someone will decide who gets how much gold, and if it is not the price system, it will be the will of the rulers, whomever they may be.

I recall an episode of *Star Trek* (I think it was in *The Next Generation* series) during which, somehow, a twentieth-century businessman winds up on the *Enterprise*. The crew is shocked by his interest in profit, buying, and selling. The crew members inform him that, in their time, things are no longer bought and sold, as there are goods aplenty to satisfy all members of society. Now, we might imagine a future in which nanotechnology repairs clothes as they wear out and builds houses essentially for free. Perhaps food will be so abundant that it is no longer an economic good. But what about starships? Can everyone who wants one have one for free? What about beach-front property in California? What if you want your own planet? As long as humans are not omnipotent and immortal, our desires will outstrip the means available to achieve them.

Economics does not hold that the desires of the consumers are pure or virtuous. It does illustrate that the market process is the only way to approximately gauge those desires. All other systems must attempt to impose the rulers' values on the ruled. Those who plan on doing the imposing have a very high regard for their own judgment, and a very low regard for that of the rest of us. To paraphrase G.L.S. Shackle, the man who would plan for others is something more than human; the planned man, something less.

Mises describes those who would coercively replace the value judgments of their fellow men by their own value judgments:

> [They] are driven by the dictatorial complex. They want to deal with their fellow men in the way an engineer deals with the materials out of which he builds houses, bridges, and machines. They want to substitute "social engineering" for the actions of their fellow citizens and their own unique all-comprehensive plan for the plans of all other people. They see themselves in the role of the dictator—the duce, the Führer, the production tsar—in whose hands all other specimens of mankind are merely pawns. If they refer to society as an acting agent, they mean themselves. If they say that conscious action of society is to be substituted for the prevailing anarchy of individualism, they mean their own consciousness alone and not that of anybody else. (*The Ultimate Foundation of Economic Science*)

A Brief History of the Austrian School

*T*HE AUSTRIAN SCHOOL of economics can trace its roots back to at least the fifteenth century, when the followers of St. Thomas Aquinas, writing and teaching at the University of Salamanca in Spain, sought to explain how individual human action created social order.

These *Late Scholastics* observed the existence of economic laws. Over the course of several generations, they discovered and explained the laws of supply and demand, the cause of inflation, the operation of foreign exchange rates, and the subjective nature of economic value. Those discoveries are among the reasons that Joseph Schumpeter called them the first real economists.

The Late Scholastics were advocates of property rights and the freedom to contract and trade. They lauded the contribution of business to society, while opposing most taxes, price controls, and regulations that inhibited enterprise. As moral theologians, they urged governments to obey ethical strictures against theft and murder.

Richard Cantillon, who had been schooled in the scholastic tradition, wrote the first general treatise on economics, *Essay on the Nature of Commerce*, in 1730. Born in Ireland, he later immigrated to France. He saw economics as an independent subject and explained the formation of prices using the method of thought experiments. He understood the market as an entrepreneurial process. The Austrian School would later adopt his theory of money creation: money enters the economy in a step-by-step fashion, disrupting relative prices along the way.

The next notable "Austrian ancestor" after Cantillon was Anne Robert Jacques Turgot, the French aristocrat who for a few years was finance minister of France. His economic writing was limited but profound. His paper "Value and Money" discussed the origins of money and the reflection in economic choice of an individual's subjective preference rankings. Turgot offered a solution to the famous diamond-water paradox that baffled later classical economists, articulated the law of diminishing returns, and criticized usury laws. He favored a classical-liberal approach to economic policy, recommending a repeal of all special privileges granted to government-connected industries. Turgot had noticed the importance of the "particular circumstances of time and place" two centuries before Hayek:

> There is no need to prove that each individual is the only competent judge of the most advantageous use of his lands and his labour. He alone has the particular knowledge without which the most enlightened man could only argue blindly. He learns by repeated trials, by his successes, by his losses, and he acquires a feeling for it which is more ingenious than the theoretical knowledge of the indifferent observer because it is stimulated by want (Turgot as quoted in Murray Rothbard's *Economic Thought Before Adam Smith*)

Turgot was the intellectual father of a long line of great French economists of the eighteenth and nineteenth centuries, most prominently Jean-Baptiste Say and Claude-Frédéric Bastiat.

Say was the first economist to think deeply about economic method. He held that economics is not about the amassing of data, but rather about the elucidation of universal components of the human condition—for example, the fact that wants are unlimited but means to aid in their satisfaction are scarce— and the tracing of the logical implications of these principles. Say discovered the productivity theory of resource pricing and the role of capital in the division of labor. He formulated the famous Say's Law: there can never be sustained overproduction or underconsumption if the market process is not hampered by artificial restrictions.

Bastiat, an influential economic journalist, argued that non-material services are subject to the same economic laws as material goods. In one of his many economic allegories, Bastiat spelled out the "broken-window fallacy" later employed to great effect by Henry Hazlitt. He held that there is a general distinction between bad economists and good economists: Bad economists look only at "what is seen," for instance, the fact that there is work for a repairman when a window is broken. Good economists look beyond this to "what is not seen," noticing that the person paying for the window repair would have spent that money on something more useful to him, if he hadn't been forced to repair the window. Human action only operates over time, and the gap between initiating an action and the final discernible ripple of effect from that action is often significant. If we desire to rearrange social relations, it won't do to simply consider the immediate effect of the reform; we must trace its influence out over time.

Despite the theoretical sophistication of this developing pre-Austrian tradition, the British school of the late eighteenth and early nineteenth centuries came to dominate economics. The British tradition (based on objective-cost and labor-productivity theories of value) ultimately led to the rise of the Marxist doctrine of capitalist exploitation.

The dominant British tradition received its first serious challenge in many years when Carl Menger's *Principles of Economics* was published in 1871. Menger, the founder of the Austrian School, resurrected the Scholastic-French approach to economics, grounding the science on the subjective valuations of individuals, rather than any objective properties of goods or labor.

Together with the contemporaneous writings of Léon Walras and William Stanley Jevons, Menger explained, for the first time, the theory of marginal utility. In addition, Menger showed how money originates in a free market when the most marketable commodity is desired, not for consumption, but for use in trading for other goods.

Menger's book was a pillar of the "marginalist revolution" in economics. When Mises said it "made an economist" out of him, he was not only referring to Menger's theory of money and prices, but also his approach to the discipline itself. Like his predecessors in this tradition, Menger was a methodological individualist, viewing economics as the science of individual choice. His *Investigations into the Method of the Social Sciences* came out twelve years after *Principles*. It battled the German Historical School, which had rejected theorizing and held that the proper scope of economics was the accumulation of historical data about the economy. To varying degrees, every Austrian since Menger has seen himself as Menger's student.

Menger was professor of economics at the University of Vienna and tutor to Crown Prince Rudolf of the House of Habsburg. Unfortunately for the Austro-Hungarian Empire, Prince

Rudolph committed suicide in 1889, before he had an opportunity to implement any of Menger's advice on liberalizing the empire's economy.

One of Menger's most prominent followers was Friedrich von Wieser, who later held the chair at the University of Vienna that had been occupied by Menger. Wieser's greatest contribution to economics was the theory of opportunity cost. He also coined the term "marginal utility" (*Grenznutzen*), and, as a teacher, was the first major economic influence on the thought of F.A. Hayek.

In Britain, Philip Wicksteed, an economist whose name is closely linked with the Austrian School, made the concept of opportunity cost central to his work, *Common Sense of Political Economy*. He also rejected the notion of economics as the study of wealth, and explored the process by which markets move toward equilibrium. Later, Ludwig von Mises would draw inspiration from Wicksteed's insistence "on the *universal* application of the conclusions which flow from our understanding of human purposefulness and rationality in the making of decisions" (Israel Kirzner, "Philip Wicksteed: The British Austrian," in *15 Great Austrian Economists*).

Menger's follower Eugen von Böhm-Bawerk took Menger's theories and applied them to capital and interest. His *History and Critique of Interest Theories*, which appeared in 1884, is a sweeping account of fallacies in the history of thought on interest. It defends the idea that the interest is not an artificially imposed construct but is an inherent part of human action. Interest is a product of the fact that time preference runs in only one direction—that, all other things being equal, we always prefer our satisfactions sooner rather than later. Frank Fetter, Ludwig von Mises, Murray Rothbard, and Israel Kirzner later expanded upon his theory.

Böhm-Bawerk's *Positive Theory of Capital* demonstrated that the normal rate of business profit is the interest rate. Capitalists save money, pay laborers, and wait until the final product is sold, collecting interest for the time period involved. He also held that capital is not homogeneous but is an intricate and diverse structure with a time dimension. A growing economy is not just a consequence of increased capital investment, but also of more roundabout processes of production.

Böhm-Bawerk engaged in a prolonged battle with the Marxists over the exploitation theory of capital, and refuted the socialist doctrine of capital and wages long before the communists came to power in Russia. Böhm-Bawerk also conducted a seminar that would later become the model for that of Mises.

Böhm-Bawerk, in the last years of the Habsburg monarchy, served three times as finance minister. In that role he advocated a balanced budget, the gold standard, free trade, and the repeal of export subsidies and other monopoly privileges.

It was his research and writing that solidified the status of the Austrian School as a unified way of looking at economic problems, and set the stage for the school to make converts in the English-speaking world. One economist who took up the Austrian banner was Frank Fetter, an American.

Fetter's *Principles of Economics* (1904) was the best systematization of Austrian thought prior to the work of Mises in the 1940s. Fetter developed the pure time preference theory of interest, achieving a unified theory of value for capital, rent, wages, and consumer goods, leaving only money outside its scope. He taught economics at Cornell, Indiana University, Stanford, and Princeton.

The final topic in classical economics for subjective value theory to reformulate was money, the institutional intersection of the microeconomic and macroeconomic approach. A young Mises, economic advisor to the Austrian Chamber of Commerce, took on the challenge.

The result of Mises's research was *The Theory of Money and Credit*, published in 1912. In that work, he demonstrated that the theory of marginal utility applies to money. He laid out his regression theorem, an elaboration of Menger's theory of the origin of money, showing that money not only originates in the market, but that it could not have done so in any other way. Drawing on the British Currency School, Swedish economist Knut Wicksell's theory of interest rates, and Böhm-Bawerk's theory of the structure of capital, Mises presented the outline of the Austrian theory of the business cycle. A year later, Mises was appointed to the faculty of the University of Vienna. Böhm-Bawerk's seminar spent a full two semesters debating Mises's book.

Mises's monetary theory received attention in the United States through the work of Benjamin M. Anderson, Jr., an economist employed at various times by Columbia, Harvard, Chase National Bank, UCLA, and Cornell. His major works included *The Value of Money*, a critique of Irving Fisher's quantity theory of money, and *Economics and the Public Welfare*, a study of the U.S. economy from World War I through the end of World War II.

World War I interrupted Mises's career for four years. He spent three of those years as an artillery officer, and one as a staff officer in economic intelligence. At the war's end, he published *Nation, State, and Economy*, arguing on behalf of the economic and cultural freedoms of minorities in the now-shattered empire, and theorizing on the economics of war.

In the political chaos after the war, the main theoretician of the socialist Austrian government was a Marxist, Otto Bauer.

Mises knew Bauer from the Böhm-Bawerk seminar. Mises engaged in an ongoing effort to convince Bauer of the wisdom of laissez-faire, eventually persuading him to back away from Bolshevik-style policies.

Mises next undertook an in-depth analysis of socialism. After writing a breakthrough paper in 1920 on the problem of calculation under socialism, he completed his second great book, *Socialism*, in 1922. A worldwide socialist commonwealth, Mises demonstrated, would result in utter chaos and a return to barbarism. Mises challenged the socialists to explain, in economic terms, precisely how their system would work—a task that the socialists had avoided up to that point. (Marx had contended that it was "unscientific" to ask such questions.) The debate between the Austrians—chiefly Mises and Hayek—and the socialists continued in a series of papers published during the '20s and '30s. Israel Kirzner holds that it was during this debate that Mises and Hayek came to understand how different their "Austrian" approach was from the emerging neoclassical mainstream.

Mises's arguments for free markets attracted a group of converts from the socialist cause, including Hayek, Wilhelm Röpke, and Lionel Robbins. Mises began holding a private seminar in his offices at the Chamber of Commerce, that was attended by Fritz Machlup, Oskar Morgenstern, Gottfried von Haberler, Alfred Schutz, Richard von Strigl, Eric Voegelin, Paul Rosenstein-Rodan, and many other intellectuals from across the European continent. Several of these scholars later held positions at leading universities in the United States: Machlup taught at Johns Hopkins and then Princeton, Rosenstein-Rodan at MIT, Haberler at Harvard, and Morgenstern at Princeton. Morgenstern, working with mathematician/physicist/computer scientist John von Neumann, did pioneering work in the area of game theory.

During the 1920s and '30s, Mises was working on two other academic fronts. He argued against the German Historical School with a series of essays in defense of the deductive method in economics, which he would later call praxeology. He also founded the Austrian Institute for Business Cycle Research, putting Hayek in charge of it.

During these years, Hayek and Mises authored several studies on the business cycle, warned of the danger of credit expansion, and predicted the coming economic crisis. The Nobel Prize committee cited Hayek's work during this period when he received the award for economics in 1974. Hayek was one of the most prominent opponents of Keynesian economics in his works on exchange rates, capital theory, and monetary reform. His popular book *The Road to Serfdom* helped revive the classical-liberal movement in America in the 1940s. His three-volume work *Law, Legislation, and Liberty* elaborated on the Late Scholastic approach to law, and applied it to criticize egalitarianism.

In the early 1930s Austria was threatened by a Nazi takeover. Hayek had already left for London in 1931, at Mises's urging. In 1934, Mises moved to Geneva to teach and write at the International Institute for Graduate Studies. Following the Anschluss, knowing Mises as an enemy of National Socialism, the Nazis confiscated Mises's papers from his apartment in Vienna and hid them for the duration of the war. After the fall of the Soviet Union, the papers were unearthed in a formerly secret archive and brought to the attention of scholars by Richard Ebeling of Hillsdale College. Ironically, Mises's ideas, through the work of Wilhelm Röpke and the statesmanship of Ludwig Erhard, had a profound influence on the postwar economic reforms that led to the "German miracle."

Meanwhile, in London, Hayek taught and researched at the London School of Economics. Among his students was a young post-graduate named Ludwig Lachmann. Hayek also profoundly influenced English economist Lionel Robbins, whose synthesis of Alfred Marshall's ideas with those of the Austrians helped to create the neoclassical mainstream that has dominated economics since that time. Robbins incorporated certain Austrian insights, especially the notion of economics as the science of employing scarce means to achieve subjectively desired ends, into Marshall's economics. The Austrian-Marshallian synthesis focused on the properties of equilibrium markets, which were taken to be a good approximation of the real world. However, at the same time, Austrian economist Hans Mayer was critiquing price theories that simply assumed equilibrium, foreshadowing Hayek's work on knowledge and prices. Austrians moved away from Robbins's formulation of economics. They began to emphasize the freedom and unpredictability of human action. Unlike Robbins's picture of a given set of fully understood means and ends, from which choices are plucked on the basis of maximizing a utility function, Austrians gradually realized that both our means and our ends only come to be understood through the market process itself. They came to view general equilibrium as a model of an unreal and unobtainable world.

In Geneva, Mises wrote his systematic work, *Nationalökonomie* (published in 1940). With war seeming to threaten even Switzerland, Mises left for the United States. Once settled in the U.S., he wrote *Bureaucracy, Omnipotent Government*, and translated, revised, and expanded *Nationalökonomie*, resulting in the publication of *Human Action* in 1949. His student Murray N. Rothbard called it: "Mises's greatest achievement and one of the finest products of the human mind in our century. It is economics made whole." The work remains, in my mind, the preeminent work of the Austrian School. However, it was not well received in the economics profession, where neoclassical and Keynesian theories dominated.

Even before Mises immigrated to the U.S., American journalist Henry Hazlitt had become his most prominent champion. Hazlitt reviewed Mises's books in the *New York Times* and *Newsweek*, and popularized Austrian ideas in such classics as *Economics in One Lesson.* Hazlitt also made original contributions to Austrian School thought, writing a detailed critique of Keynes's *General Theory,* entitled *The Failure of the "New Economics."* Hazlitt defended the work of Say, restoring him to a central place in Austrian macroeconomic theory.

In 1946, Leonard E. Read founded the Foundation for Economic Education (FEE) in Irvington-on-Hudson, New York The Foundation worked to promote free-market economics, with a heavy Austrian and Misesian influence, during times when they were especially unpopular.

Mises eventually landed at New York University. There, he gathered students around him, just as he had in Vienna. Among those attending his seminar at Washington Square (and two other locations in Manhattan) were Rothbard, Israel Kirzner, Leland Yeager, Ralph Raico, Percy Greaves, Bettina Bien Greaves, William Peterson, George Koether, Laurence Moss, George Reisman, Paul Cantor, and Hans Sennholz. Mises's New York seminar continued until two years before his death in 1973.

Murray Rothbard's treatise *Man, Economy, and State* (1962) was patterned after *Human Action,* but in some areas— monopoly theory, utility and welfare, and the theory of the state—expanded on or diverged from Mises's views. Rothbard's approach to the Austrian School picked up on Late Scholastic thought by applying economic science within a framework of a natural-rights theory of property. What resulted was a rationalist defense of a free-market, stateless social order, based on property and freedom of association and contract. Rothbard was also at work applying Austrian economics to historical periods such as the Great Depression and the colonial period of American history.

Rothbard gained new exposure for the Austrian School with his work *For a New Liberty*. A union of natural-rights theory and the economics of the Austrian School was forwarded in *The Ethics of Liberty*. Those books and several others were completed while Rothbard was producing many scholarly economic pieces, gathered in the two-volume *Logic of Action*, published in Edward Elgar's "Economists of the Century" series.

Meanwhile, Israel Kirzner extended Mises's analysis on another front. Focusing on Mises's concept of entrepreneurship as a component of all action, Kirzner developed his theory of the entrepreneur in a number of works, including *Competition and Entrepreneurship, The Meaning of the Market Process*, and *The Driving Force of the Market*. Kirzner's first book, *The Economic Point of View*, was a comparative work on economic methodology, highlighting the advantages of Mises's praxeological approach. In *An Essay on Capital*, Kirzner performed a similar exercise on the varieties of capital theory. He continued the Austrian presence at New York University, teaching there from 1957 until the spring of 2001. Extending the tradition of Böhm-Bawerk and Mises, he has gathered a weekly Austrian discussion group and tutors a new generation of Austrian scholars.

Ludwig Lachmann took Misesian thought in yet a third direction. While his work in the 1950s and 1960s flowed directly from Mises's ideas, Lachmann increasingly concerned himself with the effect of radical uncertainty on economic order. Deeply influenced by the work of British economist G.L.S. Shackle, Lachmann's work emphasized the subjective nature of expectations.

The awarding of the Nobel Prize to Hayek in 1974, and a conference on Austrian economics in South Royalton, Vermont, that same year, marked a decided upsurge of interest in the Austrian School. The founding of the Ludwig von Mises Institute in 1982, with the aid of Mises's widow, Margit von Mises, marked a further milestone in the resurgence of Austrian economics. Another organization for promoting Austrian thought, the Society for the Development of Austrian Economics, was officially founded in 1996.

Scholarly centers for the Austrian School are thriving in Paris, Rome, Madrid, Bucharest, Beijing, Tokyo, Prague, and all over Latin America. The writings of the masters appear in every major language and new translations appear just about every month. Austrian ideas have gained currency in other fields, including history, philosophy, and law. And they are increasingly popular in the mainstream financial press and brokerage houses.

Today, 130 years after its founding, the Austrian School has more adherents and a more active literature than at any previous time in its history. Dissatisfaction with the artificial, "economic man" of mainstream economics is widespread, making the future of the Austrian School look even brighter than its present.

Praxeological Economics and Mathematical Economics

The problems of prices and costs have been treated also with mathematical methods. There have even been economists who held that the only appropriate method of dealing with economic problems is the mathematical method and who derided the logical economists as "literary" economists.

—LUDWIG VON MISES, *HUMAN ACTION*

If not an economist, what am I? An outdated freak whose functional role in the general scheme of things has passed into history? Perhaps I should accept such an assessment, retire gracefully, and, with alcoholic breath, hoe my cabbages. Perhaps I could do so if the modern technicians had indeed produced "better" economic mousetraps. Instead of evidence of progress, however, I see a continuing erosion of the intellectual (and social) capital that was accumulated by "political economy" in its finest hours.

—JAMES BUCHANAN, *WHAT SHOULD ECONOMISTS DO?*

TODAY'S ECONOMIC MAINSTREAM—neoclassical economics—is thoroughly mathematical. The vast majority of papers in academic journals are dense with mathematical notation. Nonmathematical approaches to the subject are often viewed as unscientific and imprecise.

However, the success of the mathematical approach in breaking new economic ground has been minimal. Even Bryan Caplan, a critic of Austrian economics, is forced to admit, "[Mathematical approaches] have had fifty years of ever-increasing hegemony in economics. The empirical evidence on their contribution is decidedly negative."

That has led to a number of challenges to the mainstream. The part of neoclassical theory most frequently under attack has been the assumption of rational economic behavior. The neoclassical notion of rationality posits that human behavior should result in the same outcomes as a computer calculating how to employ certain "parameters" to achieve an "optimum" result. There is a great deal of fiddling around with what the parameters should be, and exactly how to categorize the optimum result. Many of the challenges to the neoclassical paradigm recommend modifying the current models with some new parameters, or adjusting what is considered optimal. Perhaps an "altruism" parameter would modify the degree of selfishness the models apparently suggest, or mixing some quantity of "social conformity" into the desired output might explain the whims of fashion better. But some of the criticism goes deeper: Mathematics, while not useless in economics, cannot convey the principles of human action.

Mises explained the fundamental gulf between praxeological economics and mathematics in *Human Action*:

> Logic and mathematics deal with an ideal system of thought. The relations and implications of their system are coexistent and interdependent. We may say as well that they are synchronous or that they are out of time. A perfect mind could grasp them all in one thought. Man's inability to accomplish this makes thinking itself an action, proceeding step by step from the less satisfactory state of insufficient

cognition to the more satisfactory state of better insight. But the temporal order in which knowledge is acquired must not be confused with the logical simultaneity of all parts of an aprioristic deductive system. Within such a system the notions of anteriority and consequence are metaphorical only. They do not refer to the system, but to our action in grasping it. The system itself implies neither the category of time nor that of causality. There is functional correspondence between elements, but there is neither cause nor effect.

What distinguishes epistemologically the praxeological system from the logical system is precisely that it implies the categories both of time and of causality.

Let us take a famous mathematical discovery, the Pythagorean theorem, as an example of what Mises is talking about. As is well known to school children everywhere, the theorem says that there is an immutable relationship between the three sides of a right triangle, where the sum of the squares of the legs is equal to the square of the hypotenuse ($a^2 + b^2 = c^2$). None of the legs of a triangle *causes* any of the other legs to be a certain length. Neither Pythagoras's equation nor any of the infinite number of triangles that it describes have any temporal relationship to each other. We needn't go into the question of whether or not mathematical forms have an existence independent of the human mind. In either case, once we apprehend the Pythagorean relationship, then the universe of right triangles, along with the relationship of their sides and all other geometric facts about them, emerge as the aspect of a completely timeless, ideal form. Although our limited minds must approach those aspects piecemeal, their existence is simultaneous with the very notion "right triangle," and none of those aspects are prior to or stand in a causal relationship to any other aspect of the ideal form.

Human action is different. Just as the idea of a right triangle implies the Pythagorean theorem, the idea of human action implies "before" and "after," "cause" and "effect." We cannot make sense of human plans unless we understand that there is a past that, for the human actor, provides the soil in which the seeds of action might be sown; there is a present during which the sowing might transpire; and there is a future in which the actor hopes to reap the fruit of any action. Similarly, we must see that the actor hopes that his action will be the cause of a desired effect, or he would not act.

Viewing the economy as if it were a mathematical form is coherent if it is seen, for instance, as the study of a limiting state—equilibrium—that the real economy may gravitate toward. But when used to explain human action it creates confusion, for it eliminates from view real human choices, the very phenomena that differentiate economics from other disciplines.

Let's look at an example. Steven Landsburg's microeconomics textbook, *Price Theory*, reminds students:

> It is important to distinguish causes from effects. For an individual demander or supplier, the price is taken as a given and determines the quantity demanded or supplied. For the market as a whole, the demand and supply curves determine both price and quantity simultaneously.

Landsburg is telling students that they must not think of prices as being determined by the actions of individuals—individuals simply take prices as a given. Instead, it is the abstract mathematical notions of supply and demand curves that "simultaneously" determine what occurs in the market.

We can agree with Landsburg that it *is* important to distinguish causes from effects. At the same time, we must contend that, from the point of view of a science of human action, he has gotten them backward. Prices and quantities only change as the *result* of human action. Where in the world can a new price come from if not a human bidding or asking above or below the market price? It is the striving of individuals to better their circumstances, in the face of an uncertain future, that drives the market process.

Landsburg is forced into his odd posture because of his desire to capture human action with mathematical equations. Those equations cannot take into account creative human decisions based on the categories of cause, effect, before, and after. What they describe is a world of timeless correlations from which causation is absent. Human intentions play no part in the model, as the model assumes all humans know all possible relevant facts about their situation, and can only accept it as a given. Faced with the prospect of acknowledging the limits of his model, Landsburg opts for eliminating human action from the economy.

The fact that supply and demand curves can give us a rough picture of market behavior is an effect of human action, and certainly not the cause of it. No one acts with the goal of bringing supply and demand into balance. People act in the market in order to profit, in the broadest sense of the word: they exchange because they feel they will be better off after the exchange than they were beforehand. That their search for profit tends to bring supply and demand into balance is a by-product of their actual goals. As Hayek says in *Individualism and Economic Order*, "the modern theory of competitive equilibrium assumes the situation to exist which a true explanation ought to account for as the effect of the competitive process."

In order to make economic theory amenable to a mathematical treatment, neoclassical economists remove the very subject matter of praxeological economics, human action, from their theories. Mises says,

> The mathematical economists disregard the whole theoretical elucidation of the market process and evasively amuse themselves with an auxiliary notion [i.e., equilibrium] employed in its context and devoid of any sense when used outside of this context. (*Human Action*)

The study of the correlations provided by mathematical descriptions of events is central to physics and chemistry because in those fields we can determine constants of correlation that allow us to make practical predictions. We feel confident that electrons will not suddenly decide that they aren't quite so attracted to protons, and that oxygen will not come to the conclusion that it would really prefer to bond with three hydrogen molecules rather than two.

Such constants are absent in human action. The subject matter of economics, in the Austrian view, is the logic of economic events, not the correlations existing between them. The study of those correlations is the subject matter of economic history and will never reveal fundamental laws of economics, because of the absence of constants. If we determine that last year a 10¢ rise in the price of bread resulted in a 2-percent reduction in demand—in neoclassical terms, we measure the *elasticity of demand* for bread—that does not tell us what will happen this year if there is another 10¢ increase.

Mathematical equations can be useful for modeling the result of people following through on previously made plans. Once a batter in a baseball game decides to swing at a pitch, we can use an equation that, based on the initial force the batter chose to apply to the bat, predicts the bat's progress. This equation will be of little use, however, in predicting whether the batter will change his mind and check his swing.

Similarly, the relative price of the two stocks in a proposed corporate merger may move in line with the predictions of a mathematical model for some time. But should market participants gain knowledge of something that alters their perception of the merger, the relative price of the stocks may differ greatly from the model's prediction. If rumors emerge indicating that the merger might fall through, the relative price of the seller might plunge. Arbitrage traders must employ their historical understanding in an attempt to grasp how other market participants will react to that news. Once that reevaluation is completed, a new risk factor for deal failure can be fed into the model and it may again function reasonably well. However, the model, cannot capture the change of perception, which is the beginning of the creation of a new plan. And it is precisely the implications of that planning that is the subject of Austrian economics. That is the moment of human choice, as the plan must aim for one goal while setting aside others, and choose some means to achieve that goal while rejecting others. Mathematical economics models the phases of markets when plans are not being created or revised, in other words, when the events that are of interest to Austrian economists, human choices, are absent.

None of the above should be taken to mean that the mathematical approach to economics is useless, only that it cannot capture the essence of human action. The British philosopher Michael Oakeshott says that we can theorize about a particular phenomenon as either a mechanical system, characterized by measurably constant responses to identical conditions, or as an intelligent activity, seen as intelligent precisely because it is not seen as the outcome of a mechanical process. In commenting on the two different approaches to the social sciences, Oakeshott says:

> [In the formulation of a mechanical] "science of society" . . . a society is understood as a process, or structure, or an ecology; that is, it is an unintelligent "going-on," like a genetic process, a chemical structure, or a mechanical system. The components of this system are not agents performing actions; they are birth-rates, age groups, income brackets, intelligence quotients, life-styles, evolving "states of societies," environmental pressures, average mental ages, distributions in space and time, "numbers of graduates," patterns of child-bearing or of expenditure, systems of education, statistics concerning disease, poverty, unemployment, etc. And the enterprise is to make these identities more intelligible in terms of theorems displaying their functional interdependencies or causal relationships. . . . It is not an impossible undertaking. But it has little to do with human [action] and nothing at all to do with the performances of assignable agents. Whatever an environmental pressure, a behaviour-style, or the distribution of gas-cookers may be said to be correlated with or to cause (a rise in the suicide rate? a fall in the use of detergents?) these are not terms in which the choice of an agent to do or say this rather than that in response to a contingent situation and in an adventure to procure an imagined and wished-for satisfaction may be understood. It is only in a categorial confusion that this enterprise could be made to appear to yield an understanding of the substantive actions and utterances of an agent. (*On Human Conduct*)

Austrian economics is the economics of people viewed as creative, intelligent agents.

Bibliography

GENERAL READING

*T*HOSE WHO WISH to ponder the policy implications of the Austrian view at greater length can't do better than picking up a copy of Henry Hazlitt's *Economics in One Lesson*. Hazlitt is one of the finest writers ever to tackle economic issues. In this book, inspired by Bastiat's conception of the seen and unseen aspects of policy, he examines a wide variety of economic interventions.

Carl Menger's *Principles of Economics* is a model of clear exposition and is packed with insights that retain their value 130 years after publication. Perhaps because Menger is laying out the basis for marginalist, subjectivist economics for the first time, he explains his concepts carefully enough that the "intelligent layman" with no economic background should be able to grasp his ideas.

Israel Kirzner's new biography, *Ludwig von Mises: The Man and His Economics* focuses on Mises's economic thought. It is another good introduction to Austrian ideas.

If you are serious about the study of Austrian economics, either Ludwig von Mises's *Human Action*, The Scholar's Edition or Murray Rothbard's *Man, Economy, and State* should be tackled next. They are both large, imposing books, but both are well written, and they are the two best sources for a systematic overview of Austrian theory. Which to choose? If you are familiar with neoclassical economics, pick Rothbard's book, as it carefully explains the points of connection and divergence between the Austrian and neoclassical approaches. If you are more philosophically inclined, start with Mises, as he spends more time on the philosophical background behind his approach. Whichever you choose first, by all means continue with the other, if time and interest permits.

For more bibliographic references, grouped by subject, see the Austrian Economics Study Guide: http://www.mises.org/study.asp. There is also a web site for this book with more information: http://www.economicsforrealpeople.com/.

Below is a list of some other recommended books, organized by the chapter(s) to which they are most relevant. For the most part, I've limited the list to things that I've read and can vouch for. There are certainly excellent books that aren't on the list simply because I'm not familiar with them.

CHAPTER ONE: WHAT'S GOING ON?
Israel Kirzner, *The Economic Point of View*.

Michael Oakeshott, *On Human Conduct*.

CHAPTER TWO: ALONE AGAIN, UNNATURALLY
Carl Menger, *Principles of Economics*.

Ludwig von Mises, *The Ultimate Foundation of Economic Science*.

CHAPTER THREE: AS TIME GOES BY
Israel Kirzner, *An Essay on Capital*.

Ludwig Lachmann, *Capital and Its Structure*.

Gerald P. O'Driscoll, Jr., and Mario Rizzo, *Economics of Time and Ignorance.*

CHAPTER FOUR: LET'S STAY TOGETHER
Leonard E. Read, *I, Pencil.*

Adam Smith, *The Wealth of Nations.*

CHAPTER FIVE: MONEY CHANGES EVERYTHING
James Buchanan, *Cost and Choice: An Inquiry in Economic Theory.*

Milton Friedman, *Monetary Mischief: Episodes in Monetary History.*

Ludwig von Mises, *The Theory of Money and Credit.*

CHAPTER SIX: A PLACE WHERE NOTHING EVER HAPPENS
Ludwig von Mises, *Human Action.*

Murray N. Rothbard, *Man, Economy, and State.*

CHAPTER SEVEN: BUTCHER, BAKER, CANDLESTICK MAKER
Israel M. Kirzner, *Competition and Entrepreneurship.*

Ludwig von Mises, "Profit and Loss," *Planning for Freedom.*

CHAPTER EIGHT: MAKE A NEW PLAN, STAN
Howard Baetjer, *Software as Capital.*

Eugen von Böhm-Bawerk, *Capital and Interest.*

Ernst Cassirer, *Language and Myth.*

Lachmann, *Capital and Its Structure.*

CHAPTER NINE: WHAT GOES UP, MUST COME DOWN
Mises, *The Theory of Money and Credit.*

Murray Rothbard, *The Case Against the Fed.*

Leland Yeager, *The Fluttering Veil.*

CHAPTER TEN: A WORLD BECOME ONE

Peter J. Boettke, *Calculation and Coordination: Essays on Socialism and Transitional Political Economy*.

F.A. Hayek, *Individualism and Economic Order*.

F.A. Hayek, *The Road to Serfdom*.

F.A. Hayek, *The Constitution of Liberty*.

F.A. Hayek, *The Fatal Conceit: The Errors of Socialism*.

Ludwig von Mises, *Socialism*.

Murray Rothbard, *Freedom, Inequality, Primitivism and the Division of Labor*.

CHAPTER ELEVEN: THE THIRD WAY

Frédéric Bastiat, *Selected Essays in Political Economy*.

Tom Bethell, *The Noblest Triumph: Property and Prosperity Through the Ages*.

Hernando de Soto, *The Mystery of Capital: Why Capitalism Triumphs in the West and Fails Everywhere Else*.

Henry Hazlitt, *Economics in One Lesson*.

Sanford Ikeda, *The Dynamics of the Mixed Economy*.

Steven Landsburg, *Price Theory*.

CHAPTER TWELVE: FIDDLING WITH PRICES WHILE THE MARKET BURNS

Hans Sennholz, *The Politics of Unemployment*.

CHAPTER THIRTEEN: TIMES ARE HARD

Anthony M. Carilli and Gregory M. Dempster, "Expectations in Austrian Business Cycle Theory: An Application of the Prisoner's Dilemma."

Roger Garrison, *Time and Money: The Macroeconomics of Capital Structure*.

Steven Horwitz, *Microfoundations and Macroeconomics: An Austrian Perspective*.

W.H. Hutt, *The Keynesian Episode*.

Mises, *The Theory of Money and Credit*.

Murray Rothbard, *America's Great Depression*.

Richard K. Vedder and Lowell E. Gallaway, *Out of Work: Unemployment and Government in Twentieth-Century America*.

CHAPTER FOURTEEN: UNSAFE AT ANY SPEED

Ronald Coase, *Essays on Economics and Economists*.

CHAPTER FIFTEEN: ONE MAN GATHERS WHAT ANOTHER MAN SPILLS

Ikeda, *The Dynamics of the Mixed Economy*.

Landsburg, *Price Theory*.

Murray Rothbard, *The Logic of Action I*.

CHAPTER SIXTEEN: STUCK ON YOU

Kirzner, *Competition and Entrepreneurship*.

Stan J. Liebowitz and Stephen Margolis, *Winners, Losers, and Microsoft*.

CHAPTER SEVENTEEN: SEE THE PYRAMIDS ALONG THE NILE

Bastiat, *Selected Essays in Political Economy*.

CHAPTER EIGHTEEN: WHERE DO WE GO FROM HERE?

John Gray, *Enlightenment's Wake: Politics and Culture at the Close of the Modern Age*.

Hans-Hermann Hoppe, "Marxist and Austrian Class Analysis."

Timur Kuran, *Private Truths, Public Lies: The Social Consequences of Preference Falsification*.

Mises, *The Ultimate Foundation of Economic Science*.

APPENDIX A: A BRIEF HISTORY OF THE AUSTRIAN SCHOOL

Benjamin M. Anderson, *Economics and the Public Welfare.*

Frank A. Fetter, *Capital, Interest, and Rent.*

F.A. Hayek, *The Fortunes of Liberalism.*

Randall G. Holcombe, ed., *15 Great Austrian Economists.*

Kirzner, *Ludwig von Mises: The Man and His Economics.*

Murray Rothbard, *Economic Thought Before Adam Smith.*

Murray Rothbard, *Classical Economics.*

APPENDIX B — PRAXEOLOGICAL ECONOMICS VS. MATHEMATICAL ECONOMICS

Mises, *The Ultimate Foundation of Economic Science.*

Landsburg, *Price Theory.*

Israel Kirzner, *The Meaning of the Market Process.*

References

Anderson, Benjamin. 1979. *Economics and the Public Welfare*. Indianapolis, Ind.: Liberty Fund.

_____. 1917. *The Value of Money*. New York: Macmillan. Reprinted by Libertarian Publishers, Grove City, Penn., n.d.

Baetjer, Howard. 1998. *Software as Capital*. Los Altimos, Calif.: IEEE Computer Society.

Bastiat, Frédéric. 1995. "What is Seen and What is Not Seen." In Bastiat, *Selected Essays in Political Economy*. Irvington-on-Hudson, N.Y.: Foundation for Economic Education.

Bethell, Tom. 1999. *The Noblest Triumph: Property and Prosperity Through the Ages*. New York: St. Martin's Press.

Boettke, Peter. 2001. *Calculation and Coordination: Essays on Socialism and Transitional Political Economy*. London: Routledge.

Böhm-Bawerk, Eugen von. 1959. *Capital and Interest*. 3 Vols. South Holland, Ill.: Libertarian Press. Includes *History and Critique of Interest and Theories* and *Positive Theory of Capital*.

Buchanan, James. 1979. *What Should Economists Do?* Indianapolis, Ind.: Liberty Press.

_____. 1979. *Cost and Choice: An Inquiry in Economic Theory.* Chicago: University of Chicago.

Callahan, Gene, and Roger W. Garrison. 2002. "A Classic Hayekian Hangover." *Ideas on Liberty* (January).

Cantillon, Richard. 1959. *Essay on the Nature of Commerce.* Henry Higgs, ed. and trans. London: Frank Cass.

Carilli, Anthony M., and Gregory M. Dempster. 2001. "Expectations in Austrian Business Cycle Theory: An Application of the Prisoner's Dilemma." *Review of Austrian Economics* 14, no. 4.

Cassirer, Ernst. 1946. *Language and Myth.* New York: Dover Publications.

Coase, Ronald. 1960. "The Problem of Social Cost." *Journal of Law and Economics* 3.

_____. 1995. *Essays on Economics and Economists.* Chicago: University of Chicago Press.

Corrigan, Sean. 2001. "Norman, Strong, and Greenspan." 14 August. <http://www.mises.org/fullarticle.asp?control=754>.

Diamond, Jared. 1997. "The Curse of QWERTY." *Discover Magazine* (April). <http://www.discover.com/archive/index.html>.

Heartland Institute. 1990. Executive Summary No. 32. "Sports Stadiums as Wise Investments: An Evaluation." 26 November. <http://www.heartland.org/studies/sports/ BAIM2-SUM.htm>.

Holcombe, Randall G., ed. *15 Great Austrian Economists*. Auburn, Ala.: Ludwig von Mises Institute.

Fetter, Frank A. 1904. *The Principles of Economics*. New York: Century.

_____. 1977. *Capital, Interest, and Rent*. Menlo Park, Calif.: Institute for Humane Studies.

Foreign Policy in Focus. 1997. *Export Promotion Programs* 2, no. 34. <http://www.fpif.org/briefs/vol2/v2n34exp_ body.html>.

Fox, Justin. 1999. "What in the World Happened to Economics?" *Fortune* 5 March.

Friedman, Milton. 1994. *Monetary Mischief: Episodes in Monetary History*. Fort Washington, Penn.: Harvest Books.

Garrison, Roger W. 2001. *Time and Money: The Macroeconomics of Capital Structure*. London: Routledge.

Gillmor, Dan. 1999. "Online Reliability will Carry a Price." *San Jose Mercury News* 18 July.

Gingrich, Newt. 2000. Book review of *Nothing Like It in the World: The Men Who Built the Transcontinental Railroad, 1863–1869*. <www.newt.org/books_ambsose.htm>.

Goldberg, Robert. 2000. "Continue the W. Revolution."
National Review Online Guest Comment, 4 November.
<http://www.nationalreview.com/comment/com-
ment110400c.shtml>.

Gottfried, Paul. n.d. "The Communitarians." <http://mises.
org/fullarticle.asp?record=312&month=13>.

Gray, John. 1997. *Enlightenment's Wake: Politics and Culture
at the Close of the Modern Age.* Essex, U.K.: Methuen Drama.

Gregerson, Steve. 2001. Quoted in "SUV Popularity Fueling
Issues on Gas Economy." By David Ivanovich and Greg
Hassell. *Houston Chronicle* 16 July. <http://www.chron.
com/cs/CDA/story.hts/special/energycrisis/gaso-
line/968488>.

Hayek, F.A. 1922. *The Fortunes of Liberalism.* Chicago:
University of Chicago Press.

_____. [1945] 1948. "The Use of Knowledge in Society." In
Hayek, *Individualism and Economic Order.* Chicago:
University of Chicago Press.

_____. 1960. *The Constitution of Liberty.* Chicago: University
of Chicago Press.

_____. 1979. *Law, Legislation, and Liberty.* Vol. 3. *The
Political Order of a Free People.* Chicago: University of
Chicago Press.

_____. 1988. *The Fatal Conceit: The Errors of Socialism.*
Chicago: University of Chicago Press.

_____. [1944] 1994. *The Road to Serfdom.* Chicago: University
of Chicago Press.

Hazlitt, Henry. [1963] 1996. *Economics in One Lesson.* San Francisco: Laissez Faire Books.

_____. 1959. *Failure of the "New Economics."* Princeton, N.J.: D. Van Nostrand.

Hoppe, Hans-Hermann. 1999. "Marxist and Austrian Class Analysis." In *Requiem for Marx*, Yuri Maltsev, ed. Auburn, Ala.: Ludwig von Mises Institute.

Horwitz, Steven. 2001. *Microfoundations and Macroeconomics: An Austrian Perspective.* London: Routledge.

Hutt, W.H. 1979. *The Keynesian Episode.* Indianapolis, Ind.: Liberty Fund.

Ikeda, Sanford. 1997. *The Dynamics of the Mixed Economy.* London: Routledge.

Kedrosky, Paul. 1995. "The More You Sell, the More You Sell." *Wired Magazine* (October). <http://www.wired.com/wired/archive/3.10/arthur.html>.

Keynes, John Maynard. 1936. *The General Theory of Employment, Interest, and Money.* New York: Harcourt, Brace.

Kirzner, Israel M. 1966. *An Essay on Capital.* New York: Augustus M. Kelley.

_____. 1973. *Competition and Entrepreneurship.* Chicago: University of Chicago Press.

_____. 1976. *The Economic Point of View*. Menlo Park, Calif.: Institute for Humane Studies.

_____. 1992. *The Meaning of the Market Process: Essays in the Development of Modern Austrian Economics*. London: Routledge.

_____. 1999. "Philip Wicksteed: The British Austrian." In *15 Great Austrian Economists*, Randall G. Holcombe, ed. Auburn, Ala.: Ludwig von Mises Institute.

_____. 2000. *The Driving Force of the Market: Essays in Austrian Economics*. London: Routledge.

_____. 2001. *Ludwig von Mises: The Man and His Economics*. Wilmington, Del.: ISI Books.

Krugman, Paul. 1998. "Baby-sitting the Economy." *Slate*, 14 August. <http://www.slate.msn.com/default.aspx?id=1937>.

_____. 2001. "Nation in a Jam." *New York Times* 13 May.

Kundera, Milan. [1984] 1999. *The Unbearable Lightness of Being*. New York: HarperCollins.

Kuran, Timur. 1995. *Private Truths, Public Lies: The Social Consequences of Preference Falsification*. Cambridge, Mass.: Harvard University Press.

Kurtz, Steve. 2001. "Sex, Economics, and Other Legal Matters." An interview with Judge Richard A. Posner. *Reason* (April). <http://reason.com/0104/int.sk.sex.shtml>.

Lachmann, Ludwig. 1978. *Capital and Its Structure.* Kansas City, Mo.: Sheed Andrews and McMeel.

Landsburg, Steven. 1999. *Price Theory.* Cincinnati, Ohio: South-Western College Publishing.

Levin, Michael. 1997. "Labeling and Consumer Choice." *Free Market* (March). <http://www.mises.org/freemarket_ detail.asp?control=142&sortorder=articledate>.

Lewin, Peter. 2002. Introduction to *The Economics of QWER-TY: History, Theory, and Policy, Essays by Stan L. Liebowitz and Stephen E. Margolis.* New York: New York University Press.

Liebowitz, Stan L., and Stephen E. Margolis. 1999. *Winners, Losers, and Microsoft.* Oakland, Calif.: Independent Institute.

Margasak, Larry. 2001. "Producing a Farm-Fresh Flop." *Associated Press* 1 June.

Menger, Carl. [1976] 1994. *Principles of Economics.* James Dingwall and Bert F. Hoselitz, trans. Grove City, Penn.: Libertarian Press.

———. 1985. *Investigations into the Method of the Social Sciences.* New York: New York University Press.

Miller, Merton, and Charles Upton. 1974. *Macroeconomics: A Neoclassical Introduction.* Chicago: University of Chicago.

Mises, Ludwig von. 1962. *The Ultimate Foundation of Economic Science: An Essay on Method.* Princeton, N.J.: D. Van Nostrand. <http://www.mises.org/ufofes.asp>.

_____. [1944] 1969. *Bureaucracy.* New Rochelle, N.Y.: Arlington House.

_____. 1980. *The Theory of Money and Credit.* Indianapolis, Ind.: Liberty Fund.

_____. 1981. *Socialism.* Indianapolis, Ind.: Liberty Fund.

_____. 1983. *Nation, State, and Economy.* New York: New York University Press.

_____. 1985. *Omnipotent Government: The Rise of Total State and Total War.* Spring Mills, Penn.: Libertarian Press.

_____. [1952] 1987. "Profit and Loss." In Mises, *Planning for Freedom.* Grove City, Penn.: Libertarian Press.

_____. [1920] 1990. *Economic Calculation in the Socialist Commonwealth.* Auburn, Ala.: Ludwig von Mises Institute. <http://www.mises.org/econcalc.asp>.

_____. [1949] 1998. *Human Action: A Treatise on Economics.* Scholar's Edition. Auburn, Ala.: Ludwig von Mises Institute. <http://www.mises.org/humanaction.asp>.

Mossberg, Walter S. 1999. "I'm Tired of the Way Windows Freezes!" *Wall Street Journal* 30 September. /www.smalltalkconsulting.com/html/windowFreezes.html>.

Noll, Roger G, and Andrew Zimbalist. 1977. "Sports, Jobs, and Taxes." *Brookings Review* 15.

Oakeshott, Michael. 1991. *On Human Conduct.* Oxford, U.K.: Clarendon Press.

O'Driscoll, Gerald P., and Mario Rizzo. 1996. *Economics of Time and Ignorance*. London: Routledge.

Postrel, Virginia. 2000. "High-Tech's Starr Report: The Consequences of a Software Culture War." *Reason* (January). <http://reason.com/0001/ed.vp.high.shtml>.

Read, Leonard. 1975. "I, Pencil." In *Free Market Economics: A Reader*, Bettina Bien Greaves, ed. Irvington-on-Hudson, N.Y.: Foundation for Economic Eduction.

Richman, Sheldon. 1998. "To Create Order, Remove the Planner." <http://www.isil.org/resources/lit/to-create-order.html>.

Rothbard, Murray N. [1970] 1991. *Freedom, Inequality, Primitivism, and the Division of Labor*. Auburn, Ala.: Ludwig von Mises Institute. <http://www.mises.org/fipandol.asp>.

_____. [1970] 1993. *Man, Economy, and State*. Auburn, Ala.: Ludwig von Mises Institute.

_____. 1994. *The Case Against the Fed*. Auburn, Ala.: Ludwig von Mises Institute.

_____. 1995. *Economic Thought Before Adam Smith: An Austrian Perspective on the History of Economic Thought*. Vol. 1. Cheltenham, U.K.: Edward Elgar.

_____. 1995. *Classical Economics: An Austrian Perspective on the History of Economic Thought*. Vol. 2. Cheltenham, U.K.: Edward Elgar.

_____. [1956] 1997. "Toward a Reconstruction of Utility and Welfare Economics." In Rothbard, *The Logic of Action One: Method, Money, and the Austrian School.* Cheltenham, U.K.: Edward Elgar. <http://www.mises. org/rothbard/ toward.pdf>.

_____. [1982] 1998. *The Ethics of Liberty.* New York: New York University Press.

_____. [1963] 2000. *America's Great Depression.* Auburn, Ala.: Ludwig von Mises Institute.

Schmookler, Andrew Bard. 1992. *The Illusions of Choice: How the Market Economy Shapes Our Destiny.* State University of New York Environmental Public Policy Series.

Sennholz, Hans F. 1987. *The Politics of Unemployment.* Spring Mills, Penn.: Libertarian Press.

Smith, Adam. [1776] 1994. *The Wealth of Nations.* New York: Modern Library.

de Soto, Hernando. 2000. *The Mystery of Capital: Why Capitalism Triumphs in the West and Fails Everywhere Else.* New York: Basic Books.

Sowell, Thomas. 2000. *Basic Economics: A Citizen's Guide to the Economy.* New York: Basic Books.

Steinert-Threlkeld, Tom. 1998. "Linux: The Back Door is Open." *ZDNet UK News* 15 September. <http://news.zdnet. co.uk/story/0,,t269-s2069361,00.html>.

Sullum, Jacob. 1997. "Safety That Kills." *Reason* (March).

_____. 1997. "Alcohol Blindness." *Reason* (October).

_____. 2001. "Parcel Delivery." *Reason* (February).

Timberlake, Richard H., Jr. n.d. "Austrian 'Inflation,' Austrian Money." *Ideas on Liberty.*

Tullock, Gordon. 1988. "Why the Austrians Are Wrong About Depressions." *Review of Austrian Economics* 2.

Vedder, Richard K., and Lowell E. Gallaway. 1993. *Out of Work: Unemployment and Government in Twentieth-Century America.* New York: New York University Press.

Vonnegut, Kurt. [1968] 1998. "Harrison Bergeron." In Vonnegut, *Welcome to the Monkey House.* New York: Delta.

_____. 1999. *Breakfast of Champions.* New York: Delta.

Wagner, Richard. 1999. "Austrian Cycle Theory: Saving the Wheat while Discarding the Chaff." *Review of Austrian Economics* 12, no. 1. <http://www.gmu.edu/jbc/fest/files/wagner>.

Wicksteed, Philip. [1910] 1933. *The Common Sense of Political Economy and Selected Papers and Reviews on Economic Theory.* Lionel Robbins, ed. London: Routledge and Kegan Paul.

Yeager, Leland B. 1997. *The Fluttering Veil: Essays on Monetary Disequilibrium.* Indianapolis, Ind.: Liberty Fund.

INDEX